FROMMER'S

COMPREHE — GUIDE

DUBLIN '93-'94

by Patricia Tunison Preston
and John J. Preston

PRENTICE HALL TRAVEL

NEW YORK • LONDON • TORONTO • SYDNEY • TOKYO • SINGAPORE

FROMMER BOOKS

Published by Prentice Hall General Reference
A division of Simon & Schuster Inc.
15 Columbus Circle
New York, NY 10023

ISBN 0-671-84760-0
ISSN 0899-286X

Design by Robert Bull Design
Maps by Geografix Inc.

FROMMER'S DUBLIN '93–'94

Editor-in-Chief: Marilyn Wood
Senior Editors: Alice Fellows, Lisa Renaud
Editors: Charlotte Allstrom, Thomas F. Hirsch, Peter Katucki, Sara
    Hinsey Raveret, Theodore Stavrou
Assistant Editors: Margaret Bowen, Lee Gray, Ian Wilker
Managing Editor: Leanne Coupe

SPECIAL SALES

Bulk purchases of Frommer's Travel Guides are available at special discounts. The publishers are happy to custom-make publications for corporate clients who wish to use them as premiums or sales promotions. We can excerpt the contents, provide covers with corporate imprints, or create books to meet specific needs. For more information write to Special Sales, Prentice Hall Travel, Paramount Communications Building, 15th floor, 15 Columbus Circle, New York, NY 10023.

Manufactured in the United States of America

This Book Is Dedicated to
Fr. Charlie Coen
Faithful Friend and Inimitable Irishman

ACKNOWLEDGMENTS

Thank you, dear people of Dublin and people of Ireland, for being your great selves. Your help, hospitality, and encouragement have made this book possible.

Thanks, in particular, to friends at Aer Lingus (John Bastable, Patrick Hanrahan, Bernie Lynch, James Lyndon, Paul Murphy, and many more); friends at the Irish Tourist Board in Dublin (Martin Dully, Matt McNulty, James Larkin, Joe Lynam, Paddy Derivan, Mary Neville, and many more), in New York (Niall Millar, Simon O'Hanlon, Orla Carey, Ruth Costelloe, and many more), and in London (Margaret Cahill); and friends at CIE/Ireland's Transport Company in Dublin (Ciaran O'Leary and many more) and in the U.S. (Brian Stack, Dennis Savage, Joe Fallon, and many more).

Thanks also to our stalwart Dublin friends over the years—Alan and Angela Glynn, Mary Crotty and Derek Sherwin, Paddy and Eithne Fitzpatrick, Margaret Doyle and the late P. V. Doyle, Brenda Weir, Vivienne Flanagan, Tony Kenny, Peter Harbison, and Mary O'Sullivan, and many more.

Thank you to Marilyn Wood, our editor-in-chief, for assigning us to write *Dublin '93–'94;* and thank you to Susan Poole for writing the first eight editions of this book, and for recommending us to take over the reins with this all-new ninth edition.

And thanks to Dublin for being our favorite city!

CONTENTS

LIST OF MAPS

INVITATION TO THE READERS

In researching this book, we have come across many wonderful establishments, the best of which we have included here. We are sure that many of you will also come across appealing hotels, inns, restaurants, guest houses, shops, and attractions. Please don't keep them to yourself. Share your experiences, especially if you want to comment on places that have been included in this edition that have changed for the worse. You can address your letters to:

Patricia and John Preston
Frommer's Dublin '93–'94
c/o Prentice Hall Travel
15 Columbus Circle
New York, NY 10023

A DISCLAIMER

Readers are advised that prices fluctuate in the course of time and travel information changes under the impact of the varied and volatile factors that affect the travel industry. Neither the author nor the publisher can be held responsible for the experiences of readers while traveling. Readers are invited to write to the publisher with ideas, comments, and suggestions for future editions.

SAFETY ADVISORY

Whenever you're traveling in an unfamiliar city or country, stay alert. Be aware of your immediate surroundings. Wear a moneybelt and keep a close eye on your possessions. Be particularly careful with cameras, purses, and wallets, all favorite targets of thieves and pickpockets.

TELEPHONE NUMBER ADVISORY

Dublin telephone numbers are currently being updated and changed from six digits to seven digits, to be completed by 1994. Although we have endeavored to present the most up-to-date numbers on these pages, many numbers will change after time of press. If you dial a number and it has changed, a recording should advise you of the new number. However, if you have any difficulty, you can dial toll free 1/800-330-330 to check the status of a number.

CHAPTER 1

INTRODUCING DUBLIN

1. CULTURE, HISTORY & BACKGROUND
- **WHAT'S SPECIAL ABOUT DUBLIN**
- **DATELINE**

2. FOOD & DRINK

3. RECOMMENDED BOOKS

Dublin embodies all that is best in the Emerald Isle—a combination of old and new vistas, a hectic yet relaxed atmosphere, and a progressive and genial citizenry. One of Europe's most picturesque capitals, Dublin sits on Ireland's east coast overlooking the Irish Sea. It is bisected by the River Liffey and sheltered on three sides by a crescent of gentle mountains. Compact and easily walkable, Dublin is a harmonious blend of past and present—narrow cobblestone lanes and wide one-way streets, medieval cathedrals and open-air markets, 18th-century town houses and multistory shopping centers, horse-drawn liveries and double-decker buses.

With over 1,000 years of history, this proud city is the nation's nucleus—politically, economically, socially, and culturally. Home of an international airport and seaport, Dublin is the seat of the Irish government, headquarters of dozens of banks, financial institutions, and major international companies, and the hub of great theaters and museums, and yet the Fair City exudes a friendly ambience, with a neighborhood pub or two on every corner.

More than a million people reside in the Dublin metropolitan area—over a quarter of the entire Irish population. Yet this is a city where conviviality is the norm, and all of the inhabitants seem to know one another. Dubliners, young and old alike, rarely walk down a single street without stopping to acknowledge someone or give a friendly wave or greeting. And, after a few days, visitors seem to fall right into the pattern of a few affable words, a nod, a wink, or a smile. Simply put, Dublin's Fair City is a cosmopolitan capital with a hometown heart.

1. CULTURE, HISTORY & BACKGROUND

GEOGRAPHY

On the western fringe of Europe, edged by the Atlantic and just across the sea from Britain, Ireland is totally surrounded by water, and so it is not surprising that the capital city of Dublin is largely defined by water. The Irish Sea and Dublin Bay border Dublin on the east and the River Liffey runs through the middle of the city in an east-west direction.

WHAT'S SPECIAL ABOUT DUBLIN

Buildings

☐ Dublin Castle, boasting a 13th-century tower, a medieval undercroft revealing excavations going back to Viking times, a 19th-century chapel, and elaborate ceremonial state apartments.

☐ Custom House, with a long classical facade overlooking the River Liffey.

☐ Four Courts, a multicolumned and domed Georgian beauty.

Museums/Art Galleries

☐ National Museum, home to such great treasures as the Tara Brooch, Cross of Cong, and Ardagh Chalice.

☐ The Royal Hospital. Patterned after Les Invalides in Paris, it's home to Ireland's museum of modern art.

☐ Chester Beatty Library, with its collection of Western, Middle Eastern, and Far Eastern manuscripts and art.

Parks/Gardens

☐ Phoenix Park. With over 1700 acres of gardens, nature trails, and forests, this is Dublin's playground.

Ace Attractions

☐ The Book of Kells. This 8th-century meticulously illuminated version of the four Gospels is Ireland's greatest artistic treasure.

☐ Merrion and Fitzwilliam Squares. Wide Georgian streets and parks lined by rows of restored brick-fronted town houses.

City Spectacles

☐ Dublinia, this re-creation of early Dublin includes a walk-through medieval maze, diorama, prototypes of 13th- to 15th-century buildings, and a 360-degree wraparound sight-and-sound show.

☐ Dublin Experience. A multimedia sound-and-light show.

Religious Buildings

☐ Christ Church Cathedral, in the heart of Dublin's Old City.

☐ St. Patrick's Cathedral, the longest church in Ireland. Among its distinguished deans was Jonathan Swift.

Literary Landmarks

☐ Dublin Writers Museum. This tribute to Dublin's great scribes contains books galore, exhibits, paintings, sculptures, and memorabilia.

☐ Joyce Tower. The 40-foot round granite seaside tower that once was home to the novelist.

Offbeat/Oddities

☐ Kilmainham Gaol Historical Museum. A jail of a museum!

☐ St. Michan's Church. The underground burial vault holds mummified bodies that show no signs of decomposition.

☐ Whitefriar Street Carmelite Church. The final resting place for St. Valentine.

☐ Heraldic Museum. A perfect place to start a search for your ancestors.

Two smaller waterways further rim the core of the city—the Royal Canal forming a semicircular ring on the north side and the Grand Canal completing the curve on the south side. Although the Dublin Mountains rise to the west of the city, most of the downtown area is flat, at sea level.

The topography of the island country is shaped like a saucer—a broad limestone plain in the center, rimmed almost completely by coastal mountains and highlands. The central plain, which is largely bogland and farmland, is broken in places by low hills. It is also dotted by hundreds of lakes and rivers, including the Shannon, which is the longest river in Ireland or Britain.

The total area of the island is 32,524 square miles, or about the size of the state of Maine. The greatest width of the country is 189 miles, and the greatest length is 302 miles. The 3,000-mile coastline follows a path of various natural indentations, resulting in a pattern that places no part of Ireland more than 70 miles from the sea.

Because of Ireland's diminutive size, Dublin is accessible by car to almost everywhere within a matter of hours—from Dublin, it's less than 100 miles to Kilkenny, Wexford, or Waterford; less than 150 miles to Limerick, Sligo, Galway, Shannon, Donegal; and less than 200 miles to Cork or Killarney.

THE PEOPLE

Ireland's greatest asset is her people—an exuberant and enthusiastic folk who are known far and wide for their hospitality. "There are no strangers in Ireland," the old Gaelic saying goes, "only friends we have yet to meet."

It won't take more than a few seconds after you arrive to see that a smile comes as naturally to the Irish as taking a breath. And when the people of Ireland want to express their welcome for you, they do it in a grand and heartfelt way. "Cead mile failte" (which means "one hundred thousand welcomes") is the customary greeting.

Not one or two welcomes, or even a few dozen—only a hundred thousand will do. And after you settle in, the Irish will beguile you with their intangible assets—from quick wit and ready conversation to lilting music and song.

Dubliners, in particular, are a special breed—well informed and interested in all that is happening in the world. They are always reading a newspaper—indeed it is amazing that such a small city can support no fewer than three morning dailies and two evening tabloids. Dubliners will draw you into conversation and eagerly strive to make you a part of their city.

IMPRESSIONS

[On the Irish] For all their wars are merry, and all their songs are sad.
—G. K. CHESTERTON (1874–1936), *THE BALLAD OF THE WHITE HORSE*

HISTORY

From "Eblana" to "Dubhlinn"

Evidence of human life in Ireland can be traced back as far as 6,000 or 8,000 B.C., but published accounts of Dublin go back only to 130–180 A.D. when the geographer Ptolemy, using the word "Eblana," pinpointed it on a map as a place of note. The present name is derived from the Irish or Gaelic "Dubhlinn," meaning "Dark Pool." The official Irish name, however, which appears on some contemporary signs, is "Baile Atha Cliath," meaning "The Town of the Hurdle Ford."

Like a lot of places in Ireland, Dublin is believed to have been visited around 448 A.D. by St. Patrick, who converted many of the inhabitants to Christianity. During the next four centuries a Christian community grew around the site of a primitive ford on the River Liffey and lived in relative peace.

The Coming of the Vikings

Although Dublin was spared the Roman and Teutonic Saxon invasions that reached neighboring England, the Vikings eventually sailed to Irish shores. The Norse built a sea fort on the banks of the River Liffey in 841 A.D., and the Danes took possession of the town 12 years later. During the 10th century, Irish kings laid claim to the settlement; and in 988 A.D., Dublin was officially recognized as an Irish city, thanks to the efforts of Mael Sechnaill II—although the Danes still kept a considerable grip. The Danish power began to wane in 1014, however, when Irish chieftain and "high king" Brian Boru was victorious at the Battle of Clontarf, but perished in the process.

Following Boru's demise, other kings exerted authority over Dublin, including the Danish King Sitric who is best remembered for helping to establish the original Christ Church Cathedral in 1038. For the next 100 years, local kings squabbled among themselves for power.

The Norman Conquerers

In the 12th century, Dermot MacMurrough, a deposed local chieftain anxious to regain his authority, enlisted the aid of a band of

warriors from western Britain. These new
arrivals, the Normans, were actually descendants of the same Viking invaders who had
attacked Ireland and other lands three centuries earlier. They had settled in northern
France, in the area known as Normandy,
and hence they were called Normans when
they eventually came to Britain with William the Conquerer. By 1162, Dermot had
complete control over Dublin and the Normans had firmly planted their feet on Irish
soil by coming to MacMurrough's aid, ulti-
mately conquering and prevailing in Ireland
for hundreds of years.

Although the Normans were generally
considered benevolent overseers, who gradually intermarried with the native population, their coming also signaled a new wave
of subjugation for the Irish.

**Eight Hundred Years of Domina-
tion** Recognizing the king of England as
their overlord, the Normans embodied the
first stage of the conquest of Ireland from
neighboring Britain. This chain of events,
which would last for over eight centuries,
officially started in 1171 when King Henry II
landed at Dublin and claimed power over
Ireland. In 1174 Henry granted a charter to
Dublin, conceding free-trading rights
throughout his dominions. In 1204 Dublin
Castle was established as the administrative
center of English power in Ireland, and in
1229 the first mayor of Dublin, Richard
Muton, was appointed. The first mint in
Dublin opened in 1251, and parliamentary
sessions were held in Dublin starting in
1297.

Throughout the Middle Ages, a succes-
sion of English kings landed briefly in
Dublin to exert their power over Ireland.
The most telling years, 1534 to 1552, came
during the reign of Henry VIII who sought
to suppress Irish Catholicism while imposing
his self-appointed supremacy as head of the
Church of England and Ireland. Monasteries were dissolved and churches were destroyed or handed over from Catholic to
Protestant clerics—hence, to this day, both
of Dublin's prime cathedrals, Christ Church
and St. Patrick's, are Protestant. Religious

DATELINE

sion of Catholic
church in Ireland.
• **1592** Elizabeth I
grants charter to
found Trinity College
in Dublin.
• **1649** Oliver
Cromwell crushes
Irish rebellion.
• **1791** Wolfe Tone
mounts an ill-fated
rebellion.
• **1803** Robert
Emmet fails in his
rebellion attempt.
• **1829** Daniel
O'Connell secures
passage of Catholic
Emancipation Act.
• **1841** Daniel
O'Connell is named
lord mayor of Dublin.
• **1867** The Fenian
uprising is put down.
• **1893** The Gaelic
League is founded.
• **1904** Abbey The-
atre is established.
• **1916** Padraic
Pearse leads an
armed rising to pro-
claim the Irish Re-
public on Easter
Monday.
• **1919** A Declara-
tion of Independence
from Britain is pro-
claimed and an Irish
provisional govern-
ment is formed with
Eamonn De Valera
as president of the
parliament.
• **1919–21** The
Anglo-Irish War is
waged, ending with
26 of Ireland's 32
counties becoming
the Irish Free State
(continues)

DATELINE

(Eire), separate from
Britain.

• **1926** Irish Free
State's first broad-
casting network
launched.

• **1927** First general
election in Irish Free
State.

• **1937** Ireland's 26
counties adopt a
new constitution,
abandoning member-
ship in British Com-
monwealth.

• **1938** Douglas
Hyde inaugurated as
Eire's first president.

• **1939** Dublin is
bombed by Germany
at start of World
War II, but Ireland
remains neutral.

• **1949** Eire formally
declares itself as the
Republic of Ireland.

• **1955** Ireland ad-
mitted into the
United Nations.

• **1963** U.S. Presi-
dent John F. Kenne-
dy visits Dublin.

• **1969** Violence
breaks out in North-
ern Ireland.

• **1972** British em-
bassy is burned in
Dublin. Ireland joins
the European Com-
munity.

• **1973–76**
Isolated car bomb
explosions break out
in Dublin.

• **1979** Pope John
Paul II celebrates
mass in Dublin's
Phoenix Park.

• **1984** U.S. Presi-
(*continues*)

persecution continued under Elizabeth I,
who in 1592 granted a charter for the
founding of Trinity College in Dublin on the
site of a suppressed former monastery.

Rebellions and Risings It is not
surprising that unrest among the oppressed
Irish began to ferment. In the mid-17th
century, an Irish rebellion was ruthlessly
crushed by Oliver Cromwell, who arrived in
Dublin in 1649 as commander-in-chief of
the English forces. This was followed in
1791 by a rebellion sparked by Wolfe Tone,
leading a society known as the United Irishmen, but was equally crushed, as was a later
rebellion led by Robert Emmet in 1803 and
an 1867 uprising led by the Irish Republican
Brotherhood, known as the Fenians.

In the midst of the failed coups, there
were also some bright spots. In 1829 the
Kerry-born Daniel O'Connell secured the
passage of the Catholic Emancipation Act, a
restoration of civil rights for Catholics. For
his efforts, in 1841, O'Connell was named
lord mayor of Dublin.

Toward the close of the 19th century,
Dublin became the center of two great
cultural movements—the Gaelic League,
founded in 1893 with the goal of restoring
the Irish language; and the Irish literary
renaissance, which ushered in the 20th century with the writings of William Butler
Yeats and the foundation of the Abbey
Theatre.

The long chronicle of England's domination over Ireland—with its string of hard-
ships and heroes, repressions and rebellions,
conflicts and compromises—finally reached
a crescendo in 1916 when the Irish Volun-
teer movement under Padraic Pearse organized an armed rising and proclaimed the
Irish Republic. The revolt, headquartered in
the General Post Office on O'Connell Street,
was put down in a week and most of the
leaders were executed, but the tide had been
turned. In 1919 a national parliament (Dail
Eireann) was convened at Dublin and con-
firmed a Declaration of Independence,
forming a provisional Irish government. The
American-born revolutionary Eamonn De
Valera was elected president of the parliament.

A Free State and Republic   Peace, alas, was still elusive. From 1919 to 1921, Ireland launched a final thrust for total independence from England, the Anglo-Irish War. It ended with only a partial victory for the Irish—the signing of a treaty establishing the Free State of Ireland (Eire) made up of 26 of the total of 32 counties, leaving the other 6 counties to remain part of Britain, and henceforth known as Northern Ireland.

DATELINE

dent Ronald Reagan visits Dublin.
• **1987**   Dublin elects its first woman lord mayor.
• **1988**   Dublin celebrates its 1,000 anniversary.
• **1990**   Ireland elects its first woman president.

In 1926 the Irish Free State's first broadcasting network was launched from Dublin and the first general election took place in the following year. In 1937 the 26 counties of Ireland adopted a new constitution, abandoning membership in the British Commonwealth. Douglas Hyde was inaugurated as Eire's first president in 1938. The following year, with the outbreak of World War II in Europe, Ireland chose to remain neutral, although German bombs twice were dropped on Dublin.

In 1949, Eire formally declared itself a republic and in 1955 it was admitted into the United Nations.

Dublin Today   Since coming into its own as the capital of a free nation, Dublin has been thrust into the world spotlight on several occasions including the visits of two U.S. presidents of Irish ancestry, John F. Kennedy in 1963 and Ronald Reagan in 1984. Pope John Paul II visited the city and celebrated an open-air mass in Phoenix Park for almost a million people in 1979.

Amid the glory, there has also been pain. Since 1969, violent events in Northern Ireland have had a chilling spin-off effect on Dublin, slowing investment developments and impeding the growth of tourism. With the exception of the burning of the British embassy in 1972 and isolated car bomb explosions in 1973–76, Dublin has rarely been drawn into the conflict, although the Dublin-based government is committed to peaceful negotiations with counterparts in Belfast.

On a brighter note, in 1972 Ireland joined the European Community, opening up many new avenues of trade and economic partnership. A new Financial Services Centre has recently been launched in Dublin, attracting dozens of international banks and investment firms.

In 1988 Dublin marked its millennium—1,000 years as an Irish

IMPRESSIONS

This city, as it is not in antiquity inferior to any city in Ireland, so in pleasant situation, in gorgeous buildings, in the multitude of people, in martial chivalry, in obedience and loyalty, in the abundance of wealth, in largeness of hospitality, in manners and civility, it is superior to all other cities and towns in that realm.
—RICHARD STANYHURST, *HOLLINSHED'S CHRONICLES*, 1577

city. The year-long program of celebration brought many welcomed improvements on the face of the city, from the restoration of historic facades to the pedestrianization of Grafton Street.

The city layout was permanently enhanced with the addition of 10 new bronze sculptures by Irish craftspersons in public places including a rendering of Dublin's legendary heroine, Molly Malone, at the juncture of Nassau and Grafton Streets, a replica of a Viking ship on Essex Quay, and a liberty bell in St. Patrick's Cathedral Park. O'Connell Street, the city's main thoroughfare, was perked up by an elaborate new 40-spout fountain with a reclining unclad female in the center, representing the River Liffey and referred to as "Anna Livia," which is the symbolic name that novelist James Joyce bestowed upon the river. Dubliners have a few good-natured names of their own for the eye-catching spectacle.

In 1987 Dublin took a progressive leap among the world's major cities by electing its first woman lord mayor, Carmencita Hederman. But, by 1990, even that feat was topped when Mary Robinson became the first woman president of Ireland, headquartered in Dublin.

POLITICS

The island of Ireland is divided into 32 counties, and into two distinct political parts: the Republic of Ireland and Northern Ireland. The republic—of which Dublin is the capital—takes up four-fifths of the land and is comprised of 26 counties.

The Republic of Ireland is a parliamentary democracy, with a duly elected president, a largely ceremonial role, and a prime minister, called the Taoiseach (pronounced tee-shock), who is the head of the government. The Irish Parliament has two houses, a House of Representatives, called the Dail (pronounced dawl), and a Senate.

The remaining six counties, designated as Northern Ireland, are part of the United Kingdom; their capital city is Belfast.

FAMOUS DUBLINERS

Samuel Beckett (1906–89) Playwright and novelist, he is one of three Irish winners of the Nobel Prize for literature (in 1969). He taught French at Trinity College, later left Ireland, served as secretary to James Joyce, became involved in the French Resistance of World War I, and worked for the Irish Red Cross. His most performed play, *Waiting for Godot,* is an example of his minimalist style—paring words and gestures to the bone. *Residence:* Born at Cooldrinagh, Foxrock, County Dublin. *Favorite Haunt:* Trinity College.

Brendan Behan (1923–64) Playwright, travel writer, and journalist, IRA activist, and raconteur, he is remembered for his boisterous behavior as well as his writings. His best works include the novel *The Borstal Boy,* and the plays *The Quare Fellow* and *The Hostage. Residence:* Mountjoy Jail where he was imprisoned for his IRA activities. *Favorite Haunts:* McDaid's Pub on Harry Street, the Palace Bar on Fleet Street, Davy Byrnes Pub on Duke Street, and Eccles Street, setting for *The Hostage.*

Dionysius Boucicault (1820–90) Well known in theaters in England and the U.S.A., this playwright and actor wrote three plays that are still performed today, *The Colleen Bawn, Arrah na Pogue*, and *The Shaughraun*. He was a pioneer in the "touring company" approach to theater. *Residence*: Born at 47 Lower Gardiner St.

Elizabeth Bowen (1899–1937) A novelist and short-story writer, she was born in Dublin but spent a major part of her life in England. Her impressions of early Dublin life are recorded in *Seven Winters. Residence*: Born at 15 Herbert Place, off Baggot Street.

Christy Brown (1932–81) Novelist and poet, he was born with severe physical disabilities, but was educated at home by his mother who taught him to write with his left foot. His autobiography, *My Left Foot*, was the basis for the Oscar-winning film of the same name. His other works include *Down All the Days* and *Wild Grow the Lillies*.

Edmund Burke (1729–97) Parliamentarian, journalist, and philosopher, he was born in Dublin, studied at Trinity, but went on to edit a literary-political journal in London. His *Reflections on the Revolution in France* is said to have spurred Thomas Paine to write *The Rights of Man*. A statue of Burke is on the west front entrance to Trinity. *Residence*: Born at 17 Arran Quay.

John Field (1782–1837) Composer and pianist, he was born in Dublin but spent most of his life in Europe and Russia. He is credited with creating the piano nocturne, made famous by Chopin. He wrote more than 20 nocturnes as well as concertos and other pieces. *Residence*: Born at 8 Golden Lane.

Oliver St. John Gogarty (1878–1957) Poet, wit, surgeon, senator, and athlete, Gogarty served as a model for the "Buck Mulligan" character in *Ulysses*, written by his friend James Joyce. His own writings include *As I Was Going Down Sackville Street, Tumbling in the Hay*, and *I Follow Saint Patrick. Residence*: Born at 5 Rutland Row (now Parnell Square). *Favorite Haunt*: The Bailey Pub, 2 Duke St.

Evie Hone (1894–1955) One of Dublin's great contemporary artists, she specialized in stained-glass work. Her stained-glass windows are featured in many churches and public buildings in Dublin, including the National and Hugh Lane Galleries, and as far away as Eton College in England. *Residence*: Born at Roebuck Grove, Rathfarnham.

Nathaniel Hone (1831–1917) An engineer who turned to art, Hone is one of Ireland's foremost and most prolific painters of the 19th century. Principally a landscape and seascape artist, he painted in a muted color range, and his works are considered a precursor to impressionism. A large collection of his works belong to the National Gallery. *Residence*: Born at Fitzwilliam Place.

Rex Ingram (1893–1950) Born Reginald Ingram Hitchcock, he left Dublin for the U.S. in 1911, becoming a film director in Hollywood, with such films to his credit as *The Four Horsemen of the Apocalypse* and *The Prisoner of Zenda*. Both Rudolph Valentino and Roman Navarro were introduced into the movie world in Ingram-directed works. *Residence*: Born at 58 Grosvenor Sq.

James Joyce (1882–1941) Although born in Dublin, he

left the city at age 22 and spent most of his life outside the country, yet he used Dublin as the setting for his masterwork, *Ulysses*. His other writings include *Portrait of the Artist as a Young Man, The Dubliners,* and *Finnegans Wake.* Although his imaginative, stream-of-consciousness, and controversial works were banned in Ireland when they were first published, he eventually was recognized as a great 20th-century novelist by his own people. *Residences:* Born at 41 Brighton Sq., Rathgar; also lived at over one dozen Dublin addresses including the following downtown locations—14 Fitzgibbon St.; 29 Hardwicke St.; 17 N. Richmond St.; 32 Glengariff Parade, off North Circular Road; and 44 Fontenoy St. Other homes were in the suburbs of Blackrock, Bray, Drumcondra, Fairview, Phibsboro, Ballsbridge, Sandymount, and Sandycove. *Haunts:* Trinity College; Eason's Bookstore; Davy Byrnes Pub; O'Connell Bridge; Aston Quay; and Grafton, Duke, Molesworth, Kildare, Dawson, Nassau, and Westmoreland Streets, and more.

Sheridan Le Fanu (1814–1873) Novelist and journalist, he is considered one of the founders of the Gothic novel. He produced 16 novels including *The House by the Churchyard, Uncle Silas,* and *In a Glass Darkly. Residence:* Born at 45 Lower Dominick St.

Hugh Leonard (1926–). Born as John Keyes Byrne, this master playwright is one of the most successful of Dublin's contemporary writers. Much of his writing is about Dublin or people and places he knows, such as *A Life* and *Da,* the Tony Award–winning story of his own father. *Favorite Haunt:* The village of Dalkey where he was born and still lives.

Thomas Moore (1779–1852) Poet and songwriter, he wrote many airs and poems that have become national favorites. Many were published in the book *Irish Melodies,* and are popular to this day, including "Believe Me If All Those Endearing Young Charms" and "The Last Rose of Summer." He also wrote biographies, including one of Lord Byron. *Residence:* Born at 12 Aungier St.

Sean O'Casey (1880–1964) Born into poverty as John Casey in Dublin, this Abbey Theatre playwright based three of his greatest works on his early life in Dublin tenements—*The Shadow of a Gunman, Juno and the Paycock,* and *The Plough and the Stars. Favorite Haunt:* The Abbey Theatre.

Patrick Pearse (1879–1916) Trained as a lawyer, he became an educator and writer, and eventually worked in the cause of Irish freedom. As commander-in-chief of the Irish Republican Brotherhood and Volunteers, he led the 1916 Rising although he was later executed for his efforts. His writings, especially his poems such as "The Rebel" and "The Mother," have brought him further acclaim in recent years. *Residence:* Born at 27 Great Brunswick St. (now Pearse Street).

George Bernard Shaw (1856–1950) Author of such works as *Man and Superman, Major Barbara, Pygmalion, Candida,* and *St. Joan,* he won the Nobel Prize for literature in 1926. Although he left school at age 15, he spent a great deal of time at the National Gallery in Dublin and later credited the institution with providing his best early education (and he bequeathed one-third of his royalties to the gallery). *Residence:* Born at 33 Synge St.

Richard Brinsley Sheridan (1751–1816) Playwright and politician, he was also a member of Parliament, but is best remembered for his comic farces such as *The Rivals* and *School for Scandal. Residence:* Born at 12 Dorset St.

Jonathan Swift (1667–1745) One of the 18th-century's great satirists, he is best remembered for his *Gulliver's Travels* and *A Modest Proposal.* From 1713 to 1745, he also served as dean of St. Patrick's Cathedral, where his self-written epitaph is inscribed. *Residence:* Born at 7 Hoey's Court, off Werburgh Street.

John Millington Synge (1871–1909) Noted Abbey Theatre playwright and one of the founders of the Irish literary revival, he is known for plays that reflect rural life in Ireland, such as *Shadow of the Glen, Riders to the Sea,* and *Playboy of the Western World. Residence:* Born in Rathfarnham, County Dublin.

Oscar Wilde (1854–1900) Well-educated, Wilde had a keen wit and was a brilliant conversationalist. As a playwright, he is best remembered for *The Importance of Being Earnest,* first produced in London. *Residences:* 15 Westland Row and 1 Merrion Sq.

William Butler Yeats (1865–1939) Poet and dramatist, Yeats was also a founding member of the Abbey Theatre. His poems, which reflect the people and scenes of his times, won him a Nobel Prize for literature in 1923. Although he also served in the Irish Senate, he rejected a knighthood in 1915. *Residence:* Born at 5 Sandymount Ave.

The American Connection

Chester Beatty Born in New York, Beatty brought his impressive collection of Far and Middle Eastern art and manuscripts to Dublin and housed them in a gallery and library named in his honor at Ballsbridge.

James Hoban The architect of the White House in Washington, D.C., Hoban patterned his design after Leinster House in Dublin, now the seat of the Irish Parliament.

Victor Herbert Born in Dublin, Herbert arrived in America in 1886 and earned the reputation of being a major American composer of light opera.

Eamonn De Valera Born in New York of an Irish mother and Spanish father, De Valera returned to Ireland as a child, became involved in the Irish struggle for freedom, and served as Irish prime minister for three terms and as Irish president twice.

Among those who have been granted the Freedom of the City of Dublin, an honor dating from the 12th century but only formalized since 1876, are at least two Americans, **Ulysses S. Grant** (1879) and **John F. Kennedy** (1963).

IMPRESSIONS

I can imagine nothing more pleasurable than continuing day after day to drive through the streets of Dublin and wave—I may come back and do it.
—JOHN F. KENNEDY ON HIS VISIT TO IRELAND, JUNE 1963

ART

Art in Ireland takes many forms. The earliest examples range from the geometric and three-dimensional figures etched onto prehistoric granite slabs and burial tombs in the countryside outside of Dublin to the delicate enamel work and manuscript illumination of the 6th century.

The Tara Brooch, the Ardagh Chalice, and the Cross of Cong are just a few of Ireland's early artistic gems. They constitute part of the collection of early Irish art housed in the National Museum in Dublin.

Ireland's greatest treasure, the Book of Kells, is housed at Trinity College in Dublin. Dating back to the late 8th or early 9th century, the Book of Kells is an elaborate version of the four Gospels of the Bible. Made of vellum, the pages are prized for their hand-lettering and colorful illustration. The distinctively Irish script is bold and well rounded, semi-uncial in shape, while the artistic ornamentation flows with elaborate interlacing, fanciful abstract designs, and charming little animals, intertwined with foliage of plants and tendrils of vines. Much of Irish art and craftsmanship has been inspired by this timeless 1,000-year-old manuscript.

Dublin is also known for its practical decorative arts, particularly the silverware, plasterwork, cut glass, hand-carved furniture, and tapestry creations that flourished in the 17th and 18th centuries. All of these items were used to fill the interiors of the great Georgian and Palladian-style houses, built for the gentry who settled in Ireland from England.

The lush Irish countryside, with its varied colors and tones and ever-changing skies, particularly lends itself to landscape painting. Among Ireland's great artists of this genre were James Arthur O'Connor and Paul Henry, the latter studied at Whistler's studio in Paris before settling down in Connemara to paint landscapes.

Ireland's leading impressionist painters were Nathaniel Hone and John Butler Yeats, father of the poet William Butler Yeats. The foremost Irish painter of the 20th century was Jack B. Yeats (the poet's brother), whose works focus on key moments and actions in the lives of individuals.

In recent years, contemporary art has flourished in Dublin, with names such as Patrick Hickey and Pauline Bewick, acclaimed for distinctive graphic arts, and Brian Bourke and Camille Souter, who contribute a modern approach to landscape art. There are no fewer than 50 art galleries in Dublin, with more springing up each day including the relatively new Irish Museum of Modern Art (IMMA), a showcase of contemporary creativity.

ARCHITECTURE

Dublin's architecture ranges from the medieval to the modern. In the historic Old City near the south bank of the River Liffey, there are the reminders of Viking and Norman times: The hub of Old Dublin is Christ Church Cathedral, dating back to A.D. 1038. This imposing stone edifice has been restored and extended through the centuries, but the original transepts and crypt remain from medieval days. Nearby is St. Patrick's Cathedral, founded in A.D. 1190 and the longest church in Ireland with a 300-foot interior, and Dublin Castle, dating back to 1204.

Although Dublin has its share of Victorian, Edwardian, and art deco influences, the predominant style of architecture in this city is undoubtedly the 18th-century Georgian period. The city's grandest buildings date from that era, including the Four Courts, Custom House, Parliament House, and the National Gallery, Museum, and Library.

In every corner of Dublin, the Georgian legacy lives—major landmarks are surrounded by sweeping avenues, graceful squares, and rows of brick-fronted town houses, each with its own unique door. Often referred to collectively as "The Doors of Dublin," these elaborate entranceways have come to symbolize Dublin in all its past and present glory. Some doors have fanlights, arches, columns, or sidelights, others have decorative brass bells or knockers. Each is painted a different color—pink, red, yellow, green, lavender, and so on—a rainbow of classic individuality.

In contrast, modern Irish architecture tends toward the glass-and-concrete genre. Among those that stand out along the Dublin skyline are the new green-tinted Financial Services Centre on Custom House Quay, a major urban renewal project being developed along the city's docks, and 30-year-old Liberty Hall, a 17-story tower of reflective glass. Considered Dublin's only high-rise of the skyscraper variety, Liberty Hall is the headquarters for the Irish Transport General Workers Union.

LANGUAGE

There are two official languages in Ireland, Gaelic (or Irish, as it is commonly known) and English. Although just about everyone speaks English in everyday communication, the Irish language is still very much in evidence in public places.

Irish is basically a Celtic language, related to Scottish Gaelic, Welsh Breton, and ancient Gaulish. The earliest known written form of Irish is Ogham, a script dating mainly from the 5th and 6th centuries. Many examples of this script can still be seen on ancient stones throughout the countryside. Ogham-inspired crafts are also for sale in many shops in Dublin.

Ireland was an Irish-speaking nation well into the 17th century, but with the growing domination by the English, the native Irish people learned English to improve their socioeconomic positions.

Today Irish is still taught in the schools and is required for some government positions. You'll hear Irish used on national radio and

IMPRESSIONS

It [Ireland] is a lovely country . . . except that the people never stop talking. Now we're in Dublin and still talking . . .
—Virginia Woolf

television at certain times of the day; articles written in Irish also appear in the daily newspapers, although most communications are overwhelmingly in English. The survival of the language is a major priority, particularly because it is intrinsically linked to the music and folklore of the land. There are certain rural parts of Ireland, classified as "Gaeltacht" regions, where Irish is still the everyday language.

Street signs in Dublin are printed in English, although many signs use both languages. Some older signs are written in Irish only, although there is invariably an English-language sign close by.

The average Dubliner speaks English and speaks it well, albeit with his or her own special lilting accent. It is often said, in fact, that the best enunciated English in the world is heard in Dublin, especially in literary and scholarly circles. Some Dubliners, on the other hand, have their own special way with words, often dropping consonants and elongating vowels, a sort of "Dublinese." The word "ha'penny" for "half-penny" (as in the city's "Ha'penny Bridge") is a good example. On the whole, however, Dublin is a thoroughly English-speaking destination.

LITERATURE

Just as the Irish are known for their gift of the gab, they are equally talented at putting pen to paper. It was G. K. Chesterton, on a visit to Dublin over 70 years ago, who said that the city was a "paradise of poets."

Ireland's earliest writings, of course, were in the Irish language. Written from the 8th to the 17th centuries, many of the earliest pieces are short poems with emphasis on nature and the sights and sounds of the sea, sky, and land. The longest poems tend to be of epic proportions, recounting the deeds of Ireland's high kings. The prose was equally varied, from the sagas of early Irish heroes to great historic annals.

Ireland's most noticeable impact on the literary world, however, has been in the genre of Anglo-Irish literature (writings by Irish men and women in English). A majority of these works, created in the last 300 years, were penned by Irish-born writers who spent most of their adult lives outside of Ireland, usually in England or other parts of Europe.

They chose to live outside of Ireland for various reasons, not the least of which was to be close to major publishing houses and theaters. Inevitably, Irish-born writers also found more freedom to write what they wanted by going abroad. Many Irish writers have been ahead of their times and mores, or perhaps too critical of established systems. Although they were often embraced as geniuses abroad, their works were initially censored or banned at home in Ireland. With the passing of time, however, most all of these literary exiles eventually earned both approval and respect in their homeland.

The contributions of these writers, both individually and collectively, continues to have a strong impact throughout the world today. Indeed critics have often wondered aloud how a country as small as Ireland could generate such an abundance of significant writing.

The names read like a literary who's who, from Jonathan Swift, the master of satire, and Oscar Wilde, the incomparable wit, to Ireland's three Nobel Prize winners, George Bernard Shaw, William Butler Yeats, and Samuel Beckett, as well as Oliver Goldsmith, Richard Brinsley Sheridan, Thomas Moore, James Stephens, George Russell (also known as A. E.), George Moore, Oliver St. John Gogarty, and James Joyce, the maverick novelist who forged new and unprecedented styles of writing.

As the home of the Abbey, the Gate, and dozens of other theaters, Dublin is also known for its compelling drama, both classic and experimental in genre, including works by John Millington Synge, Sean O'Casey, Brendan Behan, Brian Friel, John B. Keane, and Hugh Leonard. These are but a few of the most well-known names. Hundreds of other writers, both past and present, have also left their mark, both in Ireland and beyond its shores.

Best of all, contemporary Irish writers do not have to go abroad to earn recognition and acceptance. New ideas are welcomed, controversy is relished. The atmosphere in modern Ireland is conducive to creativity and the writer is a revered figure. There has even been an about-face migration of literary figures with authors from other lands, including the United States, coming to Ireland to live and write. At various times, the Irish government has even extended tax incentives to encourage more writers to be in residence.

MUSIC

Music is second nature to the Irish. Wherever they gather—be it by a hearthside, in a pub, or in the middle of Dublin's Grafton Street, music is bound to result. As a people often conquered and oppressed, the Irish have always found music to be a source of joy and self-expression.

It may come as a shock to some folks, but "Mother Macree" and "When Irish Eyes Are Smiling" are not really examples of Irish music. Such songs can best be attributed to Irish-American origins. When you come to Ireland, you'll find an entirely different repertoire, ranging from haunting patriotic melodies to spirited foot-tapping tunes.

As in most of Europe, music in Ireland can trace its beginnings back to the bards of medieval times, who traveled the countryside singing songs and telling tales, usually to the accompaniment of a harp. So important was such music that the harp was adopted as part of the coat-of-arms of Ireland in the 17th century and remains the chief symbol of the country to this day.

Although this bardic music was seldom written down, the works of one such poet, harpist, and composer, Turlough O'Carolan, have survived and provide the basis for many modern-day airs.

In addition to the harp, other instruments have come into use over

IMPRESSIONS

We are the music makers, we are the dreamers of dreams.
—ARTHUR WILLILAM EDGAR O'SHAUGHNESSY (1841–1881), "ODE"

the centuries. One of the most popular is a form of bagpipe named the uilleann pipe (pronounced *ill*-un), often referred to as the "Irish organ." First used almost 300 years ago, it is pumped with the elbow in a sitting position and produces a softer and more resonant sound than its Scottish counterpart. Other instruments used in producing the distinctive sounds of Irish music are the concertina (a smaller version of the accordion), fiddle, flute, tin whistle, and the bodhran (pronounced *bow*-rawn), a hand-held drum that can best be described as a goatskin tambourine. The Irish have also been known to improvise and use anything from a washboard to a set of spoons to make music. In recent years, groups like the Chieftains have done much to popularize authentic Irish music throughout the world.

One of the best places to hear good Irish music at any time is, of course, Dublin. No matter when you visit, scheduled and spontaneous music sessions are sure to be on tap most evenings in dozens of pubs, clubs, hotels, and theaters throughout the city.

In the scope of modern music, Dubliners have also made a considerable contribution. Pop music concert organizer, Bob Geldof, is a Dubliner, as are the members of the universally acclaimed rock group, U2, and individual performers such as Sinead O'Connor, Mary Black, and the late Phil Lynott.

RELIGION

The Irish national psyche has been significantly shaped over the centuries by Christianity, which arrived in the 5th century A.D. with the preachings of St. Patrick.

The indefatigable saint is said to have traveled the length and breadth of the country—from Dublin to the Hill of Tara, Cashel, and the smallest of towns. It was at Tara that Patrick plucked a three-leaf clover, or shamrock, from the grass to illustrate the doctrine of the Trinity. The spellbinding saint not only converted the High King Laoire to Christianity, but he made such an impression on the assembled crowd that the shamrock has been synonymous with Ireland ever since.

No sooner had the Irish embraced Christianity than they excelled in spreading the word. Ireland's first written documents date from this period, produced at great monasteries and centers of learning that sprang up in such far-flung locations as Glendalough in County Wicklow, and Clonmacnois in County Offaly. Princes, nobles, and prelates flocked from England and other nations for training.

In the same time frame, from A.D. 500 to 1000, as tiny Ireland drew scholars to its shores, it also sent missionaries abroad to educate all parts of Europe—earning Ireland the title of "Isle of Saints and Scholars." To this day, the names of Irish monks are associated with religious sites throughout the Continent, including St. Virgil (Salzburg), St. Colman (Melk), St. Kilian (Würzburg), St. Martin (Tours), and St. Columba (Bobbio).

Today the country is still overwhelmingly Christian, with over 90% of the people identifying themselves as Roman Catholic and about 5% Protestant. The remainder is a diverse mixture of everything from Jews to Hare Krishnas.

FOLKLORE

Much of Ireland's folklore and mythology can trace its origins back to a time before Dublin had even taken shape—around 350 B.C. with the coming of the Celts to Ireland from continental Europe. The natives wholeheartedly embraced the Celtic way of doing things, from a language (Gaelic), to epic-style art, music, and literature. This was the age of the horse-drawn chariots, local clans, provincial high kings, and larger-than-life heroes.

This period spawned some of the most well-known facets of Irish superstition, mythology, and legend. Over the centuries, much of this lore has been passed by word of mouth from one generation to the next. As a result, storytelling has always been considered an art among the Irish. In the days before books, newspapers, and television, storytelling was a genuine and highly respected profession. A man who would travel from area to area bringing news and telling tales was officially called a seanachie (pronounced *shan*-ah-key). He would always have a large repertoire, often up to 400 separate tales.

There are still some storytellers or seanachies in Ireland today, including a few who appear as part of traditional Irish cabarets or at local festivals.

Favorite tales often feature the heroics of Cuchulainn, legendary hurler and strong man; the saga of the *Children of Lir,* four youngsters whose stepmother changed them into white swans; the elusive place called "Tir na nOg," the land of youth; and the appearances of a woman identified as the Banshee, one who wails when death is near.

By far the most popular folk tradition focuses on the early inhabitants of Ireland, known variously as fairies, little people, or leprechauns. Legend has it that leprechauns are no more than 24 inches tall, wear bright green tunics, and live in round fairy forts hidden deep in the woods. These little people are skilled shoemakers by day. Late in the evening, when it is fully dark, they can sometimes be seen, dancing to the music of the wind singing in the trees.

It is said that each leprechaun possesses a crock of gold. If you are lucky enough to see one of these little people, you may be able to win his treasure by fixing a steely stare and keeping both eyes on him. If you blink, however, he'll disappear and so will his pot of gold. Now if you believe all of this, then you will know what Irish storytelling is all about.

NATIONAL SPORTS

Sport, in all its forms, is a year-round obsession for the Irish, and Dubliners are no exception. The choice of sporting activities available

---

IMPRESSIONS

In Ireland the inevitable never happens, and the unexpected constantly occurs.
—SIR JOHN PENTLAND MAHAFFY (1839–1919)

in the Dublin area is comparable to other countries, from golf and horseback riding to hunting, fishing, and tennis. For spectators, there is horse racing more than 250 days a year, as well as greyhound racing, soccer, rugby, polo, and other international games. What sets the Irish sporting scene apart from other countries, however, are the two native traditional games—hurling and Gaelic football.

Hurling, one of the world's fastest field sports, is played by two teams of 15, using wooden sticks and a small leather ball. Gaelic football, also played by two teams of 15, is a field game similar to rugby or soccer except that the ball is round and can be played with the hands. With huge followings in Ireland's 32 counties, these all-amateur sports are played every weekend throughout the summer, culminating in September at Dublin's Croke Park with the All-Ireland Finals, an Irish version of the Super Bowl.

2. FOOD & DRINK

In the last 25 years, Irish cuisine has undergone a healthy metamorphosis. Although recognized as one of the world's best-fed nations, for many years Ireland wallowed in a reputation for overcooked meats, water-logged vegetables, piles of potatoes, and cream-on-cream desserts. But times have changed—healthful preparation and appealing presentation of fresh natural ingredients are now the norm.

The transformation from stewed dishes to tender and flavorful main dishes of star quality has not come about by chance. It's true that the basic assets were always there—beef and lamb nurtured on Irish pastures, an abundance of freshwater fish and ocean seafood, a bounty of agrarian produce, and dairy goods straight from the local creamery—but it took the broadening influence of travel to inspire this Irish culinary revolution.

Irish chefs went abroad to continental Europe and the United States and learned the arts of French *nouvelle cuisine* and California *au courant*. At the same time, visitors came to Ireland in greater numbers and made demands for rarer meat, crisper vegetables, and more seafood on the menus.

Sparked by these dual factors, the Irish were quick to appreciate their own natural raw materials and nonfrozen ingredients—and to adapt creative ideas from abroad. In kitchens from Dublin to Donegal, a new day has dawned—and the "new Irish cuisine" reigns. And as proof, Irish chefs now bring home dozens of gold medals from the International Food Olympics.

MEALS & DINING CUSTOMS Mealtimes in Ireland are similar to those in the United States, with most hotels and restaurants offering breakfast from 6 or 7am to around 10am; lunch from noon to 2 or 3pm; and dinner from 6 or 7pm to 10 or 11pm.

Breakfast in Ireland can be continental (juice, rolls or toast, coffee or tea) or full Irish (juice, fruits, yogurt, cereal, eggs, bacon, sausage, brown bread, toast, or scones, coffee or tea, and sometimes fish). If you choose the full breakfast, you'll probably be content with a snack for lunch.

In many rural parts of Ireland, the agrarian tradition of a big dinner at midday still holds, with a light supper or "high tea" at night. In Dublin, lunch can be a light or full meal, and the evening meal is usually the main family dinner of the day. The upper-priced restaurants prefer to sell set lunches, usually three or four courses, but most other places offer snacks, sandwiches, salads, or a variety of hot and cold main dishes.

Most all Dublin restaurants have set three- or four-course dinner menus, known locally as table d'hôte, and an à la carte menu for picking and choosing. The set menus usually offer the best value, unless, of course, you want to skip an appetizer and dessert and just have a salad or soup and main course.

Dubliners tend to dine later than Americans, rarely reserving a table before 8 or 8:30pm. This means that visitors who are willing to be early birds and dine at 6:30 or 7pm can often get a table in a restaurant that might otherwise be booked out later in the evening. Dubliners like to linger over dinner in a restaurant, chatting and sipping coffee or a cordial until closing time. Consequently, waiting staff rarely present a bill unless it is asked for, so if you want to eat and run, make your intentions known.

To all of this, add morning coffee, usually around 11am, and afternoon tea around 3 or 4pm. The latter can be as simple as a cup of tea on the run in a plastic cup, or as formal as a sit-down gathering with a brewed pot of tea, finger sandwiches, pastries, and other sweets arrayed on a silver tray, and accompanied by piano or harp music in the background at some of the city's fine hotels, such as the Shelbourne, Westbury, or Gresham. After a proper afternoon tea, some visitors have been known to skip dinner!

THE CUISINE The star of most Dublin menus is seafood, formerly considered penitential fare. In particular, it is hard to equal wild Irish salmon, which is caught daily from local rivers. Served steamed or broiled with a wedge of lemon, it's pink, delicate, and sweet.

As an appetizer or "starter" (as the Irish say), salmon is slowly oak-smoked and thinly sliced with capers and lemon. Most visitors become so addicted to it that they take home at least a side of smoked salmon that can be vacuum-packaged specially for travel.

One of Ireland's most popular seafoods is the Dublin Bay prawn, a more tender version of a shrimp but a cousin to the Norway lobster in flavor. Plump and succulent, they are equally tempting served either hot with melted butter or cold with a light cocktail sauce.

Other shellfish varieties, all readily available in Dublin, include Galway Bay oysters, Kinsale and Wexford mussels, Kerry scallops, Dingle Bay lobster, and Donegal crab.

Irish beef, which is exported to all parts of the world, has always been a favorite with the natives as well as visitors. Today's menus, however, are a lot more varied than they used to be. You'll not only get your choice of steaks, but you can also order filet of beef en croûte, stir-fry beef, beef stuffed with oysters, beef flambéed in Irish whiskey, or beef sautéed in Guinness, and other creative combinations.

All the sheep that graze on the Irish hillsides produce a lot more than wool. Their offspring are the source of the lean racks and legs of lamb that are the pride of Dublin's chefs. Taste this tender meat and you'll find a dramatic improvement over the mutton stew of two decades ago.

Pork products come in many forms—from the famous Limerick ham to thick country bacon or zesty homemade sausages, all of which are featured in hefty portions as part of the standard Irish breakfast.

If you order traditional roast chicken, it will usually be the tasty free-range variety, accompanied by lean Irish bacon or ham, and a herby bread stuffing. Breast of chicken wrapped around local mushrooms or smoked salmon mousse are also popular choices.

One of Ireland's most humble foods is also one of its greatest culinary treasures—brown bread. Made of stone-ground whole-meal flour, buttermilk, and other "secret" ingredients, Irish brown bread is served on the tables of every restaurant in the country. The amazing thing is that no two recipes are exactly the same—brown bread can be light or dark, firm or crumbly, sweet or nutty, but it is always delicious, especially when the crust is crispy. For sheer ambrosia, add a little rich creamery butter or homemade raspberry jam.

In recent years, there has been a trend for some Dublin restaurants to revive and adapt traditional and regional Irish recipes to the standards of the new lighter Irish cuisine. Some dishes to try include boxty (a kind of Irish potato pancake filled with meats, vegetables, or fish); crubeens (pigs' feet); colcannon (potatoes mashed with scallions and cabbage); coddle (boiled bacon, sausages, onions, and potatoes); boiled bacon and cabbage (a precursor to the Irish-American St. Patrick's Day favorite, corned beef and cabbage); and, above all, the classic Irish lamb stew.

Irish desserts (sometimes called sweets) range from cakes (often called gâteaux), pies, and American-style cheesecakes, to a seasonal array of fruit salads, fresh strawberries, and other local garden fruit combinations. With a little effort, you can still find some of the rich traditional dishes such as trifle, a fruit salad combined with custard and sherry-soaked cake, and then topped with rich cream; and plum pudding, a rich whiskey-based soft fruitcake usually reserved for Christmas and special occasions. Other native desserts include barm brack, a light and yeasty fruitcake and raisin-filled soda cake.

For those without a sweet tooth, Irish farmhouse cheeses offer a piquant alternative. More than 60 cheeses are now produced throughout the land, and many restaurants pride themselves on the quantity and quality of their all-domestic cheeseboards.

DRINK Fine whiskey and beer are synonymous with the Emerald Isle. In fact, the Irish are credited with inventing whiskey distilling. The story goes that Irish monks concocted the first brew for medicinal purposes in the 6th century. These same monks carried the recipe to Scotland. They called their invention *uisce beathe* (pronounced *ish-ka ba*-ha), which in Gaelic means "the water of life"; shortly afterward, it was Anglicized to "whiskey." In 1608, a license to distill alcohol was granted to Old Bushmills, making it the world's oldest distillery still in operation.

Irish whiskey differs from Scotch or English whiskey in the method of distillation. The Irish use a combination of local malt and unmalted barley, which is allowed to dry naturally without the aid of heat and smoke, while the Scottish/English mode of distilling requires the use of smoke-dried malted barley. The result gives Irish whiskey a clear, smooth, and smokeless taste. Among the leading brands are John Jamison, Powers, Paddy, Tullamore Dew, Murphy, and Dunphy.

The Irish like to drink their whiskey "neat," which means without ice, water, or other mixers. It is also used as the sine qua non for Irish coffee, an after-dinner drink made by adding whiskey to a goblet of hot coffee mixed with sugar, and topping it off with a dollop of fresh cream. Mmmm . . . it's a favorite with visitors from all parts of the world.

In recent years, Irish coffee has found some competition in sweet Irish whiskey–based drinks like Bailey's Irish Cream and Irish Mist. These mostly after-dinner libations have also given rise to inventive desserts like Irish Mist soufflé and Bailey's Irish ice cream.

The most largely consumed national drink is the Dublin-brewed Guinness stout, a black, yeasty ale with a foamy head. The Irish like to drink it on draft in a large tumbler glass called "a pint." Sipping a pint of Guinness is the favorite pastime in the pubs.

First produced by Arthur Guinness in 1759, this dark brew is considered to be a healthful drink, and the advertising boldly proclaims "Guinness is good for you." The Guinness Company also makes a light lager beer called Harp and a nonalcoholic beer known as Kaliber. Other Irish beers include Smithwicks, Beamish, and Murphys.

As a country surrounded by the sea and with hundreds of lakes and rivers, Ireland has a water supply that is both pure and plentiful. In addition, several sparkling bottled waters, such as Ballygowan, Glenpatrick, and Tipperary, are readily available, rivaling Perrier and other international brands. Not surprisingly, Irish tea, strong and flavorful, is a drink that has no equal in the Emerald Isle.

3. RECOMMENDED BOOKS

General

Bennett, Douglas, *Encyclopedia of Dublin* (Dublin: Gill & MacMillan, 1991).

Byrne, Matthew, *Dublin and Her People* (Dublin: Eason & Son, 1987).

Hemp, Bill, *If Ever You Go to Dublin Town* (Old Greenwich, Conn.: Devin-Adair, 1979).

Joyce, James, *The Dubliners* (London: Grant Richards, 1914).

Joyce, James, *Ulysses* (Paris: Shakespeare & Co., 1922).

Lalor, Brian, *The Ultimate Dublin Guide/A-to-Z of Everything* (Dublin: O'Brien Press, 1991).

MacThomas, Eamonn, *Me Jewel and Darlin' Dublin* (Dublin: O'Brien Press, 1977).

Peplow, Mary, and Shipley, Debra, *Dublin for Free* (London: Grafton Books, 1987).

Preston, Patricia Tunison, *Reflections of Ireland* (New York: Smithmark, 1991, and Dublin: Eason & Son, 1992).

Architecture

Clarke, Harold, *Georgian Dublin/Irish Heritage Series* (Dublin: Eason & Son, 1978).

Costello, Peter, *Dublin Churches* (Dublin: Gill and MacMillan, 1989).

Guinness, Desmond, *Georgian Dublin* (London: Batsford, 1979); and *Portrait of Dublin* (London: Batsford, 1967).

Liddy, Pat, *Dublin, Be Proud: A Thousand Years A-Growin'* (Dublin: Chadworth Ltd., 1987).

The Arts and Literature

Arnold, Bruce, *A Concise History of Irish Art* (New York and Toronto: Oxford University Press, 1977).

Hogan, Robert, *Dictionary of Irish Literature* (Dublin: Gill & MacMillan, 1979).

Kain, Richard M., *Dublin in the Age of William Butler Yeats and James Joyce* (Norman: University of Oklahoma Press, 1962).

Kenny, Herbert A., *Literary Dublin: A History* (New York: Taplinger Publishing Co., and Dublin: Gill & MacMillan, 1974 and 1991).

Norris, David, *Joyce's Dublin* (Dublin: Eason & Son, 1982).

McCarthy, Jack, *Joyce's Dublin: A Walking Guide to Ulysses* (Dublin: Woldhound Press, 1986).

Shaw-Smith, David, *Ireland's Traditional Crafts* (New York and London: Thames & Hudson, 1984).

History and Biography

Collins, James, *Life in Old Dublin* (Cork: Tower Books, 1978).

Conlin, Stephen, *Historic Dublin: From Walled Town to Georgian Capital* (Dublin: O'Brien Press, 1986).

Cowell, John, *Where They Lived In Dublin* (Dublin: O'Brien Press, 1980).

Gilbert, John T., *History of the City of Dublin* (Dublin: Gill & MacMillan, 1978).

Moody, T. W., and Martin, F. X., *The Course of Irish History* (Cork: Mercier Press, 1987).

Mullally, Frederick, *Silver Salver: The Story of the Guinness Family* (London: Granada, 1981).

Periodicals

For the most up-to-date news on Dublin and Ireland, consider a subscription to these two periodicals, both published in Dublin:

- **Inside Ireland** is a quarterly newsletter packed with the latest details on life in Dublin and happenings all over Ireland. Now in its 15th year, this publication also provides an information service, genealogical advice, regular updates on buying property and/or retiring in Ireland, shopping news, and coupons that entitle subscribers to discounts at hotels and restaurants. It's the next best thing to having your own correspondent in Dublin, for just $35 a year. Contact Inside Ireland, Rookwood, Stocking Lane, Ballyboden, Dublin 16, Ireland (tel. 01/931906).

- ***Ireland of the Welcomes*** is a full-color bimonthly magazine, published by the Irish Tourist Board, but is not just another tourism promotion publication. It is a finely written, well-researched periodical that spotlights ongoing events and celebrations, new attractions, unique driving routes, legends and lore, flora and fauna, traditions and the arts, noteworthy trends, and interesting personalities. If you're planning a trip, it offers regular sections on "Where to Stay" and "Shopping." $18 a year. Contact Ireland of the Welcomes, P.O. Box 84, Limerick, Ireland.

CHAPTER 2

PLANNING A TRIP TO DUBLIN

Without a doubt, a sage Irishman once remarked, the next best thing to being in Dublin is planning to be in Dublin. And, to do your planning, there are some fundamental questions that you need answered: Where to get more information? When to go? How to get there? How to make the best arrangements? What to pack and prepare? What will the weather be like?

This chapter is designed to answer those questions—and more. The pages that follow will guide you in making arrangements to meet your particular needs, whether you are traveling on vacation or business, or if you have the special interests of a senior citizen, student, or disabled person.

Planning a trip to Dublin can be almost as much fun as being there.

1. INFORMATION, ENTRY REQUIREMENTS & MONEY

SOURCES OF INFORMATION

To get your planning off to a sound start, contact the following offices of the **Irish Tourist Board:**

- **New York:** 757 Third Ave., New York, NY 10017 (tel. 212/418-0800; fax 212/371-9052).
- **Toronto:** 160 Bloor St. East, Suite 934, Toronto, ON M4W 1B9 (tel. 416/929-2777; fax 416/929-6783).
- **London:** 150 New Bond St., London W1Y OAQ (tel. 071/493-3201; fax 071/493-9065).
- **Sydney:** 36 Carrington St., 5th level, Sydney, NSW 2000 (tel. 02/299-6177; fax 02/299-6323).
- **Dublin:** Baggot Street Bridge, Dublin 2 (tel. 01/765871; fax 01/764764).

ENTRY REQUIREMENTS

DOCUMENTS   For citizens of the United States, Canada, Australia, and New Zealand entering Ireland for a stay of up to 3 months, no visas are necessary, but a valid passport is required. Nationals of the United Kingdom and colonies not born in Great Britain or Northern Ireland must have a valid passport or national identity document.

CUSTOMS   When arriving in Ireland, transatlantic visitors may import 200 cigarettes, 1 liter of liquor, 2 liters of wine, and goods/gifts not exceeding the value of Ł34 ($56) per adult. If you are entering via another EC member country, then you may bring 300 cigarettes, 1.5 liters of liquor, and 5 liters of wine, plus goods to the value of Ł460 ($759) per adult traveler, provided you bought these items in another EC country. There are no restrictions on bringing currency into Ireland.

The Irish Customs system operates on a Red and Green Channel format. The Green Channel is for people who are not exceeding their duty-free allowances, and the Red Channel for those with extra goods to declare. If you are bringing in only your own clothes and personal effects, choose the Green Channel.

In addition to your luggage, you can bring in sporting equipment such as golf clubs or tennis rackets for your own recreational use while in Ireland. Prohibited goods include arms, ammunition, and explosives; narcotics; meat, poultry, plants, and their by-products; and domestic animals from outside the United Kingdom.

MONEY

CASH/CURRENCY   Ireland has its own independent currency system, even though it is now linked with several other currencies as part of the European Monetary System. The **punt** is the basic unit of currency, although most people refer to it as a **pound,** as in Britain. Do not, however, automatically assume that all pounds are equal! The value of the Irish pound is about 10% less than that of the British pound.

In dollar terms, the Irish pound has fluctuated throughout most of 1992 between $1.60 and $1.80, while the British pound has been between $1.75 and $1.90. So, it will cost you less to buy an Irish pound than a British pound. Because of this difference, British money is not legal tender in Ireland and vice versa.

The Irish pound is symbolized by a Ł sign; each unit of paper currency is called a note. The pound notes, which are printed in denominations of Ł5, Ł10, Ł20, Ł50, and Ł100, come in different sizes and colors (the larger the size, the greater the value). There are still some Ł1 notes in circulation, although these are being phased out in favor of the Ł1 coin. Each pound is divided into 100 pennies (**p**); coins come in denominations of Ł1, 50p, 20p, 10p, 5p, and 1p.

Note: The value of the Irish pound fluctuates daily, so it is best to check the exchange rate at the time of your visit. As we go to press, it is approximately Ł1 Irish = $1.65 U.S.

IRISH PUNT & U.S. DOLLAR EQUIVALENTS

Pence	U.S. $	Pounds	U.S. $
1	.0165	1	1.65
2	.033	2	3.30
3	.0495	3	4.95
4	.066	4	6.60
5	.0825	5	8.25
10	.165	7.50	12.37
25	.4125	10	16.50
50	.825	15	24.75
75	1.237	20	33.00

TRAVELER'S CHECKS Traveler's checks (spelled "cheques" in Ireland) are readily accepted in Dublin. In general, banks provide the best exchange rates, followed by bureaux de change throughout the city. Most banks and bureaux usually post exchange rates in their front windows so you can shop around for the best rate.

Hotels, restaurants, and stores also accept traveler's checks, but their rate of exchange is usually less favorable than the banks'. *Note:* Personal checks or "cheques," even when presented with your passport, are not usually accepted by banks or places of business, unless you are a member of the Eurocheque scheme or have made prior arrangements.

CREDIT CARDS Leading international credit cards, such as American Express, Carte Blanche, Diners Club, MasterCard (also known as Access or Eurocard), and VISA, are readily acceptable throughout Ireland. Most establishments display the symbols or logos of the credit cards they accept on their windows or shopfronts.

WHAT THINGS COST IN DUBLIN	U.S. $
Taxi from the airport to the city center	19.80
Express bus from airport to city center	4.12
Bus or DART minimum fare	.90
Local telephone call	.33
Double room at the Berkeley Court Hotel (deluxe)	239.00
Double room at Blooms Hotel (moderate)	165.00
Double room at Jurys Christchurch (inexpensive)	69.00
Double room at Avalon House (budget)	41.25
Lunch for one at Mitchell's Cellars (moderate)	10.72
Lunch for one at Periwinkle Seafood Bar (inexpensive)	6.60
Lunch for one at Bewley's (budget)	4.95
Dinner for one, without wine, at The Commons (deluxe)	45.37
Dinner for one at Celtic Mews Bistro (moderate)	26.40
Dinner for one at DaVincenzo (inexpensive)	13.20

	U.S. $
Pint of Guinness	3.30
Shot of Irish whiskey	2.72
Glass of wine	2.64
Coca-Cola in a café	1.23
Cup of coffee	.99
Roll of ASA 100 color film, 36 exposures	8.22
Admission to the Book of Kells at Trinity College	4.15
Admission to the National Museum	Free
Movie ticket	5.77
Ticket to the Abbey Theatre	13.20

2. WHEN TO GO — CLIMATE, HOLIDAYS & EVENTS

CLIMATE Contrary to the timeworn stereotype, Ireland does not have constant precipitation. The average annual rainfall is 30 inches in the east around Dublin and 50 inches in the western mountainous areas. In fact, the driest area is the coastal strip near Dublin.

You are certainly apt to see some rain and occasional mist during your visit, but you are also likely to experience glorious sunshine, sweeping cloud formations, and beguiling rainbows. The weather can vary dramatically from day to day; it can also change from fair to showery and back again to fair in a matter of minutes.

The reasons for Ireland's erratic weather patterns are many. Being surrounded by water is certainly a contributing factor, as is the presence of mountains all along the Irish coast. In addition, Ireland lies in an area where mild southwesterly winds prevail. Most of the country also comes under the influence of the warm drifting waters of the Gulf Stream.

On the plus side, all of these factors combine to make a mild and equable climate year-round. A former U.S. ambassador to Ireland described the country as "the land of perpetual springtime." The countryside around Dublin is always green, even in January, and palm trees and other forms of subtropical vegetation flourish side by side with the more standard forms of foliage.

Snow is a rarity in the winter, and summertime temperatures that reach into the 70s or 80s°F. are usually considered to be a heat wave by the locals.

IMPRESSIONS

. . . morning steps like a laughing girl down from the Dublin hills.
—BRENDAN KENNELLY (1936–   ), *GETTING UP EARLY*

Here are some of the average temperatures (in degrees Fahrenheit) you can expect:

Dublin's Average Mean Temperature & Rainfall

	Jan	Feb	Mar	Apr	May	June	July	Aug	Sept	Oct	Nov	Dec
Temp.(°F)	40	40	43	46	51	56	59	58	55	51	44	42
Rainfall (″)	2.6	2.0	1.9	1.8	2.2	2.0	2.3	2.9	2.8	2.6	2.7	3.1
Rainy Days	12	10	10	10	11	10	10	12	11	10	11	13

Because of its northerly situation, Ireland enjoys long daylight hours in the spring and summer months, with sunrise as early as 5am and sunset as late as 11pm. This gives a few bonus hours of daylight after dinner for a walk or a game of golf. May, June, and July have the longest days, with August, April, and September following close behind.

People frequently ask "What will the weather be like in Ireland in the month of X?" The answer most often heard on Irish radio weather reports is that the weather will be "normal." And in Ireland that means unpredictable!

Come expecting the worst; bring a raincoat, umbrella, and waterproof footwear. Then count your blessings if you never have to unpack them. And don't forget a pair of sunglasses. The Irish sun can be blindingly brilliant, especially on a long summer's evening.

Current Weather Conditions   To get the latest weather particulars and forecast for the Dublin area, dial 842-5555.

HOLIDAYS   In Ireland, the public holidays are New Year's Day (January 1); St. Patrick's Day (March 17); Easter Sunday and Monday; Summer Bank Holidays (first Monday in June and August); Autumn Bank Holiday (last Monday in October); Christmas Day; St. Stephen's Day (December 26).

Good Friday, although not a statutory public holiday, is usually observed as a holiday.

DUBLIN
CALENDAR OF EVENTS

JANUARY

☐ **International Rugby Championships.** These events, which spill into February, attract huge local crowds (and often book out hotels). The dates and venues change every year, with some games played abroad and some staged at the Lansdowne Road Stadium in Ballsbridge. Check with the Irish Tourist Board to see what the lineup is for 1993 and 1994.

FEBRUARY

✪ **DUBLIN FILM FESTIVAL** With the opening of Dublin's new Irish Film Centre by early 1993, it is anticipated that this annual event will increase in size and scope. More than 100 films are featured, with screenings of the best of Irish and world cinema, plus seminars and lectures on filmmaking.

   Where: In various movie houses throughout the city.
   When: Last week of February. **How:** For schedules and ticket information, contact the Irish Film Centre, 6 Eustace St., Dublin 2 (tel. 01/679-5744).

MARCH

✪ **ST. PATRICK'S DAY PARADE** Is there a better place to be other than marching down O'Connell Street on this Irish national holiday? There are marching bands, continuous music, floats, and delegations from all over the world.

   Where: O'Connell Street. **When:** March 17. **How:** For tickets, schedules, and information on package tours from the U.S. and Canada, contact the Irish Tourist Board.

☐ **Dog Show,** Main Hall Complex, Royal Dublin Society Showgrounds. Sponsored by the Irish Kennel Club, this event attracts canine lovers from near and far. March 17.

APRIL

✪ **DUBLIN FEIS CEOIL** Fans and players of traditional Irish music come from all parts of the world to listen and to compete in this 10-day event. You'll hear the flute, tin whistle, bodhran, concertina, and many other Irish instruments, as well as voice, orchestral, and choral performances.

   Where: Royal Dublin Society, Ballsbridge. **When:** First 10 days of April. **How:** For full information, contact Feis Ceoil Office, 37 Molesworth St., Dublin 2 (tel. 01/767365 or 934595).

☐ **Howth Jazz Festival,** Howth. There is plenty of music and fun staged in the pubs and halls of this north Dublin seaside suburb. Mid-April.

✪ **DUBLIN GRAND OPERA** Twice a year Dublin focuses on great opera, with a 1-week program of classic works presented by the Dublin Grand Opera Society.

   Where: Gaiety Theatre. **When:** Last week of April. **How:** Contact the Gaiety Theatre, South King Street, Dublin 2 (tel. 01/771717).

✪ PUNCHESTOWN SPRING HORSE RACING
FESTIVAL   Just 30 miles west of Dublin, this country racetrack offers 3 days of exciting hurdle racing in a colorful and festive atmosphere. Buses leave regularly from Busaras in downtown Dublin.

Where: Naas, County Kildare. *When:* Tuesday to Thursday of last week of April. *How:* For full details, contact the Manager, Punchestown Racecourse, Naas, County Kildare (tel. 045/97704).

MAY

✪ SPRING SHOW & GARDEN FESTIVAL   A festive week of events ranging from horse-jumping and sheepdog trials to fashion shows and culinary demonstrations, all with much social merriment.

Where: Royal Dublin Society, Ballsbridge. *When:* First week of May. *How:* For details, contact the Royal Dublin Society, Merrion Road, Ballsbridge, Dublin 4 (tel. 01/680645).

✪ FESTIVAL OF EARLY IRISH MUSIC   Visiting artists give performances and direct workshops combining 500 years of work from early to contemporary music including compositions by Handel, Bach, Monteverdi, Vivaldi, and more. The program also offers madrigals, liturgies, clapping music, sacred music, chamber music, and early Irish traditional music.

Where: Various venues throughout Dublin, including Trinity College. *When:* Last week of April, first 3 days of May. *How:* For ticket information, contact McCullough Pigott, 11–13 Suffolk St., Dublin 2 (tel. 01/773138).

JUNE

✪ FESTIVAL OF MUSIC IN GREAT IRISH
HOUSES   This is a continuous 10-day festival of classical music performed by leading Irish and international artists in some of the Dublin area's great Georgian buildings and mansions.

Where: Various venues throughout Dublin and neighboring Counties Wicklow and Kildare. *When:* Mid-June for 10 days. *How:* Contact the Festival Committee, c/o Castletown House, Celbridge, Co. Kildare (tel. 01/962021).

✪ BLOOMSDAY   Dublin's unique day of festivity, commemorating 24 hours in the life of Leopold Bloom, the central character of James Joyce's Ulysses. The whole city—including the menus at restaurants and pubs—seeks to duplicate the aromas, sights, sounds, and tastes of Dublin on June 16, 1904. Special ceremonies are held at the James Joyce Tower and Museum and there are guided walks of Joycean sights.

Where: Citywide. *When:* June 16. *How:* For full information, contact the Irish Tourist Board.

☐ **Dublin Street Carnival.** A fun-filled open-air event with music, song, face-painting, and vending. Third week of June.

✪ *BUDWEISER IRISH DERBY Although this race takes place at the Curragh racetrack in nearby County Kildare (30 miles away), it is considered to be a Dubliners' celebration. Carloads and busloads of city folk head for this fashionable event; if you're in Dublin, don't miss it.*
    Where: The Curragh, County Kildare. When: Last weekend in June or first weekend of July. How: For full information, contact the Irish Racing Board, Leopardstown Racecourse, Foxrock, Dublin 18 (tel. 01/289-2888).

JULY

☐ **City of Dublin Pipe Band Championships.** A rousing annual musical competition at various venues in Dublin. Mid-July.
☐ **Dun Laoghaire Festival.** A week-long celebration in the seafront suburb 7 miles south of Dublin, with arts and crafts, concerts, band recitals, sports events, and talent competitions. Mid-July.
☐ **Summer Schools.** Study sessions meeting in Dublin include the Irish Theatre Summer School in conjunction with the Gaiety School of Acting at Trinity College; the James Joyce Summer School at Newman House; and the International Summer Schools in Irish Studies at Trinity College and National University of Ireland. July to August.

AUGUST

✪ *KERRYGOLD DUBLIN HORSE SHOW This is the principal sporting and social event on the Irish national calendar, attracting visitors from all parts of the world. More than 2,000 horses, the cream of Irish bloodstock, are entered for this show, with jumping competitions each day, dressage, and more. Highlights include a fashionable "ladies day" (don't forget your hat!), formal hunt balls each evening, and the awarding of the Aga Khan Trophy and the Nation's Cup by the president of Ireland.*
    Where: Royal Dublin Society Showgrounds, Ballsbridge. When: First full week of August, Tuesday through Sunday, following the first Monday, except during Olympic years when it is held in mid-July. How: For ticket and schedule information, contact Royal Dublin Society, Merrion Road, Ballsbridge, Dublin 4 (tel. 01/680645).

SEPTEMBER

✪ *ALL-IRELAND HURLING & FOOTBALL FINALS Tickets must be obtained months in advance for* these two national amateur sporting events—the equivalent of the Super Bowl for Irish national sports.

Where: Croke Park. **When:** First and second weekends in September. **How:** Contact the Irish Tourist Board for information on tickets and travel packages from the United States.

OCTOBER

✪ **DUBLIN THEATRE FESTIVAL** Hailed as the major English-language event of its kind, this festival is a showcase for new plays by Irish authors and quality productions from abroad.

Where: Theaters throughout Dublin. **When:** First 2 weeks of October. **How:** For information and tickets, contact the Dublin Theatre Festival Office, 47 Nassau St., Dublin 2 (tel. 01/778439 or 679-2458).

✪ **DUBLIN CITY MARATHON** Thousands of runners from both sides of the Atlantic and the Irish Sea participate in this popular run through central Dublin.

Where: Dublin city center. **When:** Last Monday in October. **How:** For entry forms and information, contact the Dublin Marathon Office, 3 Fitzwilliam Place, Dublin 2 (tel. 01/761383 or 764647).

NOVEMBER

☐ **Design Workshops,** Rathfarnham. Arts and crafts conducted at Butterfield House. Month-long.

DECEMBER

✪ **DUBLIN GRAND OPERA** This is the second half of Dublin's twice-yearly operatic fling, with great works presented by the Dublin Grand Opera Society.

Where: Gaiety Theatre. **When:** Early December. **How:** Contact the Gaiety Theatre, South King Street, Dublin 2 (tel. 01/771717).

☐ **Christmas Horse Racing Festival,** Leopardstown Race-track. Three days of winter racing for Thoroughbreds. December 26–29.

3. HEALTH, INSURANCE & OTHER CONCERNS

HEALTH As a general rule, there are no health documents required to enter Ireland from the United States, Canada, the United Kingdom, Australia, New Zealand, or most other countries. If a traveler has visited areas where an infectious contagious disease is prevalent 14 days prior to arrival in Ireland, however, proof of immunization for such diseases may be required.

INSURANCE When planning a trip, it is wise to consider insurance coverage for the various risk aspects of travel—health and accident, cancellation or disruption of services, lost or stolen luggage. Before buying any new coverage, check your own insurance policies (automobile, medical, and homeowner) to ascertain if they cover travel abroad. Also check the membership contracts of automobile and travel clubs, and the benefits extended by credit-card companies.

If you decide you need further coverage, consult your travel agent, tour planner, or insurance agent. In many cases, tour operators that sell packages to Ireland provide insurance as part of a package or offer coverage for a small optional fee. Alternatively, you may wish to contact one of the following companies, specializing in short-term policies for travelers:

- **Access America,** 6600 West Broad St., Richmond, VA 23230 (tel. 804/285-3300 or toll free 800/424-3391).
- **HealthCare Abroad** (MEDEX), 243 Church St. NW, Suite 100D, Vienna, VA 22180 (tel. 703/255-9800, or toll free 800/666-4993).
- **Mutual of Omaha** (Tele-Trip), 3201 Farnam St., Omaha, NE 68131 (tel. 402/345-2400, or toll free 800/228-9792).
- **Travel Guard International,** 1145 Clark St., Stevens Point, WI 54481 (tel. 715/345-0505, or toll free 800/826-1300).
- **Travel Insurance Pak,** Travelers Insurance Co., 1 Tower Sq., Hartford, CT 06183-5040 (toll free 800/243-3174).
- **WorldCare Travel Assistance Association,** 605 Market St., Suite 1300, San Francisco, CA 94105 (tel. 415/541-4991, or toll free 800/666-4993).

4. WHAT TO PACK

Comfortable and casual clothing is ideal for Ireland. Slacks, sports clothes, and good walking shoes are de rigueur for both men and women; always pack a sweater or two, which you can add to or subtract from your outfits as required. It is wise for men to include a jacket and a few ties for dinnertime, especially in Dublin restaurants. Women should likewise take something dressy for evenings at the stylish restaurants.

Light rainwear or all-weather coats are advisable at any time of year; and don't forget a folding umbrella, just in case. Sunglasses can come in handy, too, especially if you'll be driving. Take a bathing suit, if you enjoy a swim and will be staying in a hotel with a heated indoor pool.

Don't panic if you forget your favorite toothpaste or hairspray. Ireland has just about everything you are used to, albeit sometimes with different brand names. Do remember to pack any prescription medicines you may need; and take along a copy of your prescription showing the generic name, just in case you need to get a refill. If you bring your hairdryer, don't forget to have a transformer and converter plugs.

---

5. TIPS FOR SPECIAL TRAVELERS

FOR THE DISABLED For the last 30 years, the **National Rehabilitation Board of Ireland,** based at 25 Clyde Rd., Ballsbridge, Dublin 4 (tel. 01/684181), has been a leader in the encouragement of providing facilities to accommodate the disabled. Consequently, some hotels and public buildings now have ramp or graded entrances, and rooms specially fitted for wheelchair access.

Unfortunately, there is still a long way to go, as many of the older hotels, guesthouses, and landmark buildings, still have steep steps both outside and within. For a list of the properties that cater to the needs of the disabled, contact the National Rehabilitation Board in advance.

In addition, the **Irish Hotels Federation** (13 Northbrook Rd., Dublin 6; tel. 01/976459) publishes an annual guide to hotels and guesthouses, with symbols indicating premises that are accessible for disabled persons or suitable with the assistance of one helper.

U.S. firms that operate tours for the disabled to Ireland include: **Evergreen Travel,** 4114 198th St. SW, Suite 13, Lynwood, WA 98036 (tel. 206/776-1184, or toll free 800/435-2288), and **Whole Person Tours,** Box 1084, Bayonne, NJ 07002-1084 (tel. 201/858-3400).

FOR SENIOR CITIZENS Seniors, who are known in Ireland as OAPs (Old Age Pensioners), enjoy a variety of discounts and privileges. Irish senior citizens ride the public transport system free of charge, but this privilege does not extend to visitors.

However, visitors can avail of other discounts, particularly on admissions to attractions and theaters. Always ask about a senior discount as special rates may not be posted. The senior discount is usually 10%.

The Irish Tourist Board/Bord Failte (see "Sources of Information," above) publishes a list of reduced rate hotel packages for seniors, "Golden Holidays/For the Over 55s." These packages are usually available in the months of March-June and September or October-November.

Some tour operators in the U.S., such as **CIE Tours,** 108 Ridgedale Ave., P.O. Box 2355, Morristown, NJ 07962-2355 (tel. 201/292-3438, or toll free 800/CIE-TOUR), give senior citizens cash discounts ranging from $75 to $100 per person on selected departures of regular tour programs throughout the year.

In addition, the following U.S. firms operate tours to Ireland specifically geared to seniors: **AARP Travel Experience with American Express,** 400 Pinnacle Way, Suite 450, Norcross, GA 30071 (tel. 404/368-5466, or toll free 800/927-0111); **Campus Holidays U.S.A.,** 242 Bellevue Ave., Upper Montclair, NJ 07043 (tel. 201/744-8724, or toll free 800/526-2915); **Holiday Travel**

Service, 2727 Henry Ave., P.O. Box 87, Eau Claire, WI 54702 (tel. 715/834-5555, or toll free 800/826-2266); and **SAGA Tours,** 222 Berkeley St., Boston, MA 02116 (tel. 617/262-2262, or toll free 800/343-0273).

FOR STUDENTS   With three revered universities—Trinity College, University College–Dublin, and Dublin City University—and many other fine schools and institutes of higher learning, Dublin is geared to students of all ages. To find out about the various year-round, semester, and summer-school academic programs, contact the Irish Tourist Board (see "Sources of Information," above) and ask for a copy of the *Study Abroad* brochure.

For information on student accommodations and discounts in Ireland, contact the **Irish Student Travel Service** (USIT), 19 Aston Quay, Dublin 2 (tel. 01/679-8833), or in the United States at 895 Amsterdam Ave., New York, NY 10025 (tel. 212/663-5435).

U.S. firms offering educational programs to Ireland include: **Academic Travel Abroad,** 3210 Grace St. NW, Washington, DC 20007 (tel. 202/333-3355, or toll free 800/556-7896); **Consortium for International Education,** 2021 Business Center Dr., Irvine, CA 92715 (tel. 714/995-1700); **Cultural Heritage Alliance,** 107-115 S. Second St., Philadelphia, PA 19106 (tel. 215/923-7060, or toll free 323-4466); and **Irish American Cultural Institute,** 2115 Summit Ave., Mail no. 5026, St. Paul, MN 55105 (tel. 612/647-5678, or toll free 800/232-3746).

6. GETTING THERE

About half of all visitors from North America to Ireland arrive via transatlantic flights directly from the U.S. into Dublin airport, 7 miles north of the city, or Shannon airport, about 140 miles southwest of the capital. The other half fly over the Atlantic first into Britain or continental Europe and then backtrack into Ireland by air or sea.

BY PLANE

FROM THE U.S.A.   The Irish national flag carrier, **Aer Lingus** (tel. toll free 800/223-6537) is the leader in providing transatlantic access into Ireland. The words *Aer Lingus* are Gaelic (with a literal meaning of "air fleet"), but are usually assumed to mean "Irish International Airlines." With bright green shamrock logos on the tails of its jets, the carrier offers year-round daily scheduled flights from New York and Boston into Dublin International Airport. Connections are available from more than 100 U.S. cities via American, TWA, or USAir.

In the high season, mid-June through August, as many as 13 round-trip Aer Lingus flights a week depart for Dublin from New York and 6 per week from Boston. As we go to press, there is a possibility that Aer Lingus will also fly to Ireland from Los Angeles and/or Chicago in 1993–94.

Scheduled flights, on a more limited basis, are also offered by

Delta Airlines (tel. toll free 800/241-4141) from Atlanta to Dublin, with feed-in connections from Delta's network of gateways throughout the United States.

If you'd like your trip over the Atlantic to be more than just another airplane ride, however, we heartily recommend Aer Lingus. You'll feel like you have arrived in Ireland from the minute you step on board—from the welcoming smiles of the cabin crew to the lilting Irish music and the hearty meals with such delicacies as Irish smoked salmon, Bewley's breads, and Golden Vale cheeses. Aer Lingus has flown the Atlantic for more than 35 years, and has an excellent record for service and year-round reliability.

In addition, many travelers opt to fly to Britain and backtrack into Dublin. Carriers serving Britain from the United States include **Air India** (tel. 212/751-6200); **Air New Zealand** (tel. toll free 800/262-1234); **American Airlines** (tel. toll free 800/433-7300); **British Airways** (tel. toll free 800/247-9297); **Continental Airlines** (tel. toll free 800/231-0856); **El Al** (tel. toll free 800/223-6700); **Kuwait Airways** (tel. toll free 800/458-9248); **Northwest Airlines** (tel. toll free 800/447-4747); **TWA** (tel. toll free 800/892-4141); **United** (tel. toll free 800/241-6522); **USAir** (tel. toll free 800/428-4322); and **Virgin Atlantic Airways** (tel. toll free 800/862-8621).

FROM BRITAIN Air service from Britain into Dublin is available via **Aer Lingus** from Birmingham, Bristol, East Midlands, Edinburgh, Glasgow, Jersey, Leeds/Bradford, London, Manchester, and Newcastle (tel. toll free 800/223-6537 in the U.S., or 081/569-5555 in Britain); **Alitalia** from Manchester (tel. toll free 800/223-5730 in

 **FROMMER'S SMART TRAVELER:
AIRFARES**

1. Be an "early bird"—book and pay for your summer trip by the end of February or March and save.
2. Travel in the off-peak months—October through April.
3. Fly midweek (Monday to Thursday) and avoid weekend surcharges.
4. Don't make last-minute changes of plans, and you'll avoid airline penalties.
5. Always ask for the lowest APEX fare.
6. Ask if there are any special once-off promotional fares limited to certain months or weeks.
7. Ask if there are reduced rate 4-day weekend fares in the off-season.
8. In the high season, check to see if charters are operating from your city.
9. Inquire about air/land packages.
10. Join the Aer Lingus Frequent Flyer/Gold Circle Club or other airlines' frequent-travel bonus-point programs.

the U.S., or 071/602-7111 in Britain); **British Midland** from London (tel. 071/589-5599 in Britain); **Brymon Airways** from Bristol and Plymouth (tel. 752/705151 in Britain); **Manx Airlines** from Blackpool, Cardiff, Isle of Man, Jersey, and Liverpool (tel. 624/824313 in Britain); **Ryanair** from Liverpool and London (tel. toll free 800/268-6755 in the U.S., or 071/435-7101 in Britain); **SAS** from Manchester (tel. toll free 800/221-2350 in the U.S., or 071/734-4020 in Britain); and **TAP Air Portugal** from Manchester (tel. toll free 800/221-7370 in the U.S., or 071/828-0262 in Britain).

FROM THE CONTINENT Major air connections into Dublin from the Continent include service from Brussels via Aer Lingus and Sabena (tel. toll free 800/952-1000); Copenhagen via Aer Lingus and SAS; Paris via Aer Lingus and Air France; Munich via Ryanair and Lufthansa (tel. toll free 800/645-3880); Rome via Aer Lingus and Alitalia; Amsterdam via Aer Lingus; Lisbon via TAP Air Portugal; and Zurich via Aer Lingus.

BEST-VALUE AIRFARES

Super APEX Airfares are always changing, with the year, with the season, and sometimes with the month (recently a round-trip fare of $299 was offered for travel during a certain week in May only).

Generally, the cheapest fare across the Atlantic to Dublin is the APEX fare—advance-purchase excursion. In the high season (June 15 to September 15), the APEX fare to Dublin, as we go to press, is $729 plus $18 tax, based on a 14-day advance purchase. In the shoulder months of May to mid-June and mid-September through October, the fare is $609 plus tax. In the off-season, January-March and November-December, the lowest fare to Dublin is $529 plus tax.

"Early Bird Fares" To get the travel season off to a brisk start each year, Aer Lingus usually offers "early bird" fares to people who will book and pay for spring/summer airfares before the end of February. In the current travel year, the "early bird" fare was as low as $529 for round-trip travel to Dublin in the off-season, $559 in the shoulder season, and $609 in the peak season. "Early bird" fares require a minimum stay of 7 days, maximum stay of 6 months, and carry a $125 penalty for changes made after February or cancellations.

Weekend Fares In the November-April period, Aer Lingus offers weekend fares for off-season mini-trips from Thursday to Sunday or Friday to Monday. These fares are usually in the region of $450 or less for round-trip from New York or Boston to Dublin. These fares also carry certain penalties and restrictions, but can be a great bargain for those who crave a long weekend in Dublin's Fair City.

Premier/First-Class Fares If the sky is the limit in your budget, treat yourself to Premier Class Service on Aer Lingus, priced at $1,244 one-way to Dublin from New York or Boston. Delta's first-class fare from Atlanta to Dublin is $2,942. Taxes are extra in both cases.

Charters Charter travel to Ireland is available in the summer months from New York, Chicago, Detroit, and Toronto. Fares average $399 to $509 plus tax, depending on airport of origin. As we go to press, the following companies operate charters to Ireland: **Eurowest Tours,** 10742 Baltimore Ave., Beltsville, MD 20705 (tel. 301/595-4774, or toll free 800/345-6625); **Round Tower Travel,** 6754 W. Diversey, Chicago, IL 60635 (tel. 312/889-7533, or toll free 800/621-7442); **Sceptre Charters,** 101-13 101 Ave., Ozone Park, NY 11416 (tel. 718/738-9400, or toll free 800/221-0924); **Transglobal Tours,** 8200 Normandale Blvd., Minneapolis, MN 55437 (tel. 612/831-1980, or toll free 800/328-6264); **Adventure Tours,** 111 Avenue Rd., Suite 500, Toronto, ON M5R 3J8 (tel. 416/967-1510, or toll free 800/268-7522 in Canada); and **Sunquest Vacations,** 130 Merton St., Toronto, ON M45 IA4 (tel. 416/485-1700, or toll free 800/268-8899).

BY FERRY

For those who fly into Britain or mainland Europe and want to travel to Ireland via sea, there are several car/passenger ferry services heading over toward Dublin.

Offering a mini-cruise atmosphere, these ferries are equipped with comfortable furnishings or cabin berths, good restaurants, duty-free shopping, and spacious lounges where you can relax in a friendly atmosphere.

The most convenient services include Holyhead, Wales, to Dublin via **B & I Line** (tel. toll free 800/221-2474 in the U.S.); Holyhead to Dun Laoghaire, 8 miles south of Dublin via **Sealink Stena Line** (tel. toll free 800/677-8585); and Le Havre, France, to Rosslare, County Wexford, about 100 miles south of Dublin, via **Irish Ferries** (tel. toll free 800/221-2472 in the U.S.).

Prices average $50 to $100 per person, depending on your route, time of travel, and other factors. It is best to check with your travel agent for up-to-date details.

One point worth noting: Since the Irish Ferries company is a member of the Eurail system, you can travel free on the ferries between Rosslare and Le Havre, if you are holding a valid Eurailpass.

BY BUS FROM BRITAIN

Even though no bridges have yet been built across the Irish Sea, there is a bus service linking Dublin with London and other leading British cities, using the B & I or Sealink ferry trips as part of the bus ride.

Operated jointly by Ireland's Bus Eireann and Britain's National Express, these **Supabus** routes operate daily, departing from and arriving at Dublin's main bus station, Busaras. One-way fares between Dublin and London start at £30 ($49.50); round-trip fares start at £45 ($74.25).

For full details on the Supabus routes, contact CIE Tours in the U.S. (tel. toll free 800/CIE-TOUR).

PACKAGE TOURS

Some people think that a package tour has to involve taking a tour with a group. Although there are many good group-tour packages, there are also many packages that do not involve group travel, such as packages designed for individuals or couples traveling together. Such packages may include airfare, a car, and hotel accommodations, or just a hotel room plus sightseeing—all for one price that is lower than if you purchased each element separately as an individual. Buying a package to Ireland can mean significant savings because you are allowing a tour operator to make your arrangements—and a tour operator can negotiate the best rates because of business volume, passing the savings on to you.

Several tour operators offer packages based in Dublin City for 3 days or more, at a price far less than if you booked just a hotel room. These packages, priced as low as $200 per person for 3 nights, include room at a first-class hotel with private bath, full Irish breakfast daily, service charges, and taxes. Depending on which package you buy, the price might also include a sightseeing tour, a theater ticket, a guidebook, and more.

In these days of fluctuating currencies, it is wise to prepay for a vacation package in U.S. dollars soon after you make reservations. Many tour operators will guarantee that there will be no increase in the land costs of a tour package as soon as the deposit is paid. So, even if the dollar weakens, your price is locked in at the original rate.

The leading firms offering package tours of Dublin and the rest of Ireland include:

Aer Lingus "Discover Ireland" Vacations (tel. toll free 800/223-6537), offering Dublin City packages, pub tours, shopping tours, golf tours, and self-drive vacations, designed for individual travelers.

CIE Tours International (tel. toll free 800/CIE-TOUR), Ireland's national tour company was established more than 60 years ago and is the leader in providing escorted vacations to Ireland, as well as Dublin City–based packages, golf tours, self-drive vacations, and Ireland/Britain combination trips. CIE also offers rail/bus touring arrangements within Ireland for individuals and for groups.

Grimes Travel (tel. toll free 800/832-7778) offers Dublin-based packages year-round, but is best known for organizing travel arrangements for the annual Dublin Marathon in October.

Other tour operators specializing in trips to Dublin and Ireland include: **Brendan Tours** (tel. toll free 800/421-8446); **Brian Moore International Tours** (tel. toll free 800/982-2299); **Lismore Tours** (tel. toll free 800/547-6673); **Lynott Tours** (tel. toll free 800/221-2474); and **Owenoak-Castle Tours** (tel. toll free 800/426-4498).

CHAPTER 3

GETTING TO KNOW DUBLIN

1. ORIENTATION
2. GETTING AROUND
• FAST FACTS: DUBLIN
3. NETWORKS & RESOURCES

Compared to other European capitals, Dublin is a relatively small metropolis and easy to get to know. The downtown core of the city, identified in Gaelic on bus destination signs as An Lar (The Center), is shaped somewhat like a pie, with the River Liffey cutting across the middle from east to west. The top half of the pie, or north side of the city, is rimmed in a semicircular sweep by the Royal Canal, and the bottom half, or south side, is equally edged in a half-circle shape by the waters of the Grand Canal.

To the north of the Royal Canal are the northside suburbs such as Drumcondra, Glasnevin, Howth, Clontarf, and Malahide; to the south of the Grand Canal are the southside suburbs of Ballsbridge, Blackrock, Dun Laoghaire, Dalkey, Killiney, Rathgar, Rathmines, and other residential areas.

A compact capital, with lots of parks and pedestrian areas, Dublin is also a very walkable city. In fact, at rush hours and other busy times, getting around on foot is usually the easiest way, as well as the fastest.

This chapter will help you to get your bearings and to determine when it is best to walk or to opt for public transportation.

1. ORIENTATION

ARRIVING

BY PLANE For visitors from North America, the fastest and most direct way to arrive is by plane, via regularly scheduled flights from New York and Boston provided by Aer Lingus, Ireland's national airline, and from Atlanta by Delta Airlines.

In the summer months, charters also operate from other U.S. and Canadian cities (see "Getting There" in Chapter 2). At presstime, it is also likely for 1993–94 that Aer Lingus will add Los Angeles and Chicago as new U.S. departure points. Alternatively, you can fly from the U.S. to London or other European cities and backtrack into Dublin airport (see "Getting There" in Chapter 2).

Airport Dublin-bound transatlantic flights from the United States, and short-haul flights from other Irish airports, and from Britain and other European cities, arrive at Dublin International Airport (tel. 01/379900), about 7 miles north of the city center.

A modern bi-level complex, the airport has 16 departure gates, two restaurants, two bars, and a duty-free shopping center. In addition, it offers a tourist information office, a bank, bureau de change, transportation desk, airline ticket desks, car-rental desks, post office, ladies' and gents' hairdressing salons, and a chapel.

Ireland's national bus company, **Bus Eireann,** provides express coach transfers between Dublin airport and the city center (Busaras, the Central Bus Station, at Store Street). Service operates daily from 7:30am until 10:50pm, with departures every 20 to 30 minutes. One-way fare is £2.50 ($4.15) for adults and £1.25 ($2.10) for children under age 12. For information, call 01/366111.

For speed and ease, a **taxi** is the best way to get directly to your hotel or guesthouse. Depending on your destination, fares average between £10 and £13 ($16.50 and $21.45). Taxis are lined up at a first-come first-served taxi rank outside of the arrivals terminal.

Major international and local **car-rental firms** operate desks at Dublin airport (for a list of firms, see "Getting Around: By Car," below). If you have never driven in Dublin before, however, it is best to take a taxi or bus and leave the driving to someone else until you get acclimated to the layout and left-side driving patterns of the city.

BY FERRY Passenger/car ferries from Britain arrive at the Dublin Ferryport (tel. 01/743293), on the eastern end of the North Docks, and at the Dun Laoghaire Ferryport (tel. 01/280-1905), about 10 miles south of the city center. There is bus and taxi service from both ports to the city center.

BY CAR If you are arriving by car from other parts of Ireland or via car ferry from Britain, all main roads lead into the heart of Dublin and are well signposted to "City Centre." If you are staying on the north side of the River Liffey, follow signs for "North Ring" and if you are staying on the south side of the River, follow signs for "South Ring." Try to time your arrival after the morning rush hour or before the evening rush hour (between 10am and 3pm) or anytime on a weekend when the city traffic is not too congested. Be sure to get directions ahead of time and have a good map handy for reference.

TOURIST INFORMATION

There are two main sources of information for visitors in Dublin City:

Dublin Tourism This is the local tourism authority charged with dispensing information about Dublin City and its environs, as well as operating a room-reservation service. There are fully staffed walk-in visitor offices at 14 Upper O'Connell St., Dublin 1 (tel. 01/747733); East Essex Street, Temple Bar, Dublin 2 (tel. 01/770160; open June to September only); Arrivals Hall, Dublin Airport (tel. 01/844-5387); and St. Michael's Wharf, Dun Laoghaire (tel. 01/280-6984).

Bord Failte (Board of Welcomes) The world headquarters for Bord Failte, otherwise known as the Irish Tourist Board, is located at Baggot Street Bridge, Dublin 2 (tel. 01/747733). Here they're equipped with a staffed information center in the main lobby. The brochure racks not only offer folders and booklets on the Dublin area, but all other parts of Ireland.

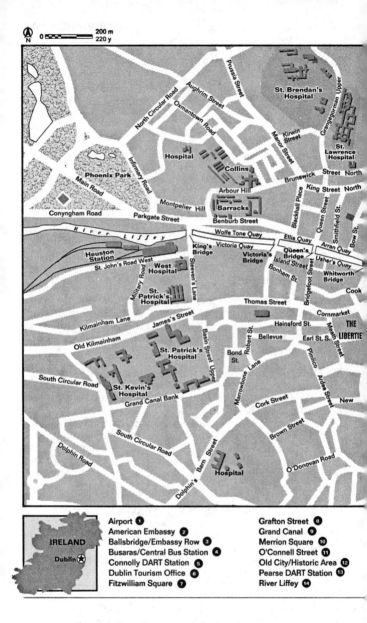

Airport ➊	Grafton Street ➑
American Embassy ➋	Grand Canal ➒
Ballsbridge/Embassy Row ➌	Merrion Square ➓
Busaras/Central Bus Station ➍	O'Connell Street ⑪
Connolly DART Station ➎	Old City/Historic Area ⑫
Dublin Tourism Office ➏	Pearse DART Station ⑬
Fitzwilliam Square ➐	River Liffey ⑭

IRELAND
Dublin ★

CITY LAYOUT

MAIN ARTERIES, STREETS & SQUARES The focal point of
Dublin is the **River Liffey,** with no fewer than 14 bridges connecting its north and south banks. On the north side of the river, the main
thoroughfare is **O'Connell Street,** a wide two-way avenue that
starts at the riverside quays and runs northward to Parnell Square.
Enhanced by statues, trees, and a modern spouting fountain,

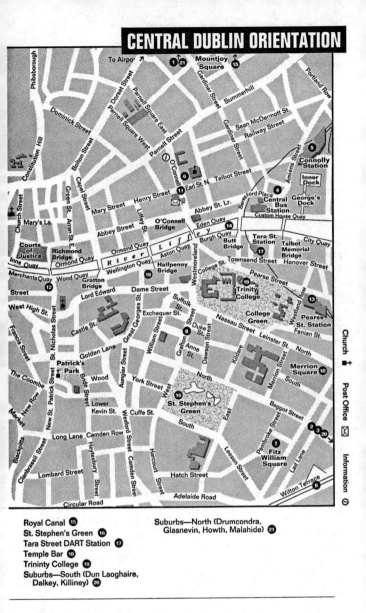

CENTRAL DUBLIN ORIENTATION

O'Connell Street of earlier days was the lifeblood of the city, and it is still important today although a little less fashionable than it used to be.

On the south side of the Liffey, **Grafton Street** is Dublin's main shopping street. Although it is narrow and pedestrianized, Grafton Street is a nucleus, surrounded by smaller and larger streets known for a variety of shops, restaurants, and hotels. At the south end of Grafton Street is **St. Stephen's Green,** a lovely park and urban oasis surrounded by rows of historic Georgian town houses, fine hotels, and restaurants.

Nassau Street, which starts at the north end of Grafton Street and rims the south side of Trinity College, is noted for its fine shops and because it leads to **Merrion Square,** another fashionable Georgian park surrounded by historic brick-fronted town houses. Merrion Square is also adjacent to Leinster House, the Irish House of Parliament, the National Gallery, and National Museum.

In the older section of the city, **High Street** is the gateway to much of medieval and Viking Dublin, from the city's two medieval cathedrals to the old city walls, and nearby Dublin Castle. The other street of note in the older part of the city is **Francis Street,** the "antiques row" of Dublin.

Finding an Address   Like London, the streets of Dublin are a maze of names, with no logical pattern or numerical grid system. Some are wide, some are narrow, a few run two ways, and many are one-way—they form rectangles, triangles, and parallel and perpendicular angles. For the most part, the larger thoroughfares are identified as streets or roads, and the smaller ones are called lanes, alleys, rows, closes, and places.

Most names are posted not on street signs but high on the corners of buildings at the end of each street. The names are usually given in English and Irish, but a few of the older ones have Irish signs only. Within each street, most buildings are numbered, but numbers are often not displayed or seldom used by the locals. "At the top of Grafton Street" is about as specific as any address can get.

For starters, always ask if an address is on the "north side" or "south side" of the River Liffey. At least, you will then be in the right direction. Another helpful guide is to acclimate yourself to the various postal zones within the city. Although there are more than 20 different zones, most of the Dublin attractions, hotels, restaurants, pubs, shops, and other activities that are of greatest interest to visitors lie within six zones—Dublin 1 and 9 on the north side of the city, and Dublin 2, 4, 6, and 8 on the south side of the city. There is a map of Dublin's postal zones in the front section of all telephone books.

Be warned, however, that there is nothing to prevent two zones from having two different streets with the same name. In other words, you'll find a "Pembroke Lane" in Dublin 2, off Baggot Street, and you'll find another "Pembroke Lane," off Raglan Road near the American embassy in Dublin 4. This only underscores the fact that a general familiarity with the postal zones can be a great help.

One rule that you can depend on for further direction is the designation of streets as "Upper" or "Lower." Streets that are "Lower" are always closer to the River Liffey.

Dubliners very often give directions that are defined by local

---

IMPRESSIONS

In a little city like Dublin, one meets every person whom one knows within a few days. Around each bend in the road there is a friend . . .
—JAMES STEPHENS (1882–1950), *THE CHARWOMAN'S DAUGHTER*

landmarks or major sights, such as "beside Trinity College" or "just off St. Stephen's Green."

Simply put, there is no dependable way to find an address in Dublin without a map.

Street Maps   With Dublin streets such a hodgepodge, a good map is essential. There are many fine maps on sale at all leading bookshops (see "Shopping A to Z" in Chapter 8).

One of the handiest maps for downtown Dublin is a pocket-size foldout laminated edition published by ERA Maptec of Dublin Ltd. It not only has a good Central Dublin map, keyed to major attractions, but it also has smaller maps focusing on Old Dublin and the Trinity College/St. Stephen's Green areas. The advantages of this map are that it can be easily and inconspicuously held in the hand, and it is weatherproof. A similar compact and foldout laminated map, with an index of streets and coverage of the suburbs, is published by Bartholomew, a division of HarperCollins. Bartholomew also puts out a large foldout color map and a small book, *Dublin: Colour Street Atlas and Guide.* All of these cost about £2 to £4 ($3.30 to $6.60).

Dublin Bus, the transport operator, publishes a very helpful *Dublin Tourist Map and Guide,* keying all major points of interest on a map of the city center. It sells for 95p ($1.60) at Dublin Bus offices, tourist offices, and bookshops.

For a free map with basic points of reference, inquire at any office of Dublin Tourism or at concierge desks at hotels. Many shops and department stores also include maps of the city center as part of their free promotional brochures.

Neighborhoods in Brief

O'Connell Street   (North of the Liffey Area) Once the fashionable and historic focal point of Dublin, this area has lost a little of its charm in recent years, but is still the core of Dublin's "north side." A wide and sweeping thoroughfare, O'Connell Street is now rimmed by shops, fast-food restaurants, and movie theaters, as well as a few great landmarks like the General Post Office and the Gresham Hotel. Within walking distance of O'Connell Street are four theaters plus the Catholic Pro-Cathedral, the Moore Street open markets, the pedestrianized shopping area of Henry Street, the new Financial Services Centre, and the Central Bus Station. Most of this area lies in the **Dublin 1** postal code.

Trinity College Area   On the south side of the River Liffey, the Trinity College complex is a 42-acre center of learning and academia in the heart of the city, surrounded by fine bookstores and shops. This area lies in the **Dublin 2** postal code.

Temple Bar Area   Wedged between Trinity College and the Old City, this section has recently been spruced up and taken a new lease on life as Dublin's "Left Bank," with a bohemian atmosphere and an assortment of unique shops, art galleries, recording studios, theaters, trendy restaurants, and atmospheric pubs. This area lies in the **Dublin 2** postal code.

Old City/Historic Area   Dating back to Viking and medieval times, this cobblestoned enclave includes Dublin Castle, the city's two main cathedrals, Christ Church and St. Patrick's, and the remnants of the city's original walls. The adjacent Liberties section, just west of High Street, takes its name from the fact that the people who lived here long ago were exempt from the local jurisdiction within the city walls. Although it prospered in its early days, the Liberties hit on hard times in the 17th and 18th centuries and is only now feeling a touch of urban renewal. Highlights here range from the Guinness Brewery and Royal Hospital to the original Cornmarket area and the still-thriving secondhand Iveagh Market. Most of this area lies in the **Dublin 8** postal zone.

St. Stephen's Green/Grafton Street Area   A visitor focal point in Dublin, this district is home to some of the city's finest hotels, restaurants, and shops. There are some residential town houses near the green, but this area is primarily a business neighborhood. This area is part of the **Dublin 2** postal zone.

Fitzwilliam and Merrion Squares Area   These two little square parks are surrounded by fashionable brick-faced Georgian town houses, each with its own distinctive and colorful doorway. Some of Dublin's most famous citizens once resided here, although today many of the houses have been turned into offices for doctors, lawyers, and other professionals. This area is part of the **Dublin 2** zone.

Ballsbridge/Embassy Row Area   Situated south of the Grand Canal, this is Dublin's most prestigious suburb, yet it is within walking distance of downtown. Although primarily a residential area, it is also the home of some of the city's leading hotels, restaurants, and the embassies of Argentina, Austria, Belgium, China, Egypt, France, Britain, Italy, Japan, Korea, Netherlands, Poland, Spain, Switzerland, Turkey, and the United States. This area is part of the **Dublin 4** zone.

Suburbs—South   Stretching southward from Ballsbridge, these towns, such as Dun Laoghaire, Dalkey, and Killiney, are on the edge of Dublin Bay. Thanks to the DART rapid transit service, they are very accessible to downtown Dublin, so they are prime residential areas and also have a fine selection of hotels and restaurants. Most of these towns are identified by name and not by postal zone.

Suburbs—North   Situated between the city center and the airport, the residential suburbs of Drumcondra and Glasnevin are close to the Botanic Gardens and offer many good lodgings en route to and from the airport. Further north, the picturesque suburb of Howth is synonymous with panoramic views of Dublin Bay, beautiful hillside gardens, and many fine seafood restaurants. Most of this area falls into the **Dublin 9** zone, although Howth and Malahide usually are not identified by postal zone.

2. GETTING AROUND

PUBLIC TRANSPORTATION

BY BUS   Dublin Bus operates a fleet of green double-decker buses throughout the city and its suburbs. Most buses originate on or near

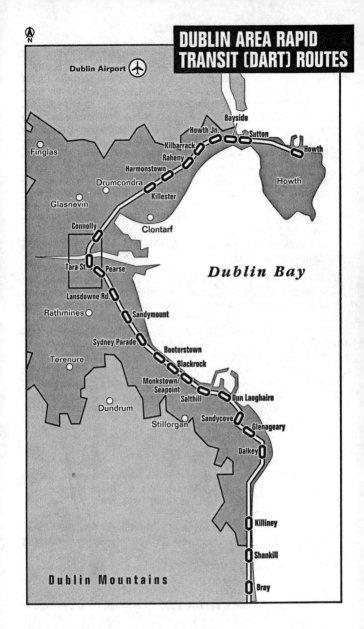

O'Connell Street, Abbey Street, and Eden Quay on the north side; and from Aston Quay, College Street, or Fleet Street on the south side. Bus stops are located every 2 or 3 blocks. Destinations and bus numbers are posted above the front windows; buses destined for the city center are marked with the Gaelic words "An Lar."

Bus service is daily throughout the city, starting at 7am (on Sunday, at 10am), with the last bus runs at 11:30pm. Frequency of service ranges from every 10 to 15 minutes for most runs, but schedules are posted on revolving notice boards at each bus stop.

For nightclubbers and disco fans, on Friday and Saturday nights there is a late express bus service from midcity (departing only from College, D'Olier, and Westmoreland Streets) out into the suburbs. Known as Nitelink, this service operates hourly from midnight to 3am and is worth considering if you are staying in any of the hotels/guesthouses in suburbs such as Ballsbridge, Dun Laoghaire, Donnybrook, Drumcondra, or Glasnevin.

Fares are calculated on distances traveled; you don't need to know what your fare will be to board—just name your destination and the driver/conductor will tell you the required amount and make the necessary change for you, although exact change is appreciated. Minimum fare is 55p (90¢); maximum fare is Ł1.10 ($1.80). Nitelink fare is a flat Ł2 ($3.30).

For more information, contact Dublin Bus, 59 Upper O'Connell St., Dublin 1 (tel. 734222).

BY DART   Although Dublin has no subway in the strict sense, there is an electrified train rapid transit system, known as DART (Dublin Area Rapid Transit). It travels mostly at ground level or on elevated tracks, linking the city center with the residential suburb of Ballsbridge, and seaside the communities of Howth on the north side and Dalkey and Dun Laoghaire to the south.

Service is swift and clean, operating every 15 minutes (and every 5 minutes during rush hours), from approximately 7am to midnight, Monday through Saturday, and from 9:30am to 11pm on Sunday. Minimum fare is approximately 55p (90¢).

Well-signposted DART boarding points are located throughout the city and its suburbs. For further information, contact DART, 35 Lower Abbey St., Dublin 1 (tel. 366222).

Discount Passes

Dublin Bus offers a variety of money-saving travel passes for people who are making frequent use of public transport including the following:

* **One-Day Bus/Rail Tickets** Unlimited travel for one person, Ł2.80 ($4.65) for bus only; Ł4 ($6.60) for combined bus and DART.
* **One-Day Family Bus/Rail Ticket** Valid for two adults and up to four children under age 16 for unlimited travel, Ł5 ($8.25) for bus only; Ł5.50 ($9) for combined bus and DART.
* **Four-Day Explorer Ticket** Valid for unlimited use by an adult traveling 4 consecutive days on Dublin bus and DART rail services, from 9:45am Monday through Friday with no restrictions on weekends, Ł10 ($16.50).
* **Weekly Bus/Rail Tickets** Valid for 7 days of unlimited travel by an adult, commencing Sunday; photo ID required; Ł10.50 ($17.35) for bus only; Ł14 ($23) for combined bus and DART.

Tickets can be purchased from Dublin Bus, 59 Upper O'Connell

St., Dublin 1 (tel. 734222), or from more than 180 bus-ticket agents throughout Dublin, including many newspaper stores.

BY TAXI It is the custom in Dublin to get a taxi by going to one of several centrally located ranks—taxi depots where available taxis line up as they wait for passengers. You'll find these taxi ranks outside all of the leading hotels, at bus and train stations, and on prime thoroughfares. Ranks are also located on Upper O'Connell Street, at College Green, and along the north side of St. Stephen's Green.

Rates are fixed by law and posted in each taxi. Minimum fare for one passenger within the city is £1.80 ($3) for any distance not exceeding 1 mile or 9 minutes; after that, it's 10p (15¢) for each additional ⅖s of a mile or 1.2 minutes. There are extra charges set as follows: 40p (65¢) for each additional passenger; 40p (65¢) for each piece of luggage; 40p (65¢) for hiring before 8am or after 8pm and all day Sunday; 80p ($1.35) for hiring at Dublin airport; and from 60p ($1) to 80p ($1.35) for certain holidays; waiting time is £5 ($8.25) per hour. These fares are valid within a 10-mile radius of the city center; fares outside of this area are "by negotiation" with the driver. All rates are subject to change in 1993–94.

You can also phone and request a cab from a specific taxi company. Among the leading companies that operate a 24-hour radio-call service are: **All Fives Taxi** (tel. 555555 and 557777); **Access Taxis** (tel. 683333); **Blue Cabs** (tel. 761111); **Co-op Taxis** (tel. 766666); **Metro Cabs** (tel. 683333); and **National Radio Cabs** (tel. 772222). For other names, look in the Golden Pages of the telephone book under "Taxicabs." The extra charge for a ride initiated by a phone request is 75p ($1.25) per mile or a maximum of £1.15 ($1.90) to the pickup point.

BY CAR Rentals All major international car-rental firms are represented in Dublin, as are many Irish-based companies, with desks at the airport and/or full-service offices downtown.

To arrange a rental, all you need is a valid driver's license from your country of residence; some companies enforce age restrictions, renting only to those over 23 or 25 years of age and under 70 or 75 years of age.

Renting a car can be expensive, especially in the peak months of July and August. Depending on the season, rates average £40 to £60 ($66 to $99) per day for a small subcompact standard shift car to £125 to £150 ($206 to $247) for a large automatic car. Most weekly rates range from £200 to £700 ($330 to $1,155), depending on the size of the car, the season, and if it is standard shift or automatic.

Car-rental rates quoted by most companies may include 10% government tax (VAT), but do not include CDW (collision damage waiver) insurance or gas. Gasoline, referred to as petrol by the Irish, is sold by the liter, with 1 liter to .26 gallon. Costs average 68p ($1.15) per liter of unleaded petrol or £2.72 ($4.55) for 1 gallon; and 70p ($1.15) per liter of regular petrol or £2.80 ($4.65) for an imperial gallon.

Unless you are going to be doing a lot of driving from Dublin to neighboring counties, it is not logistically or economically advisable to rent a car. In fact, getting around the city center and its environs is much easier without a car.

International firms represented in Dublin include:

- **Avis/Johnson & Perrott** (tel. toll free 800/331-1084 in the U.S.), with offices at 1 Hanover St. East, Dublin 1, (tel. 01/774010), and Dublin airport (tel. 01/370204).
- **Budget** (tel. toll free 800/472-3325 in the U.S.), at Dublin airport (tel. 01/370919).
- **Hertz** (tel. toll free 800/654-3001 in the U.S.), Upper Leeson Street, Dublin 4 (tel. 01/602255) and at Dublin airport (tel. 01/429333).
- **National/Murray's Europcar** (tel. toll free 800/CAR-EUROPE in the U.S.), Baggot Street Bridge, Dublin 4 (tel. 01/681777), and at Dublin airport (tel. 01/378179).
- **Thrifty** (tel. toll free 800/367-2277 in the U.S.) at Dublin airport (tel. 01/425199).

The leader among the Irish-based firms is **Dan Dooley Rent-a-Car** (tel. toll free 800/331-9301 in the U.S.), 42/43 Westland Row, Dublin 2 (tel. 01/772723) and at Dublin airport (tel. 01/428355).

Parking During normal business hours, free parking on Dublin streets is limited, and marked accordingly by signs. Never park in bus lanes or along a curb with double yellow lines. Fines for parking illegally are £10 to £15 ($16.50 to $24.75); if a car is towed away, it costs £150 ($248) to retrieve it.

If driving is a necessity, you can normally find some metered parking in midtown areas such as St. Stephen's Green and Baggot Street; rates range from 20p to 50p (35¢ to 85¢) per hour. Certain parking areas require drivers to display a parking disc (on sale at most shops for 20p, or 35¢, per hour) in the front window of a car.

The most reliable and safe places to park are at surface parking lots or in multistory car parks in central locations such as Kildare Street, Lower Abbey Street, and Marlborough Street. Parking lots usually charge 50p (85¢) per hour, up to 4 hours, with a maximum of £4.50 ($7.45) for all day. Multistory car parks charge from 60p to 80p ($1 to $1.35) per hour, with a maximum of £3.50 to £8 ($5.80 to $13.20) for 24 hours, depending on location. Evening charges from 6pm to midnight average £2 ($3.30) for the entire period.

Driving Rules The most important rule to remember is that traffic keeps to the left-hand side of the road; and passing is done from the right. Do not drive in bus lanes.

The speed limit within the city is 30 m.p.h. and seat belts must be worn at all times by driver and passenger(s). Pedestrians have the right of way at specially marked zebra-striped crossings; as a warning, there are usually two flashing lights at these intersections.

Ireland has a strict law against drinking while "under the influence." Do not drink and drive.

BY BICYCLE The steady flow of Dublin traffic rushing down one-way streets may be a little intimidating for most bicyclists, but there are many opportunities for more relaxed pedaling in residential areas and suburbs, along the seafront, and around Phoenix Park. The Dublin Tourism office can supply you with bicycle-touring information and suggested routes.

Daily rental charges average Ł7 ($11.55) per day or Ł30 ($50) per week. In the downtown area, bicycles can be rented from the **Bike Store,** 58 Lower Gardiner St., Dublin 1 (tel. 725931); **C. Harding for Bikes,** 30 Bachelor's Walk, Dublin 1 (tel. 732455; and **Mr. Bike Ltd.,** 57 Upper Dorset St., Dublin 1 (tel. 745212).

FAST FACTS: DUBLIN

Airport See "Orientation" in this chapter.

American Express The American Express office is centrally located opposite Trinity College, just off College Green, at 116 Grafton St., Dublin 2 (tel. 01/772874). The office changes money, sells traveler's checks, operates a travel agency, and accepts mail for clients. Hours for most services are Monday through Friday 9am to 5pm, Saturday 9am to noon; the foreign exchange operates Monday through Saturday 9am to 5pm and Sunday from 11am to 4pm. In an emergency, traveler's checks can be reported lost or stolen by dialing in Ireland toll free 1-800/626-0000.

Area Code The area code for telephone numbers within Dublin City and County is 01.

Babysitters With advance notice, most hotels and guesthouses will arrange for babysitting.

Bookstores See "Shopping A to Z" in Chapter 8.

Business Hours Banks are open Monday through Wednesday and Friday from 10am to 12:30pm and from 1:30pm to 3pm, Thursday from 10am to 12:30pm and from 1:30 to 5pm. Bar hours are Monday through Saturday from 10:30am to 11:30pm in the summertime, closing a half hour earlier in winter. On Sunday bars open from 12:30 to 2pm and 4 to 11pm all year. Most business offices are open from 9am to 5pm, Monday through Friday. Stores and shops are open from 9am to 5:30pm Monday through Wednesday and Friday and Saturday, and from 9am to 8pm on Thursday. Some bookshops and tourism-oriented stores also open Sunday from 11am or noon until 4 or 5pm. In the peak tourism season (May through September), many gift and souvenir shops post Sunday hours.

Car Rentals See "Getting Around" in this chapter.

Climate See "When to Go" in Chapter 2.

Currency See "Information, Entry Requirements, and Money" in Chapter 2.

Currency Exchanges A currency exchange service in Ireland is signposted as a "bureau de change." There are bureaux de change at all banks and at many branches of the Irish Post Office system, known as "An Post." A bureau de change operates daily during flight arrival and departure times at Dublin airport; a foreign currency note exchanger machine also is available on a 24-hour basis in the main Arrivals Hall. In addition, many hotels and travel agencies offer bureau de change services, although the best rate of exchange is usually given at banks.

Dentist For dental emergencies, contact the Irish Dental Council, 57 Merrion Sq., Dublin 2 (tel. 762226 or 762069), for a recommendation. You can also look under "Dental Surgeons" in the Golden Pages of the telephone book. A while-you-wait denture-repair service is operated by McDonagh Bros., 106 Marlborough St., Dublin 1 (tel. 729721).

Doctor In an emergency, most hotels and guesthouses will contact a house doctor for you. You can also ask for a recommendation from the Irish Medical Organization, 10 Fitzwilliam Place, Dublin 2 (tel. 7627273), or consult the Golden Pages of the telephone book under "Doctors–Medical."

Documents Required See "Information, Entry Requirements, and Money" in Chapter 2.

Driving Rules See "Getting Around" in this chapter.

Drugstores In Ireland, drugstores are called chemists shops or pharmacies. Centrally located drugstores include Crowley's Pharmacy at 25 Nassau St., Dublin 2 (tel. 679-6262), and 6 Lower Baggot St., Dublin 2 (tel. 785612); Hamilton Long and Co., 5 Lower O'Connell St., Dublin 1 (tel. 743352); and O'Connell's Pharmacy, 6 Henry St., Dublin 1 (tel. 731077) and 55 Lower O'Connell St., Dublin 1 (tel. 730427). Additional suggestions are given under "Chemists–Pharmaceutical" in the Golden Pages of the telephone book.

Electricity The standard electrical current in Ireland is 220 volts AC (50 cycles). Hotels usually have 220/110 volt sockets for shavers; 110 voltage is suitable only for use of electric shavers. Some shavers and hairdryers have a built-in transformer that can be set for 220 volts or 110 volts. To use small appliances, a plug adaptor may be needed too, to fit Ireland's three-pin flat or two-pin round wall sockets. If required, small transformers and adaptors should be purchased before departure to Dublin.

Embassies/Consulates The American embassy is located at 42 Elgin Rd., Ballsbridge, Dublin 4 (tel. 01/688777); Canadian embassy, 65/68 St. Stephen's Green, Dublin 2 (tel. 01/781988); British embassy, 33 Merrion Rd., Dublin 4 (tel. 01/695211); Australian embassy, Fitzwilton House, Wilton Terrace, Dublin 2 (tel. 01/761517).

Emergencies In Dublin, for police, fire, or other emergencies, dial **999**.

Etiquette Dubliners still observe chivalrous practices, such as males holding doors for females and younger folk giving up a seat on a bus for a senior citizen. The Irish are inquisitive and will try to draw you into conversation; be polite and soft-spoken and you will fit right in. Avoid discussions of religion or politics, especially criticisms of Irish religious practices or politics in Northern Ireland. Common courtesies prevail; never use a demanding or demeaning tone of voice, avoid "pushiness," and always stand in line or a "queue" patiently.

Eyeglasses For 1-hour service on glasses or contact lenses, try Specsavers, Unit 9, GPO Arcade, Henry Street, Dublin 1 (tel. 728155) or look in the Golden Pages of the telephone book under "Opticians–Ophthalmic."

Hairdressers/Barbers The leading hairstyling names for

women and men are Peter Mark, with more than two dozen locations throughout Dublin and its suburbs, including 74 Grafton St., Dublin 2 (tel. 714399) and 11A Upper O'Connell St., Dublin 1 (tel. 745589); and John Adam, with shops at 13A Merrion Row, Dublin 2 (tel. 610354), 112A Baggot St., Dublin 2 (tel. 611952), and 39 Capel St., Dublin 1 (tel. 730081). Also consult the Golden Pages under "Hairdressers–Ladies" and "Hairdressers–Men."

Holidays See "When to Go" in Chapter 2.

Hospitals For emergency care, two of the most modern health care facilities are St. Vincent's Hospital, Elm Park, Dublin 4 (tel. 269-4533), on the south side of the city; and Beaumont Hospital, Beaumont, Dublin 9 (tel. 379964), on the north side.

Hotlines In Ireland, hotlines are called "helplines." Some examples are for emergencies, police, or fire, dial **999;** Rape Crisis Centre (tel. 614911); Samaritans (tel. 727700); Alcoholics Anonymous (tel. 538998); and Narcotics Anonymous (tel. 300944).

Information For information on finding a telephone number, dial 1190; for visitor information, see "Information, Entry Requirements, and Money" in Chapter 2.

Language See "Language" in Chapter 1.

Laundry/Dry Cleaning Most hotels provide same-day or next-day laundry and/or dry cleaning services. If you wish to make your own arrangements, two centrally located choices are Craft Cleaners, 12 Upper Baggot St., Dublin 2 (tel. 688198), and Grafton Cleaners, 32 S. William St., Dublin 2 (tel. 679-4409). More are listed under "Dry Cleaners" in the Golden Pages of the telephone book.

Libraries For research materials and periodicals, try the National Library of Ireland, Kildare Street, Dublin 2 (tel. 765521); Dublin's Central Library, ILAC Centre, Henry St., Dublin 1 (tel. 734333); the Central Catholic Library, 74 Merrion Sq., Dublin 2 (tel. 761264); or the City Archives, City Hall, Dame Street, Dublin 2 (tel. 679-6111). To view rare books, visit Trinity College Library, College Green, Dublin 2 (tel. 772941); Marsh's Library, St. Patrick's Close (off Upper Kevin Street), Dublin 8 (tel. 543511); and the Chester Beatty Library, 20 Shrewsbury Rd., Ballsbridge, Dublin 4 (tel. 269-2386).

Liquor Laws Individuals must be age 18 or over to be served alcoholic beverages in Ireland. Ireland has very strict laws and penalties regarding driving while intoxicated, so don't drink and drive. Bars, known as pubs or public houses, are open in the summertime from 10:30am to 11:30pm, closing a half hour earlier in winter. On Sunday bars are open from 12:30 to 2pm and 4 to 11pm all year. Restaurants with liquor licenses are permitted to serve alcohol during normal opening hours for meals. Hotels and guest-houses with licenses can serve during normal hours to the general public; overnight guests, referred to as residents, can be served after closing hours. Alcoholic beverages by the bottle can be purchased at liquor stores, pubs displaying "off-license" signs, and at some supermarkets.

Lost Property Most hotels have a lost property service, usually under the aegis of the housekeeping department. For items lost in public places, contact the police (known as garda) headquarters, Harcourt Square, Dublin 2 (tel. 732222).

Luggage Storage/Lockers There are no lockers at

Dublin airport or at train stations for security reasons, but most hotels and guesthouses will check and store luggage for you, as a courtesy if you have been a guest, under the supervision of the concierge. Some hostels, such as Avalon House and Kinlay House, do provide lockers for guests.

Mail In Ireland, mail boxes are cylindrical in shape and are painted green with the word "post" on top. For airmail service to the U.S., it costs 52p (85¢) for a letter and 38p (65¢) for a postcard. It takes about 5 days to a week for delivery. The best way to receive mail while in Dublin is to have it sent c/o your hotel or guesthouse. Otherwise, you can have mail sent to the main post office—this service is called poste restante, and should be addressed to your name, c/o GPO Counter, General Post Office, Dublin 1. All poste restante mail—which can be collected within normal opening hours—will be held for 2 weeks, then returned to sender if unclaimed. There is no charge for this service, which can be used for up to 3 months.

Maps See "Street Maps," above, in this chapter.

Money See "Information, Entry Requirements, and Money" in Chapter 2.

Newspapers/Magazines Dubliners devour newspapers. The three morning Irish dailies, all published in Dublin, are the *Irish Times* (not published on Sunday), *Irish Independent,* and *Irish Press.* In the afternoon, two tabloids—*Evening Herald* and *Evening Press*—hit the stands. In addition, the *International Herald Tribune* is on sale at many newsstands and in major hotels. Newspapers from other European capitals can also be purchased at Eason & Son, 40 Lower O'Connell St., Dublin 1. The leading magazine for upcoming events and happenings is *In Dublin,* published every 2 weeks.

Photographic Needs For photographic equipment, supplies, and repairs, visit Dublin Camera Exchange, 9B Trinity St., Dublin 2 (tel. 679-3410), Camera Exchange, 63 S. Great George's St., Dublin 2 (tel. 784125); and City Cameras, 23A Dawson St., Dublin 2 (tel. 762891). For fast developing, try the Camera Centre, 56 Grafton St., Dublin 2 (tel. 775594), or One Hour Photo, 5 St. Stephen's Green, Dublin 2 (tel. 718578), 110 Grafton St., Dublin 2 (tel. 774472), and at the ILAC Centre, Henry Street, Dublin 1 (tel. 728824).

Police A law enforcement officer in Ireland is called a Garda Siochana (Guardian of the Peace); in the plural, it's Gardai (pronounced *gar*-dee) or simply referred to as "Guards." Dial **999** in an emergency. Except for special detachments, Irish police are unarmed and wear dark blue uniforms.

Post Office The main post office, called the General Post Office (GPO), is located on O'Connell Street, Dublin 1 (tel. 728888). Hours are Monday through Saturday 8am to 8pm, Sunday and holidays 10:30am to 6pm. Branch offices, identified by a sign, "Oifig An Post/Post Office," are open Monday through Saturday only, 8am to 5:30pm or 6pm.

Radio/TV RTE (Radio Telefis Eireann) is the national broadcasting authority and controls two TV channels—RTE 1 and Network 2; three radio stations—RTE 1, 2FM, and Radio na Gaeltachta (all Irish-language programming). Besides RTE programming, there are other smaller local stations. By 1993, it is expected that a third television channel, TV 3, will commence broadcasting as an independent station. In addition, television programs from Britain's BBC-TV (British Broadcasting Corporation) and ITN-TV (Independent) can be picked up by most receivers in the Dublin area. BBC Radio 1, 2, and 3 can also be heard in the area. Satellite programs, via CNN, SKY News, and other international operators, are also fed into the Dublin area.

Religious Services Although Ireland is a predominantly Catholic country, many other beliefs are represented in Dublin. Lists of services are usually available from any hotel concierge or in Saturday's *Irish Times*. Some centrally located houses of worship include: Roman Catholic—St. Mary's Pro-Cathedral, Marlborough Street, Dublin 1 (tel. 745441), and St. Teresa's Carmelite Church, Clarendon Street, off Grafton Street, Dublin 2 (tel. 718466); Church of Ireland/Episcopal/Anglican—St. Patrick's Cathedral, Patrick Street, Dublin 8 (tel. 754817), and Christ Church Cathedral, Christ Church Place, Dublin 8, (tel. 778099); Baptist—Grace Baptist Church, 28A Pearse St., Dublin 2 (tel. 962857); Christian Science—First Church of Christ Scientist, 21 Herbert Park, Dublin 4 (tel. 683695); Lutheran—St. Finian's, 23 Adelaide Rd., Dublin 2 (tel. 766548); Methodist—Abbey Street Church, Lower Abbey Street, Dublin 1 (tel. 742123); Presbyterian—Abbey Church, Lower Abbey Street, Dublin 1 (tel. 742810); Jewish—Dublin Hebrew Congregation, 37 Adelaide Rd., Dublin 2 (tel. 761734).

Restrooms Public restrooms are usually called toilets or are marked with international symbols, but some of the older ones still carry the Gaelic words *Fir* (men) and *Mna* (women). The newest and best-kept restrooms are found at shopping complexes and at multistory car parks—and cost 10p (15¢) to enter. In addition, free use of restrooms is available to customers of sightseeing attractions, museums, hotels, restaurants, pubs, shops, theaters, and department stores. Gas stations normally do not have public toilets.

Safety Although Ireland enjoys a relatively low-crime rate with little physical violence, Dublin is a major city and normal precautions should prevail. In recent years, the city has been prey for pickpockets, purse snatchers, car thieves, and drug traffickers. To alert visitors to potential dangers, the Garda Siochana (police) department publishes a small leaflet, *A Short Guide to Tourist Safety*, available at tourist offices and other public places. The booklet advises you not to carry large amounts of money or important documents like your passport or airline tickets when strolling around the city (leave them in a safety-deposit box at your hotel). Do not leave rented cars, cameras, binoculars, or other expensive equipment unattended or unlocked. Be alert and aware of your surroundings, and do not wander in lonely areas alone at night.

Shoe Repairs Two reliable shops in midcity are O'Connell's Shoe Repair, 3 Upper Baggot St., Dublin 2 (no phone), and Rapid Shoe Repair, Sackville Place, off Lower O'Connell St., Dublin 1 (no phone).

Taxes As in many European countries, sales tax is called VAT (value-added tax) and is often included in the price quoted to you and on price tags. VAT rates vary—for hotel and restaurant bills, it is 12.5%; for car rentals, 10%; for souvenirs and gifts, 10% to 21%.

Happily, there's no tax on books or children's clothing. VAT charged on services such as hotel stays, meals, car rentals, and entertainment, cannot be refunded to visitors, but the VAT charged on products such as souvenirs is refundable to visitors. For full details on VAT refunds for purchases, consult "The Shopping Scene" in Chapter 8.

Taxis See "Getting Around" in this chapter.

Telephone/Telex/Fax In recent years, the telephone system in Ireland (Telecom Eireann) has been dramatically updated and modernized, bringing it up to world-class efficiency. All hotels and most guesthouses have individual direct-dial telephones in each guest room, making communications within Ireland and beyond as simple as dialing or touching a few numbers. The dial tone is a long uninterrupted ring; the ringing sound is a short series of two-beat rings, and the busy signal (called an engaged tone) is a series of long one-beat rings.

For information (directory inquiries), dial 1190. For operated-assisted and collect international calls (except Britain), dial the prefix 114 first (to Britain, dial 10 first), then the area code and number. For direct-dial calls to the U.S., dial the international access code (00), then the country code (1), followed by area code and number.

Local calls cost 20p (33¢) for the first 5 minutes, 16p (26¢) for each additional 5 minutes or portion thereof.

Making a call from a public phone has become easier in the last few years, thanks to the installation of Cardphones throughout the city. With a Cardphone, you insert a prepaid computerized card instead of coins to make a call for local, national, and international calls. Callcards can be purchased at Telecom Eireann offices, post offices, and many retail outlets such as newsstands. Each callcard entitles the holder to a specific number of call units: a 10-unit card costs Ł2 ($3.30); 20 units, Ł3.50 ($5.80); 50 units, Ł7.50 ($12.40); and 100 units, Ł15 ($24.75). If you intend to make calls from public phone booths, these cards are well worth buying.

The Dublin area (01 area code) has its own telephone directory and a separate Golden Pages classified directory. Both books offer extremely helpful information in the opening pages. Most hotels and guesthouses have telex and/or fax machines and allow guests to use them for a small charge. Otherwise, post offices or Telecom Eireann offices will transmit such messages and telegrams for a fee.

Telephone Number Advisory Dublin telephone numbers are currently in a state of transition, from six digits to seven digits. By 1994, all numbers will be expanded to seven digits. Although we have endeavored to present the most up-to-date numbers on our pages, many numbers will be changing after presstime; if you dial a number and it has changed, a recording should advise you of the new number. However, if you have any difficulty, you can dial toll free 1/800-330-330 to check on the status of a number.

Time Ireland follows Greenwich mean time (1 hour earlier than central European time) from November through March; and British standard time (the same as central European time) from April through October. This means that Ireland is five time zones earlier than the eastern U.S. (when it is noon in New York, it is 5pm in Ireland).

Tipping   Most hotels and guesthouses add a service charge to the bill, usually 12.5% to 15%, although some smaller places add only 10% or nothing at all. This amount is collected on behalf of those who provide services, such as porters, housekeepers, and other behind-the-scenes staff. Always check to see what amount, if any, has been added to your bill. If it is 12.5% to 15%, you may feel that is sufficient and there is no need for further gratuities. However, if a lesser amount has been added or if staff members have provided exceptional service, then it is appropriate to give additional cash gratuities. For restaurants, the policy is usually printed on the menu—either a gratuity of 10% to 15% is added to your bill, or, in some cases, no service charge is added, leaving it up to you. Always ask if you are in doubt. If nothing has been added, then tip as you would in the U.S.—an average of 15% according to the service provided. If a gratuity of 15% has been added, you may feel that is sufficient, and if only 10% to 12.5% has been added, then you may want to leave an additional 2.5% to 5% in change. For porters or bellmen, tip 50p to £1 (85¢ to $1.65) per piece of luggage. For taxi drivers, hairdressers, and other providers of service, tip as you would at home, an average of 10% to 15%, with a minimum tip of 50p (85¢). As a rule, bar staff do not expect a tip, except if table service is provided.

Transit Info   Phone 734222, Monday through Saturday, from 9am to 7pm.

Water   Tap water in Dublin is considered safe to drink. If you prefer bottled water, it is readily available at all hotels, guesthouses, restaurants, and pubs.

Weather   Phone 842-5555.

Yellow Pages   The classified section of the Dublin telephone book is called the Golden Pages.

3. NETWORKS & RESOURCES

FOR STUDENTS   Located in the heart of the city, **Trinity College,** College Green, Dublin 2 (tel. 772941), is a focal point for students of all ages and all nationalities. Everyone is welcome to walk through the open gates and archways onto the cobbled quadrangle, stroll from building to building, or consult the bulletin boards for open activities. Other universities in the Dublin area include **University College–Dublin,** Belfield, Dublin 4 (tel. 269-3244), and **Dublin City University,** Glasnevin, Dublin 9 (tel. 704-5000).

Information for the student community of Dublin is also posted at the office of the **Union of Students in Ireland/Irish Student Travel Service** (USIT), 19 Aston Quay, Dublin 2 (tel. 679-8833).

FOR GAY MEN & LESBIANS   Information on meetings and

social activities is often listed in such publications as *Hot Press* and *In Dublin* magazine, available at all newsstands. In addition, the following organizations are helpful:

Gay Switchboard, Carmichael House, North Brunswick Street, Dublin 7 (tel. 721055), offers nondirective counseling, support, and information.

Reach (tel. 961843) is a phone support group for Christian gay people.

Lesbian Line, 64 Lower Mount St., Dublin 2 (tel. 613777), operates a nondirective listening line for women and organizes discussion groups.

FOR WOMEN Among the organizations to contact are: **Dublin Well Woman Centre,** 73 Lower Leeson St., Dublin 2 (tel. 610083 or 610086), a professional health care center for women; and **Rape Crisis Centre,** 70 Lower Leeson St., Dublin 2 (tel. 614911), which operates a 24-hour helpline and support services.

DUBLIN ACCOMMODATIONS

From legendary old-world landmarks like the Shelbourne and Gresham to sleek glass-and-concrete high-rises such as Jurys and the Westbury, Dublin offers a contrasting variety of places to stay, priced to suit every budget.

All hotel accommodations in Dublin and throughout Ireland are inspected, registered, and graded into categories (A* is the highest rating, followed by A, B*, B, and C) by the Irish Tourist Board, a government agency. Surprisingly, for a capital city, Dublin only has about 50 registered hotels, about half of which fall into the A* (deluxe) or A (first-class) category. This rather limited supply of hotels, however, is supplemented by a fine array of smaller inns, classified as guesthouses, many of which are in the A grade.

Hotels, as a rule, offer full services, restaurants, coffee shops, bars, lounges, shops, currency exchanges, concierge desks, and more, while guesthouses provide more limited facilities—they may serve only breakfast, may or may not have a bar license or a wine license, and often do not have elevators (because of the historic nature of their structures). The Irish Tourist Board publishes a list of all registered and inspected premises in every category, with a summary of services and minimum/maximum charges.

The lodgings described on the following pages are the places that we consider to offer the best facilities and value. Unless otherwise noted, they offer all rooms with private bath or shower. All are centrally heated, although the majority do not have air conditioning, since Dublin has a fairly equable climate and air conditioning is a feature of only the newest properties. Almost all of these lodgings provide car parking for customers, whether in secure garages or adjacent parking lots. This service is free for overnight guests.

RATES All room charges quoted include 12.5% government tax (VAT), but do not include service charge, usually between 10% and 15%, with the majority of hotels adding 12.5%. These rates are in effect at presstime, but will probably increase slightly in 1993–94. Some hotels also charge slightly higher prices during special events, such as the Dublin Horse Show. For the best deals, try to reserve a room in Dublin over a weekend, and ask if there is a reduction or a weekend package in effect. Some hotels cut their rates by as much as 50% on Friday and Saturday nights, when business traffic is low.

Rates shown are for room only, unless otherwise indicated. Although the price of a fully cooked breakfast is also specified for most premises, continental breakfasts (juice, baked goods, and tea or coffee) are always available, at about half the price of a full breakfast.

We have classified hotels and guesthouses into categories of location and price. The price levels are an indication of what it costs for a double room for two people per night including tax but not service charge.

> Very Expensive—Ł150 and up ($250 and up)
> Expensive   —Ł120 to Ł150 ($200 to $250)
> Moderate   —Ł60 to Ł120 ($100 to $200)
> Inexpensive   —Ł30 to Ł60 ($50 to $100)
> Budget   —Under Ł30 ($50)

RESERVATIONS   Reservations for most of the hotels can be made through toll-free 800 numbers in the United States. For those properties that do not have a U.S. reservation number, the fastest way to reserve is by telephone or fax. Fax is preferable since you then have a printed confirmation. You can then follow up by sending a deposit check (usually the equivalent of one night's room rate) or giving your credit-card number.

If you arrive in Dublin without a reservation, the staff at the Dublin Tourism offices will gladly find you a room via a computerized reservation service known as Gulliver.

BED-&-BREAKFAST HOMES   In addition to hotels and guest-houses, Dublin has hundreds of private homes that rent rooms to visitors on a nightly basis. Usually referred to as "bed and break-fasts," these homes are also inspected and registered by the Irish Tourist Board, but are not graded. The number of rooms available at each house varies, but it is usually three to five, which may or may not have a private bath or shower.

Because the facilities offered vary greatly from house to house, the Irish Tourist Board publishes an up-to-date list, indicating the time of year that rooms are available, the number of rooms in each house (and the number with private facilities), the rates, and other pertinent information. These houses can be booked through any tourist office in Dublin or Ireland or by phoning or writing to individual owners. Nightly per person rates average Ł14 to Ł17 ($23 to $28) with private bath and Ł11 to Ł13 ($18 to $21) without private bath. These rates include a full Irish breakfast and there is no service charge. For a list of homes available in advance of your visit, contact the Irish Tourist Board (see "Sources of Information" in Chapter 2).

A FEW TIPS   Many older Dublin hotels and guesthouses consider the lobby level as the ground floor (not the first floor); the first floor is the next floor up or what Americans would call the second floor. So, if your room is on the first floor, that means it is one flight up.

Elevators, readily available in hotels but not so plentiful in guesthouses, are called lifts. Remember to press "G" for the main floor or lobby, not "1."

Concierges or hall porters, as they are sometimes called, are the equivalent of bell captains in the United States—they arrange all types of services from taking luggage or delivering packages to your room, to obtaining theater tickets, booking a self-drive or chauffeur-driven car, selling postage stamps and mailing letters and cards, dispensing tourist literature, or reserving taxis. Many of Dublin's concierges consider their craft a real art form and are members of the prestigious international organization known as Les Clefs d'Or. Be prepared to be pampered!

1. HISTORIC OLD CITY/ LIBERTIES

INEXPENSIVE

JURYS CHRISTCHURCH INN, Christchurch Place, Dublin 8. Tel. 01/475-0111, or toll free 800/843-6664 in the U.S. Fax 01/475-0488. 172 rms. A/C TV TEL **Bus:** No. 21A, 50, 50A, 78, 78A, or 78B.

$ Rates: Ł42–Ł50 ($69–$82.50) per room. Service charge 12.5%. Breakfast extra. AE, CB, DC, MC, V.

Slated to open in May of 1993, this Ł7 ($11.5) million development is a first for the city's historic district, an area heretofore without lodgings of an international standard. It is a brand-new purpose-built four-story hotel, designed in keeping with the area's Georgian/Victorian architecture and heritage, situated across from Christ Church Cathedral and adjacent to the Lord Edward restaurant. Although it is a sister hotel to the deluxe Jurys in Ballsbridge, this new inn is geared to the cost-conscious traveler, without frills but with emphasis on quality accommodations—fully fitted bedrooms, all with private bath and contemporary furnishings. Each room can sleep at least three people. Facilities include a moderately priced restaurant, pub lounge, and a multistory car park.

BUDGET

KINLAY HOUSE, 2-12 Lord Edward St., Dublin 8. Tel. 01/679-6644. Fax 01/679-7437. Telex 91797. 37 rms (17 with bath). **Bus:** No. 49, 50, 54, 65, or 77.

$ Rates (including continental breakfast): Ł16.50–Ł17 ($27.25–$28.05) single sharing bath; Ł23–Ł24 ($37.95–$39.60) double sharing bath; Ł25–Ł26 ($41.25–$42.90) double with bath; Ł7.50–Ł10.50 ($12.40–$17.35) per person in dorm-style rooms. MC, V.

Located in a restored 1890s building adjacent to Christ Church

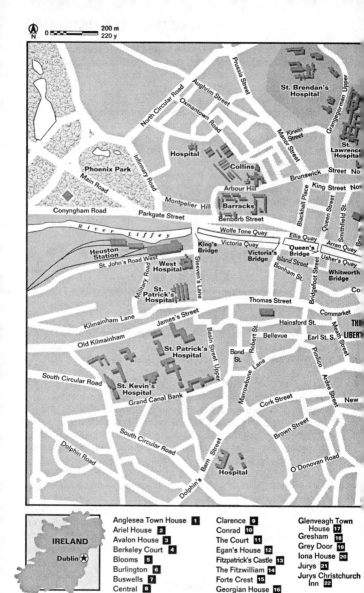

Map Legend

Anglesea Town House **1**	Clarence **9**	Glenveagh Town House **17**
Ariel House **2**	Conrad **10**	Gresham **18**
Avalon House **3**	The Court **11**	Grey Door **19**
Berkeley Court **4**	Egan's House **12**	Iona House **20**
Blooms **5**	Fitzpatrick's Castle **13**	Jurys **21**
Burlington **6**	The Fitzwilliam **14**	Jurys Christchurch Inn **22**
Buswells **7**	Forte Crest **15**	
Central **8**	Georgian House **16**	

IRELAND

Dublin ★

Cathedral and opposite City Hall at the corner of historic Fishamble Street, this property is one of the best in the hostel category of accommodations. Ideal for students or travelers on a tight budget, it offers clean and comfortable accommodations in two-, four-, and six-bed rooms, and one 20-bed dorm. Facilities include a coffee shop, study, TV lounge, self-catering kitchen, launderette, recreation/meeting room, pay phones, bicycle hire and parking, luggage storage, lockers, bureau de change, and craft shop.

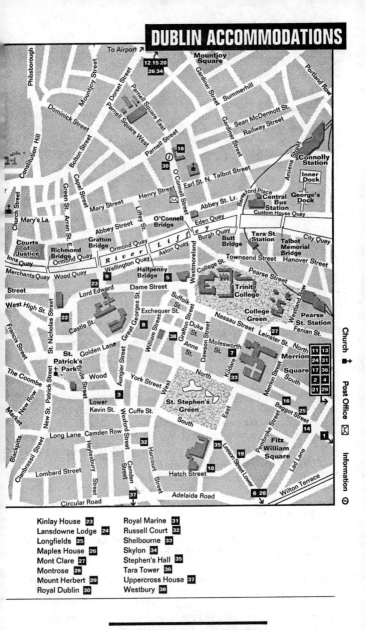

DUBLIN ACCOMMODATIONS

2. TEMPLE BAR/ TRINITY COLLEGE

MODERATE

BLOOMS, Anglesea St., Dublin 2. Tel. **01/715622.** Fax 01/715997. Telex 31688. 86 rms. TV TEL **Transportation:**

DART to Tara Street Station or bus no. 21A, 46A, 46B, 51B, 51C, 68, 69, or 86.

$ Rates: Ł80–Ł90 ($132–$148.50) single; Ł100–Ł110 ($165–$181.50) double. Service charge 12.5%. Breakfast Ł8 ($13.20) extra. AE, DC, MC, V.

Lovers of Irish literature will feel at home at Blooms. Named after Leopold Bloom, a character in James Joyce's *Ulysses,* this hotel is in the heart of Dublin, near Trinity College and in the southern edge of the artsy Temple Bar district. The bedrooms are modern and functional—if a bit smallish—with useful extras like garment presses and hairdryers, as well as electric shoe shiners and ice machines on all floors.

Dining/Entertainment: For formal dining in the continental style, reserve a table at the Trinity Room restaurant, or for more informal fare, try Yesterday's Bar, with a pubby decor of dark woods and brass. For late-night entertainment, there is the new basement-level nightclub known simply as M.

Services: Concierge, 24-hour room service, valet/laundry service.

Facilities: Enclosed private car park, meeting room, foreign currency exchange.

CENTRAL, 1-5 Exchequer St., Dublin 2. Tel. 01/679-7302.

Fax 01/679-7303. 70 rms, 2 suites. TV TEL MINIBAR

$ Rates: Ł55–Ł70 ($90.75–$115.50) single; Ł70–Ł95 ($115.50–$156.75) double; Ł150–Ł175 ($247.50–$288.75) suite. Service charge 12.5%. Breakfast Ł7.50 ($12.40) extra. AE, DC, MC, V.

Situated midway between Trinity College and Dublin Castle at the corner of Exchequer and Great George's Streets, this century-old five-story hotel was renovated and refurbished in 1991. The public areas retain a Victorian atmosphere, enhanced by an impressive collection of contemporary Irish art. The guest rooms, cheerfully decorated with colorful Irish-made furnishings, offer such extras as a trouser press, hairdryer, and coffee/tea maker.

Facilities and services include a Victorian-style dining room, two bars, concierge, and room service. There is no on-premises parking, but a public lot is nearby.

CLARENCE, 6/8 Wellington Quay, Dublin 2. Tel. 01/776178.

Fax 01/777487. 66 rms. TV TEL **Bus:** No. 51B, 51C, 68, 69, or 79.

$ Rates (including full breakfast): Ł34–Ł45 ($56–$74.25) single; Ł55–Ł69 ($90.75–$113.85) double. Service charge 15%. AE, DC, MC, V.

Picturesquely situated between the south bank of the River Liffey and the artsy Temple Bar district, this Regency-style hotel has an ideal location but has been in need of new capital for some time. As we go to press, it has been sold to an investment group that includes the four members of the Irish rock band U2. It is reported that a Ł2 ($3.3) million refurbishment program will give the property a new look and a new nightclub, while retaining the overall genteel 1930s ambience, but rates may go up accordingly. For fans of U2, this will be "the

**FROMMER'S SMART TRAVELER:
ACCOMMODATIONS**

1. Try to be in Dublin over a weekend and ask if there is a special reduced weekend rate, which can be as much as 50% off midweek rates.
2. Avoid Dublin during rugby-match weekends or special events or holidays, such as the Dublin Horse Show or Spring Show, when surcharges may apply.
3. If it is not posted, ask if the service charge is included and how much—so you avoid overtipping (or undertipping) the staff.
4. If you are staying for 3 days or more, inquire about package deals including meals, available from a tour operator/travel agent in the United States or the hotel directly. You could save 30% or more off rack rates.
5. Ask about discounts for seniors, schoolteachers, union employees, or commercial rates that some international businesses enjoy.
6. In some older hotels or guesthouses, rooms that are smaller, without a good view, or at the back of the house often cost less—ask if any are available.
7. If you are staying a week or more, ask about long-term discounts.
8. At small family-run guesthouses, ask if there is a discount for payment in cash.

place" to stay in Dublin. Current facilities include a grill room and lounge bar.

3. ST. STEPHEN'S GREEN/ GRAFTON STREET

VERY EXPENSIVE

CONRAD, Earlsfort Terrace, Dublin 2. Tel. 01/765555, or toll free 800/HILTONS in the U.S. Fax 01/765424. Telex 91872. 188 rms, 9 suites. A/C TV TEL MINIBAR **Transportation:** DART to Pearse Station or bus no. 11A, 11B, 13, or 14A.

$ Rates: Ł125 ($206.25) single; Ł150 ($247.50) double; Ł310–Ł550 ($511.50–$907.50) suite. Service charge 15%. Breakfast Ł9 ($14.85) extra. AE, CB, DC, MC, V.

A member of the international subsidiary of Hilton Hotels and one of the city's newest deluxe hotels, this modern seven-story high-rise is situated opposite the National Concert Hall and across from the southeast corner of St. Stephen's Green. In keeping with the posh standards of this chain, the spacious public areas are rich in marble, brass, contemporary art, and lots of leafy plants.

Each guest bedroom is outfitted with contemporary furnishings, dark woods, and pastel tones, with a marble bathroom, electronic safety lock, executive desk, and two or three telephone lines.

Dining/Entertainment: The Alexandra, a clubby room known for a range of gourmet continental and Irish fare (see "St. Stephen's Green/Grafton Street" in Chapter 5) has earned a following in its own right. The hotel also offers Plurabelle, a brasserie-style restaurant; the Lobby Lounge, for traditional afternoon tea or drinks with piano background music; and Alfie Byrne's, a pub named for a former lord mayor of Dublin and serving light meals.

Services: 24-hour room service, concierge, valet, shoeshine, express checkout.

Facilities: Fully equipped business center, meeting rooms, foreign currency exchange, car parking garage, hairdressing salons.

SHELBOURNE, 27 St. Stephen's Green, Dublin 2. Tel. 01/766471, or toll free 800/CALL-THF in the U.S. Fax 01/616006. Telex 93653. 164 rms. TV TEL MINIBAR **Transportation:** DART to Pearse Station or bus no. 10, 11A, 11B, 13, or 20B.

$ Rates: Ł140 ($231) single; Ł195 ($321.75) double. Service charge 15%. Breakfast Ł11.75 ($19.40) extra. AE, CB, DC, MC, V.

★ With a fanciful brick and white-trimmed facade enhanced by wrought-iron railings and flower-filled window boxes, this grand six-story hostelry stands out on the north side of St. Stephen's Green. Built in 1824, it was named after the earl of Shelbourne by its original owner, Richard Burke. Now a Forte Exclusive hotel, it has played a significant role in Irish history (the new nation's constitution was signed in room 107 in 1921), and it has often been host to international leaders, stars of stage and screen, and literary giants. The public areas, replete with glowing fireplaces, Waterford chandeliers, and equestrian-themed original art, are popular rendezvous spots for Dubliners.

Constantly being updated and refurbished, this luxurious landmark offers up-to-date guest rooms of varying sizes, furnished with antique and period pieces; the front units overlook the bucolic setting of St. Stephen's Green.

Dining/Entertainment: The main dining room, The Aisling, offers Irish and continental cuisine (see "St. Stephen's Green/Grafton Street" in Chapter 5), while the Horseshoe Bar is ideal for a convivial drink and the Lord Mayor's Lounge is favored by the locals for a proper afternoon tea.

Services: 24-hour room service, concierge.

Facilities: Foreign currency exchange, meeting rooms, private enclosed car park.

VERY EXPENSIVE/EXPENSIVE

STEPHEN'S HALL, 14-17 Lower Leeson St., Earlsfort

Terrace, Dublin 2. Tel. 01/610585, or toll free 800/223-6510 in the U.S. Fax 01/610606. 37 suites. TV TEL **Transportation:** DART to Pearse Station or bus no. 14A, 11A, 11B, 13, 46A, 46B, or 86.

$ Rates: Ŀ85 ($140.25) single, Ŀ130 ($214.50) double in 1-bedroom suite; Ŀ95 ($156.75) single, Ŀ150 ($247.50) double for 2-bedroom suite; Ŀ105 ($173.25) single, Ŀ170 ($280.50) double for penthouse/town house suite. No service charge. Breakfast Ŀ6 ($9.90) extra. AE, DC, MC, V.

With a gracious Georgian exterior and entranceway, this is Dublin's first all-suite hotel, situated on the southeast corner of St. Stephen's Green, within a half block from the National Concert Hall. It's ideal for visitors who plan an extended stay or who seek to do their own cooking or entertaining. Furnished in a contemporary motif, each suite contains a hallway, sitting room, dining area, kitchen, bathroom, and one or two bedrooms. The luxury penthouse suites, on the upper floors, offer views of city, while the ground-level town house suites have private entrances.

Services: Concierge, maid service.
Facilities: Restaurant/coffee shop, underground parking.

WESTBURY, Grafton St., Dublin 2. Tel. 01/679-1122, or toll free 800/223-6800, 800/223-0833, or 800/44-UTELL in the U.S. Fax 01/679-7078. Telex 91091. 200 rms, 6 suites. A/C TV TEL **Transportation:** DART to Tara Street or Pearse Station or bus no. 10, 11A, 11B, 13, or 20B.

$ Rates: Ŀ120–Ŀ130 ($198–$214.50) single; Ŀ135–Ŀ190 ($222.75–$313.50) double; Ŀ230–Ŀ380 ($379.50–$627) suite; Ŀ480 ($792) penthouse suite. Service charge 15%. Breakfast Ŀ9 ($14.85) extra. AE, CB, DC, MC, V.

A tasteful hybrid of modern and traditional design, this relatively new midtown hotel blends a sleekly contemporary facade with a serene interior of soft pastel tones and antique furnishings. Wedged in a cul-de-sac off the lower end of Grafton Street, it sits in the heart of the city's fashionable shopping district and near all the major sights. As the chic brainchild of the late hotelier P. V. Doyle, it created quite a stir a decade ago as the first new purpose-built hotel of deluxe caliber erected in downtown Dublin in more than 50 years. It quickly earned international recognition as one of the first two Irish members of the Leading Hotels of the World.

The guest rooms, many with half-canopy or four poster beds, are furnished with dark woods, brass trim, and floral designer fabrics. Many of the suites have Jacuzzi baths.

Dining/Entertainment: Choices include a top-class French/Irish restaurant, the Russell Room (see "St. Stephen's Green/Grafton Street" in Chapter 5); The Sandbank, a nautical-style pub serving fresh seafood; Charlie's Coffee Shop for a quick meal; and the Terrace Bar and Lounge, a favorite venue for afternoon tea or a drink with piano music in the background.

Services: 24-hour room service, concierge, express checkout.
Facilities: Hairdressing salon, an arcade of 20 shops, under-

ground parking, fitness room, meeting rooms, foreign currency exchange.

MODERATE

BUSWELLS, 25 Molesworth St., Dublin 2. Tel. 01/764013 or 613888, or toll free 800/473-9527 in the U.S. Fax 01/762090. 67 rms. TV TEL **Transportation:** DART to Pearse Station or bus no. 10, 11A, 11B, 13, or 20B.

$ Rates: ₤55 ($90.75) single; ₤86 ($141.90) double. Service charge 15%. Breakfast ₤6.50 ($10.75) extra. AE, DC, MC, V.

Centrally located 2 blocks from Trinity College and opposite the National Museum, Library, and Art Gallery, and Leinster House, this vintage four-story hotel has long been a meeting point for artists, poets, scholars, and politicians. Originally two Georgian town houses (1736), it was launched as a hotel in 1928 by Nora O'Callaghan Duff and William Duff, and has been managed by three generations of the same family ever since. The public rooms are replete with period furniture, intricate plasterwork, Wedgwood flourishes, old prints, and memorabilia.

Recently refurbished, all the bedrooms have been updated with contemporary decor and Victorian touches, plus added amenities of tea/coffee makers and hairdryers. Facilities and services include a restaurant, two bars, concierge, and room service.

RUSSELL COURT, 21-23 Harcourt St., Dublin 2. Tel. 01/784066. Fax 01/781576. 21 rms. TV TEL **Bus:** No. 62.

$ Rates: ₤51–₤70 ($84.15–$115.50) single; ₤76–₤82 ($125.40–$135.30) double. Service charge 12.5%. Breakfast ₤5.25 ($8.70) extra. AE, DC, MC, V.

Slightly off the beaten track, yet just a block south of St. Stephen's Green, this little hotel was formed from joining together of two Georgian town houses. The public areas are decorated with some art deco motifs, but much of the 18th-century charm remains. Guest rooms are contemporary, with light woods and pastel fabrics. Facilities include a restaurant, bar, and nightclub.

BUDGET

AVALON HOUSE, 55 Aungier St., Dublin 2. Tel. 01/750001. Fax 01/750303. 42 rms (7 with bath), 3 dorms. **Bus:** No. 16, 16A, 19, or 22.

$ Rates (including continental breakfast): ₤17.50 ($28.90) single; ₤25 ($41.25) double; ₤11 ($18.15) per person in four-bedded room; ₤7 ($11.55) per person in dorm-style room. AE, MC, V.

(S) With a four-story red sandstone facade, this strikingly ornate Victorian building was erected in 1879 as a medical school, later used for commercial offices, and then completely gutted and transformed into a hostel in 1992. Great care was taken in the restoration to preserve original turf fireplaces, some of the more artistic wallpaper, and the wide windows, while installing the most modern equipment for showers, toilets, and other guest facilities. Accommodations are offered in single, two-, three-, four-, and eight-bed rooms. Geared for students and budget-conscious travelers, it is situated next to the Whitefriar Street Church (see "More Attractions" in Chapter 6) and less than 2 blocks from St. Stephen's Green; it is equally positioned close to St. Patrick's Cathedral (see "The Top Attractions" in Chapter 6) and other sights in the older section of the city.

Facilities include a coffee shop, study/reading room, bureau de change, TV lounge room, international pay phones, lockers, luggage storage, self-catering kitchen, and guest laundry.

4. FITZWILLIAM/ MERRION SQUARES

EXPENSIVE

MONT CLARE HOTEL, Merrion Sq., Clare St., Dublin 2. Tel. 616799, or toll free 800/44-UTELL in the U.S. Fax 01/615663. Telex 91471. 74 rms. A/C TV TEL MINIBAR **Transportation:** DART to Pearse Station or bus no. 5, 7A, 8, or 62.
$ Rates: Ł105–Ł150 ($173.25–$247.50) single; Ł120–Ł150 ($198–$247.50) double. Service charge 12.5%. Breakfast Ł8.50 ($14) extra. AE, DC, MC, V.

Overlooking the northwest corner of Merrion Square, this vintage six-story brick-faced hotel was thoroughly restored and refurbished in recent years. It has a typically Georgian facade, matched tastefully inside by period furnishings of dark woods and polished brass. The guest rooms, decked out in contemporary style, offer every up-to-date amenity including hairdryer, tea/coffee maker, and trouser press.

Dining/Entertainment: Named for one of Ireland's great writers, the main restaurant, Goldsmith's, has a literary theme. There is also a traditional lounge bar.

Services: 24-hour room service, concierge.

Facilities: Foreign currency exchange, meeting rooms, enclosed parking lot.

MODERATE

GREY DOOR, 22/23 Upper Pembroke St., Dublin 2. Tel. 01/763286. Fax 01/763287. 7 rms. TV TEL **Transportation:** DART to Pearse Station or bus no. 46A, 46B, or 86.
$ Rates: Ł55 ($90.75) single; Ł83 ($136.95) double. Service charge 12.5%. Breakfast Ł6.95 ($11.50) extra. AE, DC, MC, V.

An offshoot of the successful restaurant of the same name (see "Fitzwilliam/Merrion Squares" in Chapter 5), this small guesthouse offers the elegance of a Georgian home with the comforts of a modern inn. The bedrooms are furnished with dark woods and designer fabrics, many incorporating the characteristically Georgian high ceilings and tall multipaned windows, as well as extras such as trouser press, hairdryer, coffee/tea maker, and complimentary daily newspaper. Located on a street known for its profusion of handsome brick town houses, it is conveniently placed between Lower Leeson Street and Quinn's Lane, less than a block from the southwest corner of Fitzwilliam Square and within walking distance of St. Stephen's Green. No car park.

LONGFIELDS, 10 Lower Fitzwilliam St., Dublin 2. Tel. 01/761367, or toll free 800/223-1588 in the U.S. Fax 01/761542. 26 rms. TV TEL MINIBAR **Transportation:** DART to Pearse Station or bus no. 10.

$ Rates: Ŀ85 ($140.25) single; Ŀ99 ($163.35) double. Service charge 12.5%. Breakfast Ŀ6.50 ($10.75) extra. AE, DC, MC, V.

Melded from two 18th-century Georgian town houses, this classy little hotel sits on one of Dublin's most fashionable thoroughfares, lined with colorful doorways and decorative fanlights. It is named after Richard Longfield, also known as

---

Ⓕ **FROMMER'S COOL FOR KIDS: ACCOMMODATIONS**

Fitzpatrick's Castle (see p. 78) Located in the scenic suburb of Killiney, this hotel imparts a fairy-tale atmosphere for all ages and is a special delight for youngsters, with its authentic dungeon, turrets and towers, and suits of armor on display. It also sits on 9 acres, with plenty of room for children to roam and run, and offers an indoor swimming pool, gym, and other sports facilities.

Jurys Hotel and Towers (see p. 72) Although this hotel attracts an international business clientele, it also welcomes families, especially on weekends, because of its indoor/outdoor swimming pool and the informal atmosphere of its Coffee Dock restaurant.

Jurys Christchurch (see p. 61) New for Dublin, this hotel has been built with families in mind, offering reasonably priced rooms that can sleep at least three people. The location—close to Christ Church and St. Patrick's Cathedrals, Dublinia, and other Old City attractions, is ideal for having children within walking distance of historic sights.

Stephen's Hall (see p. 66) As Dublin's only all-suite hotel, this place offers units with one or two bedrooms and full cooking facilities, ideal for families.

Clarence (see p. 64) Teens find it cool that this hotel is owned by the rock group U2.

Viscount Longueville, who originally owned this site and was a member of the Irish Parliament two centuries ago. Totally restored and refurbished several years ago, it combines Georgian-style decor and reproduction period furnishings of dark woods and brass trim. Bedrooms offer extra touches such as desks, clock radios, and hairdryers. Facilities include a restaurant with bar, room service, meeting room, and foreign currency exchange, but no car park. It is positioned almost equally between Merrion and Fitzwilliam Squares, at the corner of Lower Baggot Street.

MODERATE/INEXPENSIVE

THE FITZWILLIAM, 41 Upper Fitzwilliam St., Dublin 2. Tel. 01/600448. Fax 01/767488. 12 rms. TV TEL **Transportation:** DART to Pearse Station or bus no. 10.

$ Rates (including full breakfast): Ł29–Ł36 ($47.85–$59.40) single; Ł44–Ł65 ($72.60–$107.25) double. Service charge 10%. AE, DC, MC, V.

Appropriately named for the wide thoroughfare that it overlooks, this cozy guesthouse is a restored and refurbished 18th-century Georgian home, sitting at the corner of Lower Baggot Street, almost midway between Fitzwilliam and Merrion Squares. The entrance parlor has a homey atmosphere, with a marble fireplace and antique furnishings, while the bedrooms are outfitted with every contemporary amenity, including hairdryers and clock radios. Facilities include a restaurant.

GEORGIAN HOUSE, 20 Lower Baggot St., Dublin 2. Tel. 01/618832. Fax 01/618834. 18 rms. TV TEL **Transportation:** DART to Pearse Station or bus no. 10.

$ Rates (including full breakfast): Ł32–Ł45 ($52.80–$74.25) single; Ł50–Ł71 ($82.50–$117.15) double. Service charge 10%. AE, DC, MC, V.

Located midway between Merrion and Fitzwilliam Squares and less than 2 blocks east of St. Stephen's Green, this four-story 200-year-old brick town house sits in the heart of Georgian Dublin, within walking distance of most major attractions. The bedrooms are smallish, but offer all the essentials and a colorful decor with pine furniture. As at most guesthouses, there is no elevator, but there is an enclosed car park behind the house, and a full-service restaurant specializing in seafood, the Ante Room (see "Fitzwilliam/Merrion Squares" in Chapter 5), in the basement. Plans call for the addition of 14 more rooms at the back of the house by 1993.

5. BALLSBRIDGE/EMBASSY ROW

EXPENSIVE

BERKELEY COURT, Lansdowne Rd., Ballsbridge, Dublin 4. Tel. 01/601711, or toll free 800/223-6800, 800/223-0888, or 800/44-UTELL in the U.S. Fax 01/617238. Telex 30554. 197

rms, 10 suites. TV TEL **Transportation:** DART to Lansdowne Road or bus no. 5, 7A, 8, 46, 63, or 84.

$ Rates: Ł115–Ł130 ($189.75–$214.50) single; Ł130–Ł145 ($189.75–$239.25) double; Ł185–Ł375 ($305.25–$618.75) suite; Ł1,350 ($2,227.50) penthouse suite. Service charge 15%. Breakfast Ł9 ($14.85) extra. AE, CB, DC, MC, V.

The flagship of the Irish-owned Doyle Hotels group and the first Irish member of Leading Hotels of the World, the Berkeley Court (pronounced "Barkley") is nestled in a residential area near the American embassy on well-tended grounds that were once part of the botanic gardens of University College. A favorite haunt of diplomats and international business leaders, the hotel is known for its posh lobby decorated with fine antiques, original paintings, mirrored columns, and Irish-made carpets and furnishings. The guest rooms, which aim to convey an air of elegance, have designer fabrics, semicanopy beds, dark woods, and bathrooms fitted with marble accoutrements. The suites have more classic furnishings and a sprinkling of antiques; the 7,500-foot penthouse suite offers two bedrooms, dining room, sitting room with grand piano, kitchen, meeting room, lounge, study/library, and full-time butler service.

Dining/Entertainment: Choices include the formal Berkeley Room for gourmet dining; the plant-filled and skylit Conservatory for casual meals; the Royal Court, a Gothic-style bar with carved paneling and trim for drinks; and the Court Lounge, a proper setting for afternoon tea or a relaxing drink.

Services: 24-hour room service, concierge, laundry service, and express checkout.

Facilities: Foreign currency exchange, meeting rooms, boutiques, a health center with indoor swimming pool, and ample outdoor parking.

JURYS HOTEL, Pembroke Rd., Ballsbridge, Dublin 4. Tel. 01/650000, or toll free 800/843-6664 in the U.S. Fax 01/605540. Telex 93723. 390 rms. A/C TV TEL **Transportation:** DART to Lansdowne Road Station or bus no. 5, 7A, 8, 46, 63, or 84.

$ Rates: Main hotel, Ł99 ($163.35) single; Ł120 ($198) double. Towers wing (with continental breakfast), Ł145 ($239.25) single; Ł175 ($288.75) double. Service charge 12.5%. Breakfast Ł9.25 ($15.30) extra. AE, CB, DC, MC, V.

Setting a progressive tone in a city steeped in tradition, this unique hotel welcomes guests to a skylit three-story atrium-style lobby with a marble and teak decor. Situated on its own grounds opposite the American embassy, this sprawling property is actually two interconnected hotels in one—a modern eight-story high-rise, formerly an Inter-Continental, and a new 100-unit tower with its own check-in desk, separate elevators, and private entrance, as well as full access to all of the main hotel's amenities.

The guest rooms in the main wing, recently refurbished, offer dark wood furnishings, brass trim, designer fabrics, and well-fitted bathrooms. The Towers section—a first for the Irish capital—is an exclusive wing of oversize concierge-style rooms with bay windows.

Each unit has computer-card key access, stocked minibar, three telephone lines, well-lit work area with desk, reclining chair, tile-and-marble bathroom, walk-in closet, and either a king- or queen-size bed. Decors vary, from contemporary light woods with floral fabrics, to dark tones with Far Eastern motifs. Towers guests also enjoy exclusive use of a private hospitality lounge with library, boardroom, and access to complimentary continental breakfast, daily newspapers, and coffee/tea service throughout the day.

Dining/Entertainment: There are two top-class restaurants, the Embassy Garden and the Kish, plus the Coffee Dock, Dublin's only around-the-clock coffee shop (for descriptions of all three, see "Ballsbridge/Embassy Row" in Chapter 5). This is also the home of Jurys Cabaret Show, Ireland's longest-running evening entertainment (see "The Performing Arts" in Chapter 9); a turn-of-the-century themed pub, the Dubliner, and the skylit and plant-filled Pavilion Bar, overlooking the indoor-outdoor pool.

Services: 24-hour room service, concierge, foreign currency exchange, valet/laundry service, safety-deposit boxes, and express checkout.

Facilities: Heated indoor/outdoor pool, therapeutic hot whirlpool, hairdressing salons, craft/clothes shop, meeting rooms, Aer Lingus ticket office, car-rental desk, and outdoor parking.

EXPENSIVE/MODERATE

BURLINGTON, Upper Leeson St., Dublin 4. Tel. 01/ 605222, or toll free 800/223-0888 in the U.S. Fax 01/608496. 477 rms. TV TEL **Bus:** No. 10 or 18.
$ **Rates:** Ŀ79–Ŀ86 ($130.35–$141.90) single; Ŀ95–Ŀ125 ($156.75–$206.25) double. Service charge 15%. Breakfast Ŀ8 ($13.20) extra. AE, CB, DC, MC, V.

A favorite headquarters for conventions, meetings, conferences, and group tours, this is the largest hotel in Ireland, situated 1 long block south of the Grand Canal in a fashionable residential section within walking distance of St. Stephen's Green and off the main (N11) road to the southeast of Ireland. A member of the Irish-owned Doyle group, it's a modern, smartly furnished seven-story property, constantly being updated and refurbished. The bedrooms are outfitted with brass-bound oak furniture and designer fabrics. There is a good proportion of interconnecting units, ideal for families.

Dining/Entertainment: There are two restaurants, the Sussex, the large main dining room, and the Diplomat for more intimate specialty dining, and a coffee shop for light meals. In addition, the skylit Conservatory pub and the Presidents Bar, a split-level lounge off the main lobby, both offer drinks and snacks; and Annabel's is the basement-level nightclub (see "The Club & Music Scene" in Chapter 9). From May to early October, the main ballroom offers Doyle's Irish Cabaret, a 3-hour cabaret dinner show featuring Irish music and song (see "The Performing Arts" in Chapter 9).

Services: 24-hour room service, concierge, valet/laundry service.

Facilities: Foreign currency exchange, meeting rooms, underground and outdoor parking, arcade of shops, and hairdressing salons.

MODERATE

ANGLESEA TOWN HOUSE, 63 Anglesea Rd., Ballsbridge, Dublin 4. Tel. 01/683877. Fax 01/683461. 7 rms. TV TEL **Transportation:** DART to Lansdowne Road Station or bus no. 46, 63, or 84.

$ Rates (including full breakfast): Ł50 ($82.50) single; Ł80 ($132) double. Service charge 10%. AE, MC, V.

A true bed-and-breakfast experience is the keynote of this 1903 Edwardian-style guesthouse. Located in the Ballsbridge section of the city, close to the Royal Dublin Showgrounds, the Chester Beatty Library, and the American embassy, it is furnished with visitor comfort in mind— rocking chairs, settees, a sun deck, and lots of flowering plants, as well as all the modern conveniences in every guest room. You can count on a warm welcome from hostess Helen Kirrane and a breakfast of homemade goodies.

ARIEL HOUSE, 52 Lansdowne Rd., Ballsbridge, Dublin 4. Tel. 01/685512. Fax 01/685845. 28 rms. TV TEL **Transportation:** DART to Lansdowne Road Station or bus no. 5, 7A, 8, 46, 63, or 84.

$ Rates: Ł37.50 ($61.90) single; Ł60–Ł80 ($99–$132) double. Service charge 10%. Breakfast Ł7.50 ($12.40) extra. MC, V.

As Dublin guesthouses go, this one is the benchmark, opened more than 25 years ago by Dublin-born and San Francisco-trained Michael O'Brien. With an historic mid-19th-century mansion as its core, this bastion of hospitality has been expanded and enhanced continually over the years to its present capacity. Guests are welcome to relax in the drawing room, rich in Victorian style, with Waterford glass chandeliers, an open fireplace, and delicately carved cornices and roses complementing the theme of the era.

The bedrooms are individually decorated, with period furniture, fine oil paintings and watercolors, and real Irish linens, as well as modern extras such as hairdryers. Facilities include a conservatory-style dining room that serves breakfast, morning coffee, and afternoon tea, a wine bar, and a private car park. It is conveniently located 1 block from the DART station and across the street from the Berkeley Court Hotel.

MONTROSE, Stillorgan Rd., Dublin 4. Tel. 01/269-3111, or toll free 800/223-0888 or 800/44-UTELL in the U.S. Fax 01/269-1164. Telex 91207. 190 rms. TV TEL **Bus:** No. 10, 46, 46A, 46B, or 63.

$ Rates: Ł48–Ł54 ($79.20–$89.10) single; Ł68–Ł75 ($112.20–$123.75) double. Service charge 15%. Breakfast Ł6 ($9.90) extra. AE, CB, DC, MC, V.

Nestled on its own palm tree–lined grounds in a residential neighborhood, across from the Belfield campus of Dublin's University College and close to the Irish National TV Studios, this modern four-story hotel sits beside the main road (N11) to the southeast of Ireland. The largest hotel on the southern outskirts of the city, it is a 10-minute drive from downtown, and offers ample outdoor car parking. Guest rooms are modern and functional, with colorful Irish-made furnishings; front rooms have balconies.

Dining/Entertainment: Facilities include a full-service bi-level restaurant, the Belfield Room, plus a grill room and skylit lounge bar.

Services: Concierge, room service, laundry service.

Facilities: Health center, meeting rooms, souvenir shop, and full-service bank.

TARA TOWER, Merrion Rd., Dublin 4. Tel. 01/269-4666, or toll free 800/223-0888 or 800/44-UTELL in the U.S. Fax 01/269-1027. Telex 90790. 100 rms. TV TEL **Transportation:** DART to Booterstown Station or bus no. 5, 7, 7A, or 8.

$ Rates: Ł48–Ł54 ($79.20–$89.10) single; Ł68–Ł75 ($112.20–$123.75) double. Service charge 15%. Breakfast Ł6 ($9.90) extra. AE, CB, DC, MC, V.

Positioned along the coast road between downtown Dublin and the ferryport of Dun Laoghaire, this modern seven-story hotel offers wide-windowed views of Dublin Bay, just 10 minutes from the city center in a residential area. It's an ideal place to stay for car renters, as there is ample parking space; and for those who prefer to use public transport, it's within easy walking distance of major bus routes and a DART station. The guest rooms offer every modern convenience and attractive Irish-made furnishings.

Dining/Entertainment: There is a conservatory-style restaurant and a Joycean-themed lounge bar.

Services: Concierge, room service, laundry service.

Facilities: Foreign currency exchange, souvenir shop, meeting rooms.

INEXPENSIVE

GLENVEAGH TOWN HOUSE, 31 Northumberland Rd., Ballsbridge, Dublin 4. Tel. 01/684612. Fax 01/684559. 11 rms. TV TEL **Transportation:** DART to Lansdowne Road Station or bus no. 5, 7, 7A, 8, or 45.

$ Rates (including full breakfast): Ł33 ($54.45) single; Ł45 ($74.25) double. Service charge 10%. AE, MC, V.

Fashioned into a guesthouse by the Cunningham family, this converted three-story Georgian residence is situated between the Grand Canal and the American embassy. Sitting on a quiet tree-lined street, it offers a homey atmosphere with a glowing fireplace in the sitting room, high ceilings, and tall windows bedecked with floral drapery. The guest rooms are decorated in a modern vein, with light woods, lots of frilly pastel fabrics, and all the modern conveniences such as hairdryers. There is a private car park for guests' use.

LANSDOWNE LODGE, 4 Lansdowne Terrace, Shelbourne Rd., Ballsbridge, Dublin 4. Tel. 01/605755 or 605578. Fax 01/605662. 12 rms. TV TEL **Transportation:** DART to Lansdowne Road Station or bus no. 5, 7, 7A, 8, or 45.

$ Rates (including full breakfast): Ł35–Ł39 ($57.75–$64.35) single; Ł49–Ł57 ($80.85–$94.05) double. No service charge. MC, V.

With a lovely two-story brick town house facade, this guesthouse enjoys a very convenient location, between Lansdowne and Haddington Roads, and adjacent to the Lansdowne Road Football Stadium and within a block of the DART station and major bus routes. Owner Finbarr Smyth offers a variety of individually styled bedrooms with armchairs and homey furnishings including decorative bed coverings and framed paintings; some rooms are on the ground floor. The grounds include a garden and private car park for guests.

MOUNT HERBERT, 7 Herbert Rd., Ballsbridge, Dublin 4. Tel. 01/684321. Fax 01/607077. Telex 92173. 144 rms. TV TEL **Transportation:** DART to Lansdowne Road Station or bus no. 5, 7, 7A, 8, 46, 63, or 84.

$ Rates: Ł31.95–Ł41.95 ($52.75–$69.25) single; Ł34–Ł44 ($56.10–$72.60) double. Service charge 10%. Breakfast Ł3 ($4.95) extra. AE, DC, MC, V.

Although technically classified as a guesthouse, this three-story, much-expanded property is more like a small hotel.
Originally the family home of Lord Robinson, it is a gracious residence set in its own grounds and gardens in a residential neighborhood near the DART station and major bus routes. Operated by the Loughran family, it offers bedrooms of various vintages and sizes, but all have standard amenities, including a trouser press. Guest facilities include a restaurant, wine bar, sauna, indoor solarium, exercise room, gift shop, and guest car park.

UPPERCROSS HOUSE, 26/30 Upper Rathmines Rd., Rathmines, Dublin 6. Tel. 01/975486, 975361, or 975890. Fax 01/975486. 14 rms. TV TEL **Bus:** No. 14, 14A, 15, 15A, 15B, 47, 47A, 47B, or 83.

$ Rates (including full breakfast): Ł28–Ł30 ($46.20–$49.50) single; Ł46–Ł50 ($75.90–$82.50) double. No service charge. AE, MC, V.

Built 100 years ago when Rathmines was known as Dublin's Uppercross because it was a prime location for well-to-do family residences and business premises, this guesthouse is a harmonious combination of three adjacent two- and three-story Georgian town houses. Located 2 miles south of the city center, it is operated by the Mahon family who offer a variety of rooms with individualized furnishings and basic amenities including a hairdryer and coffee/tea maker. Facilities include a bistro-style restaurant.

6. O'CONNELL STREET

MODERATE

GRESHAM, 23 Upper O'Connell St., Dublin 1. Tel. 01/746881, or toll free 800/44-UTELL in the U.S. Fax 01/787175. Telex 32473. 202 rms, 6 suites. TV TEL **Transportation:** DART to Connolly Station or bus no. 40A, 40B, 40C, or 51A.

$ Rates: £90 ($148.50) single; £110 ($181.50) double; from £150 ($247.50) suite. Service charge 12.5%. Breakfast £8 ($13.20) extra. AE, CB, DC, MC, V.

Centrally located on the city's main business thoroughfare, this Regency-style hotel is one of Ireland's oldest (1817) and best-known lodging establishments, now a member of the Ryan Hotel group. Although much of the visitor emphasis in Dublin has shifted south of the River Liffey in recent years, the Gresham is still synonymous with stylish Irish hospitality and provides easy access to the Abbey and Gate Theatres, Point Depot, and other northside attractions. The lobby and public areas are a panorama of marble floors, molded plasterwork, and crystal chandeliers.

With high ceilings and individual decors, the guest rooms vary in size and style, with heavy emphasis on deep blue and pink tones, soft lighting, tiled bathrooms, and period furniture including padded headboards and armoires. The front upper floors also offer a selection of one-of-a-kind luxury terrace suites.

Dining/Entertainment: Choices include the bi-level Aberdeen Restaurant for elegant formal meals (see "O'Connell Street" in Chapter 5) and Toddy's, a trendy pub/lounge offering light meals all day (see "O'Connell Street" in Chapter 5). Another bar, Magnums, attracts a late-night crowd.

Services: Concierge, 24-hour room service, valet laundry service.

Facilities: Meeting rooms, private parking garage, ice machines, foreign currency exchange.

ROYAL DUBLIN, 40 Upper O'Connell St., Dublin 1. Tel. 01/733666, or toll free 800/528-1234 in the U.S. Fax 01/733120. Telex 32568. 120 rms. TV TEL **Transportation:** DART to Connolly Station or bus no. 36A, 40A, 40B, 40C, or 51A.

$ Rates: £62–£75 ($102.30–$123.75) single; £76–£96 ($125.40–$158.40) double. No service charge. Breakfast £6.50 ($10.75) extra. AE, DC, MC, V.

Romantically floodlit at night, this modern five-story hotel is positioned near Parnell Square at the north end of Dublin's main thoroughfare, within walking distance of all the main theaters and northside attractions. Completely refurbished in 1991, it combines a contemporary skylit lobby full of art deco overtones with adjacent lounge areas that were part of an original building dating back to 1752. These Georgian-themed rooms impart an old-world ambience, rich in high molded ceilings, ornate cornices, crystal chandeliers, gilt-edged mirrors, and open fireplaces. The bedrooms are strictly modern with light woods, pastel fabrics, and three-sided full-length windows that extend out over the busy street below. Corridors are extremely well lit, with individual lights at each doorway.

Dining/Entertainment: Choices include the Café Royale Brasserie (see "O'Connell Street" in Chapter 5); Raffles Bar, a skylit clubby room with portraits of Irish literary greats, for snacks or drinks; and the Georgian Lounge for morning coffee or afternoon tea beside the open fireplace.

Services: 24-hour room service, concierge, valet/laundry service.

Facilities: Bureau de change, underground car park, car-rental desk, meeting rooms.

7. SUBURBS — SOUTH

EXPENSIVE/MODERATE

FITZPATRICK'S CASTLE, Killiney Hill Rd., Killiney, Co. Dublin. Tel. 01/284-0700 or toll free in the U.S. 800/367-7701 or 800/223-5695. Fax 01/285-0207. Telex 30353. 88 rms. TV TEL **Transportation:** DART to Dalkey Station or bus no. 59.
$ Rates: Ł61–Ł79 ($100.65–$130.35) single; Ł81–Ł120 ($133.65–$198) double. Service charge 15%. Breakfast Ł7.50 ($12.40) extra. AE, CB, DC, MC, V.

★ With a fanciful Victorian facade of turrets, towers, and battlements, this restored 1741 gem is Dublin's only deluxe castle hotel and an ideal choice for those who want to live like royalty for a few days. A 15-minute drive from the center of the city, it is situated between the villages of Dalkey and Killiney, on 9 acres of gardens and hilltop grounds, with romantic vistas of Dublin Bay.

Two generations of the Fitzpatrick family pamper guests with 20th-century comforts in a regal setting which includes medieval suits of armor, Louis XIV–style furnishings, Irish antiques, original oil paintings, and specially woven shamrock-patterned green carpet. Most of the guest rooms have four-poster or canopy beds, and many have balconies with sweeping views of Dublin and the surrounding countryside. In spite of its size and exacting standards, the castle never fails to exude a friendly family-run atmosphere.

Dining/Entertainment: Choices include a gourmet restaurant known as Truffles (see "Suburbs—South" in Chapter 5), the Castle Grill for informal meals, the Cocktail Bar, for a relaxing drink in a posh setting, and The Dungeon, for a pub/nightclub atmosphere.

Services: 24-hour room service, concierge, laundry service, courtesy minibus service to downtown and to the airport.

Facilities: Complete health center with indoor pool, gym, saunas, squash and tennis courts; hairdressing salon; helipad; guest privileges at nearby 18-hole golf course; garden; and extensive outdoor parking.

ROYAL MARINE, Marine Rd., Dun Laoghaire, Co. Dublin. Tel. 01/280-1911, or toll-free 800/44-UTELL in the U.S. Fax 01/280-1089. Telex 91277. 104 rms. TV TEL **Transportation:** DART to Dun Laoghaire Station or bus no. 7, 7A, or 8.
$ Rates: Ł80–Ł100 ($132–$165) single; Ł90–Ł120 ($148.50–$198) double. Service charge 15%. Breakfast Ł8 ($13.20) extra. AE, DC, MC, V.

A tradition along the seafront since 1865, this four- and five-story landmark hotel sits on a hill overlooking the harbor, 7 miles south of Dublin City. A favorite with British visitors, it's a good place to stay for ready access to the Holyhead/Dun Laoghaire ferry which travels across the Irish Sea to and from Wales.

Basically a Georgian building, with a wing of modern bedrooms, the Royal Marine was recently refurbished and renovated by the Ryan group. The public areas have been beautifully restored, with original molded ceilings and elaborate cornices, crystal chandeliers, marble-mantled fireplaces, and antique furnishings. The guest rooms, many of which offer wide-windowed views of the bay, carry through the Georgian theme, with dark woods, traditional floral fabrics, four-poster and canopy beds; some of the newer rooms have light woods and pastel tones. All units have up-to-date facilities including hairdryer and garment press. The 4 acres of grounds include a flower garden and a gazebo, yet the entrance to the hotel is just a half block from Dun Laoghaire's main thoroughfare.

Dining/Entertainment: There is a dining room with wide-windowed views of the bay and a lounge bar with frequent piano music.

Services: 24-hour room service, concierge, valet/laundry service.

Facilities: Meeting rooms, garden, and ample outdoor parking.

MODERATE

THE COURT, Killiney Bay Rd., Killiney, Co. Dublin. Tel. 01/285-1622, or toll free in the U.S.A. 800/228-5151. Fax 01/285-2085. Telex 33244. 86 rms. TV TEL **Transportation:** DART to Killiney Station or bus no. 59.

$ Rates: Ł46–Ł55 ($75.90–$90.75) single; Ł81–Ł112 ($133.65–$184.80) double. Service charge 12.5%. Breakfast Ł7 ($11.55) extra. AE, DC, MC, V.

Situated on 4 acres of gardens and lawns overlooking Dublin Bay, this three-story multigabled Victorian-style hotel offers a relaxing country inn atmosphere, yet it is within 20 minutes (12 miles) of downtown Dublin. Best of all, guests who stay here don't even have to rent a car because there is a DART station adjacent to the grounds. The bedrooms, most of which have lovely views of the bay, are decorated with Victorian flair, full of scalloped headboards, tasseled lampshades, Queen Anne–style tables and chairs, gilt-framed paintings, brass lamps, quilted fabrics, and floor-to-ceiling drapery. This hotel is affiliated with the Quality/Choice lodging group.

Dining/Entertainment: Choices include a Victorian-themed restaurant with views of the bay, a coffee shop, and a conservatory-style lounge bar.

Services: Concierge, room service, laundry service.

Facilities: Meeting rooms, snooker room, gardens, and ample outdoor parking.

8. SUBURBS — NORTH

MODERATE

FORTE CREST, Airport Rd., Dublin Airport, Co. Dublin. Tel. 01/379211, or toll free 800/225-5843 in the U.S. Fax

01/425874. Telex 32849. 195 rms. TV TEL **Bus:** 41, 41C, or Express Airport Coach.

$ Rates: Ł79–Ł85 ($130.35–$140.25) single; Ł94–Ł100 ($155.10–$165) double. Service charge 15%. Breakfast Ł7.50 ($12.40) extra. AE, DC, MC, V.

Formerly known as the Dublin International Hotel, this is the main lodging on the grounds of the airport, situated 7 miles north of city center. With a modern three-story brick facade, it has a sunken skylit lobby, with a central courtyard surrounded by guest rooms. The bedrooms are contemporary and functional, with windows looking out into the courtyard or toward distant mountain vistas. Each unit is equipped with standard furnishings plus full-length mirror, hairdryer, coffee/tea-making equipment, and trouser press. About one-fourth (45) of the higher-priced rooms have a minibar.

Dining/Entertainment: Choices include the Garden Room restaurant for Irish cuisine, Sampans for Chinese food (dinner only), and the Heritage Bar for drinks and snacks.

Services: 24-hour room service, concierge, valet/laundry service, and courtesy coach between hotel and airport.

Facilities: Meeting rooms, gift shop, and ample outdoor parking.

SKYLON, Upper Drumcondra Rd., Dublin 9. Tel. 01/ 379121, or toll free 800/223-0888 or 800/44-UTELL in the U.S. Fax 01/372778. Telex 90790. 92 rms. TV TEL **Bus:** No. 3, 11, 16, 41, 41A, or 41B.

$ Rates: Ł48–Ł54 ($79.20–$89.10) single; Ł68–Ł75 ($112.20–$123.75) double. Service charge 15%. Breakfast Ł6 ($9.90) extra. AE, CB, DC, MC, V.

With a modern five-story glass-and-concrete facade, this hotel stands out on the city's north side, situated midway between downtown and the airport. Set on its own grounds in a residential neighborhood next to a prominent teacher-training college, it is just 10 minutes from the heart of the city via several major bus routes that stop outside the door. The guest rooms have all the latest amenities, with colorful Irish-made furnishings.

Dining/Entertainment: For full-service dining, it's the Rendezvous Room, a modern plant-filled restaurant with an Irish/continental menu; and for drinks, try the Joycean-themed pub.

Services: Concierge, room service, laundry service.

Facilities: Meeting rooms, gift shop, and ample outdoor parking.

INEXPENSIVE

EGAN'S HOUSE, 7/9 Iona Park, Glasnevin, Dublin 9. Tel. 01/303611 or 305283. Fax 01/303312. 23 rms. TV TEL **Bus:** No. 3, 11, 13, 13A, 19, 19A, 16, 41, 41A, or 41B.

$ Rates: Ł18.70–Ł25.50 ($30.85–$42.10) single; Ł32–Ł40.50 ($52.80–$66.85) double. Service charge 10%. Breakfast Ł5.50 ($9.10) extra. MC, V.

Located on the north side of the city between Botanic and Lower Drumcondra Roads, this two-story red-brick Victorian guesthouse is in the center of a pleasant residential neighborhood, within walking distance of the Botanic Gardens. Operated by John and Betty Egan, it offers bedrooms in a variety of sizes and styles including ground-floor rooms, with all the modern conveniences including hairdryers and coffee/tea makers. The comfortable public rooms have an assortment of traditional dark woods, brass fixtures, and antiques. Car parking is provided for guests.

IONA HOUSE, 5 Iona Park, Glasnevin, Dublin 9. Tel. 01/ 306217. Fax 01/306732. 11 rms. TV TEL **Bus:** No. 3, 11, 13, 13A, 19, 19A, 16, 41, 41A, or 41B.

$ Rates (including full breakfast): Ł23–Ł25.50 ($37.95–$42.10) single; Ł46–Ł51 ($75.90–$84.15) double. No service charge. MC, V. **Closed:** Dec–Jan.

S A sitting room with a glowing open fireplace, chiming clocks, brass fixtures, and dark wood furnishings sets a tone of welcome for guests to this two-story red-brick Victorian home. Built around the turn of the century and operated as a guesthouse since 1963 by John and Karen Shouldice, it is located in a residential neighborhood, midway between Lower Drumcondra and Botanic Roads, within walking distance of the Botanic Gardens. The guest rooms offer modern hotel-style appointments and contemporary Irish-made furnishings. Facilities include a lounge, small patio, and outdoor parking for guests.

MAPLES HOUSE, 79/81 Iona Rd., off St. Alphonsus Rd., Drumcondra, Dublin 9. Tel. 01/728382 or 303049. Fax 01/303874. 21 rms. TV TEL **Bus:** No. 3, 11, 13, 13A, 19, 19A, 16, 41, 41A, or 41B.

$ Rates (including full breakfast): Ł30 ($49.50) single; Ł50 ($82.50) double. No service charge. AE, DC, MC, V.

Situated in a quiet residential district 10 minutes north of the city center and 15 minutes from the airport, this classic two-story Edwardian brick building was established as a guesthouse almost a half century ago and is still operated by the Smith family. The welcoming lobby is bedecked with oil paintings, ornate statuary, Waterford crystal chandeliers, and a one-of-a-kind Victorian rococo sideboard. The bedrooms offer every modern comfort including hairdryers and tea/coffee makers. Facilities range from a Victorian-style grill/restaurant and lounge to a meeting room and car park. This lodging is well positioned within walking distance of the Botanic Gardens, between Botanic and Lower Drumcondra Roads.

DUBLIN DINING

From formal old-world hotel dining rooms to casual bistros and wine bars, Dublin has a great variety of restaurants, in all price categories. As befits a European capital, there is plenty of continental fare, with a particular leaning toward French and Italian influences, plus a fine selection of international eateries, with recipes that come from as far away as Scandinavia, Russia, the Mediterranean, India, China, and even California.

Best of all, Dublin has been in the forefront of the culinary revolution that has enveloped Ireland in the last 25 years (see "Food and Drink" in Chapter 1). Traditional Irish dishes such as boxty and colcannon are taking pride of place in some restaurants, and still other dining rooms are giving a haute cuisine twist to time-honored dishes, with low-fat ingredients and lighter sauces, creating a "new Irish" cuisine.

With Dublin Bay at its doorstep and the Atlantic waters nearby, Dublin is also a great seafood mecca. There are many fine restaurants that specialize in piscine delights—from Dublin Bay prawns and wild Irish salmon to trout, black sole, crab, lobster, plaice, and other local varieties. You can blow the budget at a top-of-the-line seafood enclave or opt for a simple order of fish-and-chips at a take-out counter—and still savor the freshest of "fruits de mer."

So get ready for some good eating in Dublin's Fair City.

RESERVATIONS Except for self-service eateries and informal cafés, most all Dublin restaurants encourage reservations. The more expensive restaurants absolutely require reservations, since there is little turnover—once a table is booked, it is yours for the whole lunch period or for the evening until closing. Friday and Saturday nights (and Sunday lunch) seatings are often booked out a week or more in advance at some places, so have a few choices in mind if you are booking at the last minute.

Here's a tip for Americans who don't mind dining early. If you stop into or phone a top restaurant and find that it is booked out from 8pm or 8:30pm onward, ask if you can dine early (at 6:30pm or 7pm), with a promise to leave by 8pm, and you will sometimes get a table. A few restaurants are even experimenting with "early bird" menus, with reduced prices, to attract people for early evening seating. Dublin restaurateurs are just beginning to learn that it is a lot more profitable to have more than one seating a night.

Table d'Hôte vs. à la Carte

In most Dublin restaurants, two menus are offered: **table d'hôte**—a set three- or four-course lunch or dinner, with a variety of choices, for a fixed price; and **à la carte**—a menu offering a wide choice of appetizers (starters), soups, main courses, salads or vegetables, and desserts (sweets), each individually priced. With the former, you pay the set price whether you take each course or not, but, if you do take each course, the total price offers very good value. With the latter, you choose what you want and pay accordingly. If you are just a salad and main course person, then à la carte will probably work out to be less expensive, but if you want all the courses and the trimmings, then stick with the table d'hôte.

In the better restaurants, the table d'hôte menu is pushed at lunchtime, particularly for the business clientele. In the evening, both menus are readily available. In the less expensive restaurants, coffee shops, and cafés, you can usually order à la carte style at any time, whether it be a soup and sandwich for lunch or steak and salad at night.

Here is a tip for those on a budget: If you want to try one of Dublin's top-rated restaurants, but can't afford the dinner prices, then have your main meal in the middle of the day by trying the table d'hôte menu. You'll experience the same great cuisine at half the price of a nighttime meal.

PRICES   Meal prices at Dublin restaurants include 12.5% government tax, but service charge is extra. In about two-thirds of Dublin's restaurants, a set service charge is added automatically to your bill—this can range from 10% to 15%. In the remaining restaurants, it is now the custom not to add any service charge, leaving the amount of the tip up to you. Needless to say, this diversity of policy can be confusing for a visitor, but each restaurant normally prints its policy on the menu. If it is not clear, ask.

In the cases when no service charge is added, then you should tip as you normally would in the U.S.—up to 15% depending on the quality of the service. If 10% to 12.5% has already been added to your bill, then you should leave an appropriate amount that will total 15% if service has been satisfactory.

We have classified our favorite Dublin restaurants into categories of location and price. The price levels are based on what it costs for a complete dinner (or lunch, if dinner is not served) for one person including tax and tip, but not wine or alcoholic beverages.

Very Expensive	—	Ł35 ($57.75) and up
Expensive	—	Ł25 to Ł35 ($41.25 to $57.75)
Moderate	—	Ł10 to Ł25 ($16.50 to $41.25)
Inexpensive	—	Ł5 to Ł10 ($8.25 to $16.50)
Budget	—	Under Ł5 ($8.25)

Money-saving tip: Some Dublin restaurants, in all categories of price, offer a fixed-price three-course tourist menu during certain hours and days. These menus offer limited choices, but are usually lower in price than the restaurant's regular table d'hôte menu. Look for a tourist menu with a green Irish chef symbol in the window; there will also be a copy of the menu displayed and the hours when the prices are in effect. As we go to press, the tourist-menu prices, which are set nationally, are as follows:

Three-course meal at £6 ($9.90) or under
Three-course meal at £8.25 ($13.60) or under
Three-course meal at £12 ($19.80) or under

SOME DINING TIPS If you are fond of a cocktail or beer before or during your meal, be sure to check in advance if a restaurant has a "full license"—some restaurants are only licensed to sell wine.

Don't be surprised if you are not ushered to your table as soon as you arrive at a restaurant. This is not a delaying tactic—many of the better dining rooms carry on the old custom of seating you in a lounge or bar area while you sip an apéritif and peruse the menus. Your waiter then comes to discuss the choices and take your order. You are not called to the table until the first course is about to be served. It's a relaxed way of dining, designed to avoid having you sit at a table with empty dishes or glasses—and just another Irish way of making guests feel welcome.

1. HISTORIC OLD CITY/ LIBERTIES

EXPENSIVE

LORD EDWARD, 23 Christchurch Place, Dublin 8. Tel. 542420.
Cuisine: SEAFOOD. **Reservations:** Required. **Bus:** No. 21A, 50, 50A, 78, 78A, or 78B.
$ Prices: Bar lunch £2.95–£11.95 ($4.90–$19.75); dinner appetizers £2.45–£11.75 ($4.05–$19.40); dinner main courses £9.55–£15.75 ($15.75–$26). AE, DC, MC, V.
Open: Lunch Mon–Fri noon–2:45pm; dinner Mon–Sat 5–10:45pm.

Established in 1890 and situated in the heart of the Old City opposite Christ Church Cathedral, this cozy upstairs dining room claims to be Dublin's oldest seafood restaurant. The menu is a piscine lover's delight, with a dozen different preparations of sole including au gratin and Véronique; seven variations of prawns from thermidor to Provençal; and fresh lobster prepared au naturel or in sauces; plus all types of fresh fish, from salmon and sea trout to plaice and turbot—served grilled, fried, meunière, or poached. Vegetarian dishes are also available. At lunchtime, light snacks and simpler fare are served in the bar.

EXPENSIVE/MODERATE

OLD DUBLIN, 90/91 Francis St., Dublin 8. Tel. 542028 or 542346.

   Cuisine: SCANDINAVIAN/RUSSIAN. **Reservations:** Recommended. **Bus:** No. 78A, 78B, or 21A.

$ Prices: Set lunch Ł12 ($19.80); 3-course dinners Ł19–Ł25 ($31.35–$41.25). AE, DC, MC, V.

   Open: Lunch Mon–Fri 12:30–2:15pm, dinner Mon–Sat 7–11pm.

Located in the heart of Dublin's antiques row, this shopfront restaurant is also on the edge of the city's medieval quarter, once settled by Vikings. So it is not surprising that many recipes featured here reflect this background, with a long list of imaginative Scandinavian and Russian dishes. Main courses include novgorod, a rare beef thinly sliced and served on sauerkraut, with fried barley, mushrooms, garlic butter, sour cream, and caviar; salmon kulebjaka, a pastry filled with salmon, dill herbs, rice, egg, mushrooms, and onion; sole Dragamiroff, prepared with prawn and Mornay sauce and garnished with mussels; golubtze, stuffed cabbage leaves, cooked with fresh tomatoes, garlic, onions, and veal consommé; and curried satsivi, seasonal vegetables pan-fried with garlic, curry, peppercorns, and savory rice or kasha barley.

 FROMMER'S SMART TRAVELER: RESTAURANTS

1. If the service charge is not posted, ask if there is any, and what amount has been added to your bill.
2. Patronize the most expensive restaurants for lunch—a set lunch costs about half the price of dinner and the daily menu is often very similar.
3. If you prefer salad or soup and main course only, order from the à la carte menu; if you want three or four courses, the best buy is the table d'hôte set-price meal.
4. Ask if a restaurant offers a reduced price "early bird" menu for dining before 7:30 or 8pm.
5. Check if a restaurant has a fixed-price tourist menu and save at least 25% off normal fixed-price meals.
6. If you drink wine, order a house wine by the carafe; it is much cheaper than ordering a bottle.
7. Order daily specials—they usually offer the best value as well as fresh seasonal ingredients.
8. Look for special offers advertised in the *Irish Times* and other papers—some restaurants offer "dinner for two" specials and other deals.
9. If you are attending a show, ask about pre- or post-theater dinner menus, which offer excellent value.

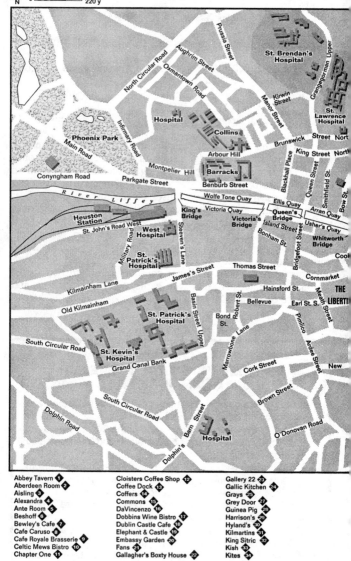

Abbey Tavern ❶	Cloisters Coffee Shop ⑫	Gallery 22 ㉓
Aberdeen Room ❷	Coffee Dock ⑬	Gallic Kitchen ㉔
Aisling ❸	Coffers ⑭	Grays ㉕
Alexandra ❹	Commons ⑮	Grey Door ㉗
Ante Room ❺	DaVincenzo ⑯	Guinea Pig ㉙
Beshoff ❻	Dobbins Wine Bistro ⑰	Harrison's ㉚
Bewley's Cafe ❼	Dublin Castle Cafe ⑱	Hyland's ㉚
Cafe Caruso ❽	Elephant & Castle ⑲	Kilmartins ㉛
Cafe Royale Brasserie ❾	Embassy Garden ⑳	King Sitric ㉜
Celtic Mews Bistro ❿	Fans ㉑	Kish ㉝
Chapter One ⓫	Gallagher's Boxty House ㉒	Kites ㉞

INEXPENSIVE

GALLIC KITCHEN, Back Lane, Dublin 8. Tel. 544912.
   Cuisine: INTERNATIONAL/FAST FOOD. **Reservations:** Not
accepted. **Bus:** No. 21A, 50, 50A, 78, 78A, or 78B.
$ Prices: Appetizers Ł1.95–Ł4 ($3.25–$6.60); main courses
Ł5–Ł7 ($8.25–$11.55). No credit cards.

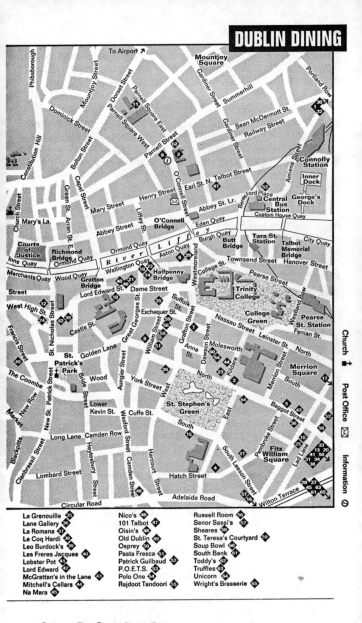

La Grenouille	Nico's	Russell Room
Lane Gallery	101 Talbot	Senor Sassi's
La Romana	Oisin's	Sheares
Le Coq Hardi	Old Dublin	St. Teresa's Courtyard
Leo Burdock's	Osprey	Soup Bowl
Les Freres Jacques	Pasta Fresca	South Bank
Lobster Pot	Patrick Guilbaud	Toddy's
Lord Edward	P.O.E.T.S.	Truffles
McGrattan's in the Lane	Polo One	Unicorn
Mitchell's Cellars	Rajdoot Tandoori	Wright's Brasserie
Na Mara		

Church ■→ Post Office ⊠ Information ⊙

Open: Fri–Sun 10am–5pm.

⭐ Situated at Mother Redcaps Market opposite Christ Church Cathedral, this small enterprise specializes in elegant fast food. Instead of the usual burger or sandwich dispensed at such flea market settings, you can nibble on salmon en croûte, casserole of pork with apple, breast of chicken stuffed with pine nuts, or pastries with fillings such as mousse of sole and salmon or sweet buttery vegetables. There is also a great selection of pâtés, quiches, oven-fresh crispy sausage rolls, vegetable and meat pies, and baked goods, ranging from traditional brown bread and yeasty poppy rolls, to circular spud cakes or rich chocolate cheesecake.

BUDGET

LEO BURDOCK'S, 2 Werburgh St., Dublin 8. Tel. 540306.
  Cuisine: FISH-AND-CHIPS/FAST FOOD. **Reservations:** Not accepted. **Bus:** No. 21A, 50, 50A, 78, 78A, or 78B.
  $ Prices: 70p–£2.50 ($1.15–$4.15). No credit cards.
  Open: Mon–Fri 12:30–11pm, Sat 2–11pm.

Established in 1913, this is a quintessential Dublin "take-away" fish-and-chips shop. Situated at the corner of Castle and Werburgh Streets, it is just a stone's throw from Christ Church Cathedral and other Old City landmarks. Types of fish vary, from ray and cod to whiting, but it is always fresh, light, and flaky, and the chips are said to be among the crispest in town, whether you order "a single" or a "large chip." There is no seating at the shop, but you can recline on a nearby bench or stroll down to the park at St. Patrick's Cathedral.

THE CLOISTERS COFFEE SHOP, High St., Dublin 8. Tel. 679-1855.
  Cuisine: INTERNATIONAL/SELF-SERVICE. **Reservations:** Not accepted. **Bus:** No. 21A, 78A, or 78B.
  $ Prices: 90p–£3.75 ($1.50–$6.20). No credit cards.
  Open: Daily 11am–5pm.

Housed in St. Audeon's Catholic church, this is one of a handful of new eateries springing up in surprising settings. It is cleverly decorated in a monastic theme, with church choir benches and pews and refectory-style tables. The menu features an ever-changing selection of freshly prepared sandwiches, salads, quiches, lasagnes, and traditional sausage rolls, as well as home-baked scones and cakes.

2. TEMPLE BAR/ TRINITY COLLEGE

EXPENSIVE

LES FRERES JACQUES, 74 Dame St., Dublin 2. Tel. 679-4555.
  Cuisine: FRENCH. **Reservations:** Recommended. **Transportation:** Bus no. 50, 50A, 54, 56, and 77.
  $ Prices: Appetizers £4.50–£7.50 ($7.45–$12.40); lunch main courses £6.50–£16 ($10.75–$26.40); dinner main courses £15–£18.95 ($24.75–$31.30). AE, MC, V.
  Open: Lunch Mon–Fri 12:30–2:30pm; dinner Mon–Fri 7–10:30pm, Sat 7–11pm.

Well situated between Crampton Court and Sycamore Street opposite Dublin Castle and next to the Olympia Theatre, this upstairs bistro brings a slice of haute cuisine and ambience to the lower edge of the trendy Temple Bar district. The menu offers creative main courses such as filet of beef in red wine and bone marrow sauce; duck suprême on a sweet-corn pancake in tangy ginger sauce; rosette of spring lamb in meat juice sabayon and tomato coulis with crispy potato straws; veal on rainbow pasta with garlic-and-basil sauce; and grilled lobster from the tank flamed in whiskey.

MODERATE

COFFERS, 6 Cope St., Dublin 2. Tel. 715900.
> **Cuisine:** CONTINENTAL/IRISH. **Reservations:** Recommended. **Transportation:** DART to Tara Street Station or bus no. 21A, 46A, 46B, 51B, 51C, 68, 69, or 86.
> **$ Prices:** Appetizers Ł2–Ł5 ($3.30–$8.25); lunch main courses Ł5–Ł8 ($8.25–$13.20); dinner main courses Ł6–Ł12 ($9.90–$19.80). AE, MC, V.
> **Open:** Lunch Mon–Fri 12:15–2:30pm; dinner Mon–Sat 6–11pm.

This little restaurant, tucked in the heart of the Temple Bar district off Crown Alley, offers a homey fireside atmosphere and down-to-earth prices. The menu blends European flair with Irish ingredients, with dishes such as pannequets of salmon stuffed with mushrooms and herbs; médaillons of beef in garlic butter, escalope of pork with mushroom sauce; duck in peach, cream, and Madeira sauce; and lamb chops in a honey-and-rosemary sauce. On many evenings, there are special three-course pre- and post-theater dinners offered at very affordable prices.

FANS, 60 Dame St., Dublin 2. Tel. 679-4263.
> **Cuisine:** CHINESE. **Reservations:** Recommended. **Bus:** No. 21A, 78A, or 78B.
> **$ Prices:** Appetizers Ł1.90–Ł12 ($3.15–$19.80); lunch main courses Ł4–Ł7 ($6.60–$11.55); dinner main courses Ł6.50–Ł9.50 ($10.75–$15.70). MC, V.
> **Open:** Lunch daily 12:30–2:15pm; dinner daily 6:30–11:30pm.

If you crave a little Chinese food with imagination and a cut above the usual fast-food variety, then this is a good place to know. With a stylish decor of red, gold, and black tones, it is not typically Dublin, but it is worth a look. All the usual Chinese favorites are on the menu, with an emphasis on hot and spicy Cantonese cooking as well as dim sum, curries, and chow mein.

HARRISON'S, 29 Westmoreland St., Dublin 2. Tel. 679-9373.
> **Cuisine:** IRISH/INTERNATIONAL. **Reservations:** Recommended. **Transportation:** DART to Tara Street Station or bus no. 5, 7A, 8, 15A, 15B, 15C, 46, 55, 62, 63, 83, or 84.
> **$ Prices:** Appetizers Ł1.95–Ł3.95 ($3.25–$6.55); lunch main courses Ł3.50–Ł4.95 ($5.80–$8.20); dinner main courses Ł5.95–Ł11.95 ($9.85–$19.75). AE, DC, MC, V.

Open: Mon–Fri noon–10:30pm, Sat–Sun 5–10:30pm.

Ⓢ Situated 1 block south of the Liffey between Burgh Quay and Fleet Street, this modern art deco restaurant occupies a spot that was formerly Harrison and Co. Confectioners, dating back to 1896 and mentioned in James Joyce's *Ulysses*. A plaque outside the front door attests to this honor and the interior decor carries through the theme with Joycean art and memorabilia. The menu blends a variety of influences, from chicken curry or Kiev, to flamed duck with blueberry sauce, paupiettes of lemon sole, prawns Provençal, and scallops with white wine and Cheddar sauce. Steaks are also featured here, with several cuts of filet or sirloin steaks individually cooked to order with a choice of sauces. Other choices include vegetarian plates, pastas, and several house specials such as Irish stew. Lunch items include chicken pancakes or spicy chicken drumsticks, steak-and-kidney pie, chili, lasagne, and vegetarian tagliatelle.

NICO'S, 53 Dame St., Dublin 2. Tel. 773062.
   Cuisine: IRISH/ITALIAN. **Reservations:** Recommended. **Bus:** No. 21A, 78A, or 78B.
$ **Prices:** Appetizers Ł1.50–Ł5.50 ($2.50–$9.10); lunch main courses Ł5.50–Ł7.95 ($9.10–$13.15); dinner main courses Ł6.95–Ł10.95 ($11.50–$18.10). AE, DC, MC, V.

Ⓕ FROMMER'S COOL FOR KIDS: RESTAURANTS

Beshoff *(see p. 92)* or **Leo Burdock's** *(p. 88)* For real Dublin experiences in fast-food eating, these take-out places sell finger-licking fish-and-chips, instead of chicken or the usual kid's fare.

The Cloisters Coffee Shop *(see p. 88)*, **St. Teresa's Courtyard Café** *(see p. 99)*, or **Dublin Castle Café** *(see p. 92)* These three eateries give kids the chance to eat (and talk out loud) in a church.

Elephant & Castle *(see p. 91)* The decor pleases the small fry, with elephants and "Popeye" cartoon characters on the walls, and the food is fast and tasty, especially the "Elephant burger," with a half-dozen ingredients on top.

Pasta Fresca *(see p. 98)* Kids feel at home at this place, with its informal atmosphere, variety of tasty pastas, and well-stocked salad bar.

Hyland's *(see p. 113)* Families enjoy the nautical atmosphere of this restaurant, situated opposite the harbor at Howth. The menu also pleases young appetites, from ribs and pastas to Irish stew, as well as lots of just-caught fresh fish.

Open: Lunch Mon–Fri 12:30–2:30pm; dinner Mon–Sat 6pm–12:30am.

Located at the corner of Temple Lane on the edge of the Temple Bar district, this is one of the busiest restaurants in town, serving Italian food in an Irish style, often with a pianist playing Puccini music in the background. Featured dishes include veal scaloppine, pastas, scampi, and chicken cacciatore, as well as generous cuts of salmon and steaks.

MODERATE/INEXPENSIVE

ELEPHANT & CASTLE, 18 Temple Bar, Dublin 2. Tel. 679-3121.
Cuisine: CALIFORNIAN/INTERNATIONAL. **Reservations:** Not required. **Transportation:** DART to Tara Street Station or bus no. 21A, 46A, 46B, 51B, 51C, 68, 69, or 86.
$ Prices: Appetizers Ł2.25–Ł5.75 ($3.75–$9.50); lunch main courses Ł4.50–Ł7.95 ($7.45–$13.15); dinner main courses Ł5.50–Ł10.50 ($9.10–$17.35). AE, DC, MC, V.
Open: Sun–Thurs 11:30am–11:30pm, Fri–Sat 11:30am–midnight.

Located in the heart of the Temple Bar district, this is an informal and fun restaurant, with simple pinewood tables and benches, and a decor blending modern art with statues of elephants and cartoon figures. The menu is eclectic, offering choices such as spicy Asian curries scented with lemongrass and paired with sweet basmati rice; guacamole and tortilla chips; sesame chicken with spinach and cucumber; fettuccine with shrimp, sun-dried tomatoes, and saffron; linguine with goat cheese, tomato, broccoli, and thyme; and rare sliced steak with cracked pepper, watercress, and ginger vinaigrette; as well as smoked salmon salads, sandwiches, Stilton burgers, and a house special "Elephant burger" with curried sour cream, bacon, scallions, Cheddar, and tomato.

GALLAGHER'S BOXTY HOUSE, 20-21 Temple Bar, Dublin 2. Tel. 772762.
Cuisine: TRADITIONAL IRISH. **Reservations:** Recommended. **Transportation:** DART to Tara Street Station or bus no. 21A, 46A, 46B, 51B, 51C, 68, 69, or 86.
$ Prices: Appetizers Ł1.50–Ł4.50 ($2.50–$7.45); lunch main courses Ł1.95–Ł3.50 ($3.25–$5.80); dinner main courses Ł4.50–Ł9.50 ($7.45–$15.70). MC, V.
Open: Mon–Fri 11am–11pm, Sat–Sun 12:30–11pm.

Although native Irish cooking is sometimes hard to find in Dublin restaurants, this is one spot that keeps the traditions alive, with a particular emphasis on Irish stew, bacon and cabbage, and a dish called boxty. Boxty is an Irish potato pancake grilled and rolled with various fillings, such as beef, lamb, chicken, fish, or combinations such as bacon and cabbage. The menu features all types of boxty as well as salmon and steaks. At lunchtime, there are hearty sandwiches served on open wedges of brown bread.

INEXPENSIVE

BESHOFF, 14 Westmoreland St., Dublin 2. Tel. 778026.
   Cuisine: SEAFOOD/FISH-AND-CHIPS. **Reservations:** Not
   required downstairs; recommended upstairs. **Transportation:**
   DART to Tara Street Station or bus no. 5, 7A, 8, 15A, 15B, 15C,
   46, 55, 62, 63, 83, or 84.
$ Prices: Lunch or dinner appetizers Ł1.50–Ł1.95 ($2.50–$3.25);
   lunch or dinner main courses Ł3.50–Ł7.50 ($5.80–$12.40);
   fast-food counter all items Ł1.90–Ł3.50 ($3.15–$5.80). No credit
   cards for fast food; MC, V for restaurant.
   Open: Downstairs Sun–Thurs 11:30am–11pm, Fri–Sat
   11:30am–3am; upstairs daily noon–10pm.

Little wonder that the Beshoff name is synonymous with fresh
fish in Dublin—Ivan Beshoff settled here in 1913 from Odessa,
Russia, and started a fish business which has now developed
into this top-notch fish-and-chips eatery. With an atmosphere
reminiscent of an Edwardian oyster bar, it offers both self-
service on the ground floor and waitress service upstairs.

The atmosphere is informal and the menu is simple—crisp chips
(french fries) are served with a choice of fresh fish, from the "original
recipe" of cod, to more classy variations using salmon, shark, prawns,
turbot, and other local seafare—some days as many as 20 varieties of
fish. The potatoes are grown on a 300-acre farm in Tipperary and
freshly cut each day. In the upstairs restaurant, you can also get
fisherman's platters, smoked-fish salads, salmon steaks, scampi,
stuffed trout, and fried chicken. A second shop, for fast food only, is
located at 5/6 Upper O'Connell St. in the International Food Court
(tel. 743223).

BUDGET

DUBLIN CASTLE CAFE, Palace St., off Dame St., Dublin 2.
   Tel. 679-3713.
   Cuisine: INTERNATIONAL/SELF-SERVICE. **Reservations:**
   Not required. **Bus:** No. 50, 54 50A, 56A, or 77.
$ Prices: Most items Ł1–Ł3.50 ($1.65–$5.80).
   Open: Mon–Sat 11am–4pm.

Visitors to the Church of the Most Holy Trinity at Dublin Castle are
surprised to find this bustling enterprise tucked into the basement-
level crypt. With whitewashed stone walls, colorful paned windows,
and scalloped alcoves and arches, it provides a medieval setting for a
snack or light lunch. The menu consists of homemade soups, pâtés,
quiches, lasagnes, sausage rolls, stuffed baked potatoes, salads, and
sandwiches, as well as cakes and sweets. The crypt also holds an
interesting gift shop for browsing.

3. ST. STEPHEN'S GREEN/ GRAFTON STREET

VERY EXPENSIVE/EXPENSIVE

AISLING, 27 St. Stephen's Green, Dublin 2. Tel. 766471.
   Cuisine: IRISH/CONTINENTAL. **Reservations:** Required.

Transportation: DART to Pearse Station of bus no. 10, 11A, 11B, 13, or 20B.

$ Prices: Set lunch Ł14.50 ($23.95); dinner appetizers Ł2–Ł10 ($3.30–$16.50); dinner main courses Ł12.50–Ł20 ($20.65–$33). AE, CB, DC, MC, V.

Open: Lunch daily 12:30–2:30pm; dinner Mon–Sat 6:30–10:30pm, Sun 6:30–10pm.

Overlooking St. Stephen's Green, this is the signature restaurant of the fashionable Shelbourne Hotel and a place to be seen and to see the movers and shakers of Dublin society and the international jet set. Using the best of fine linens, silver, and crystal, it presents a formal setting for beautifully presented portions of chateaubriand, rack of lamb, prime ribs cut to order, filet of wild salmon, whole sole on the bone, or roast duckling à l'orange. If your budget won't stretch for a meal, at least have a drink in the equestrian-themed Horseshoe Bar across the lobby.

ALEXANDRA, Earlsfort Terrace, Dublin 2. Tel. 765555.

Cuisine: CONTINENTAL. **Reservations:** Required. **Transportation:** DART to Pearse Station or bus no. 14A or 62.

$ Prices: Set lunch Ł16.50 ($27.25); dinner appetizers Ł2.60–Ł10.50 ($4.30–$17.35); dinner main courses Ł13.90–Ł17.75 ($22.95–$29.30). AE, DC, MC, V.

Open: Lunch Mon–Fri noon–3pm; dinner Mon–Sat 7–10:45pm.

Tucked behind the main lobby of the posh Conrad Hotel, this restaurant exudes the aura of a private club, with dark wood-paneled walls, a glowing hearth, and fine crystal, china, and silver plate settings. The imaginative menu changes often, but usually features dishes such as chateaubriand with a bouquet of fresh vegetables; coquilles St-Jacques; chicken with smoked salmon and whiskey sauce; black sole with capers; lobster with tagliatelle pasta; rack of lamb persillade with courgettes in a light garlic juice; roasted veal mignon with glazed baby onions, mushrooms, and ginger-cream sauce; or baked filets of brill with black-pepper crust, vegetable spaghetti, and red wine sauce. It is conveniently situated just off St. Stephen's Green, opposite the National Concert Hall.

THE COMMONS, 85-86 St. Stephen's Green, Dublin 2. Tel. 780530 or 780539.

Cuisine: CONTINENTAL. **Reservations:** Required. **Transportation:** DART to Pearse Station or bus no. 14A or 62.

$ Prices: Set lunch Ł16 ($26.40); set dinner Ł27.50 ($45.40). AE, MC, V.

Open: Lunch Mon–Fri 12:30–2:15pm; dinner Mon–Sat 7–10pm.

Nestled on the south side of St. Stephen's Green, this relatively new restaurant occupies the basement level of Newman House (see "More Attractions" in Chapter 6), the historic seat of Ireland's major university and comprised of two elegant town houses dating back to 1740. The interior of the dining rooms is a blend of Georgian architecture, cloister-style arches, and original contemporary artworks with Joycean influences. For an apéritif in fine weather, there is a lovely stone courtyard terrace surrounded by a "secret garden" filled with lush plants and trees. The inventive menu changes daily, but often offers dishes such as pan-fried tuna with red wine; roast spring lamb Provençal with thyme and honey; grilled filet of sole coated with almonds and breadcrumbs in olive oil dressing; roast partridge stuffed with pistachio nuts on a tarragon vinegar sauce; and grilled filet of beef with Guinness and oyster sauce.

RUSSELL ROOM, off Grafton St., Dublin 2. Tel. 679-1122.
   Cuisine: FRENCH/IRISH. **Reservations:** Required. **Transportation:** DART to Pearse Station or bus no. 10, 11A, 11B, 13, or 20B.
$ Prices: Set lunch £18.50 ($30.55); dinner appetizers £3.30–£8.70 ($5.45–$14.35); dinner main courses £7.40–£28.95 ($12.25–$47.80). AE, CB, DC, MC, V.
   Open: Lunch daily 12:30–2:30pm; dinner daily 7–10:30pm.

Located on the upper lobby level of the Westbury Hotel in the heart of the city's main shopping area, this spacious and wide-windowed dining room overlooks the bustling activity of Grafton Street. The decor is relaxing, with a blend of light peach and green linens and fine silver, set off by crystal lighting, trellis dividers, and lots of leafy plants. The menu features the best of Irish ingredients, with main courses ranging from lobster Newburg, filet of wild salmon topped with Dublin Bay prawns, and crêpes fruits de mer, to chateaubriand, rack of lamb; chicken Kiev, duck with orange-and-brandy sauce, and filet of veal in lemon-and-ginger sauce.

EXPENSIVE

OISIN'S, 31 Upper Camden St., Dublin 2. Tel. 753433.
   Cuisine: IRISH. **Reservations:** Recommended. **Bus:** No. 55 or 83.
$ Prices: Set dinner £25 ($41.25). AE, DC, MC, V.
   Open: Sept–May, dinner Tues–Sat 6:30–10:30pm; June–Aug, dinner daily 6:30–10:30pm.

Although this restaurant is situated slightly off the beaten track, it is only about 3 blocks southwest of St. Stephen's Green and well worth a detour. Housed in a small shopfront building and named after a legendary Irish folk hero, it is the brainchild of Feargal and Angela O hUiginn, a young couple who apply haute cuisine standards to traditional Irish dishes. The homey decor features Irish art and wall hangings as well as musical instruments, such as a guitar, fiddle, and banjo, all of which are usually pressed into service as hosts and guests join in a spontaneous session of Irish music as the meal ends.

The menu, which is printed in Irish and English using Celtic uncial script, offers traditional dishes such as Irish stew with dumplings or pheasant pie, as well as breast of duck with brambleberry sauce; pigeon breast with Guinness mustard sauce; Wellington steak with Irish whiskey cream; stuffed filet of lamb with apple-mint sauce; salmon in pastry; and black sole with mushrooms and caper butter. Other local favorites, such as crubeens, Dublin coddle, boxty, colcannon, and champ, are offered as appetizers or accompaniments.

POLO ONE, 5/6 Molesworth Place, off Molesworth St., Dublin 2. Tel. 766442.

Cuisine: CALIFORNIA/CONTINENTAL. **Reservations:** Recommended. **Transportation:** DART to Pearse Station or bus no. 10, 11A, 11B, 13, or 20B.

$ Prices: Set lunch Ł14.95 ($24.70); dinner appetizers Ł4–Ł6 ($6.60–$9.90); dinner main courses Ł14.50–Ł16.50 ($23.95–$27.25). AE, DC, MC, V.

Open: Lunch Mon–Sat 12:30–3pm; dinner Mon–Sat 7:30–11pm.

Fancifully decorated with modern artwork and skylights, this trendy restaurant is wedged in a laneway between Dawson and Kildare Streets, almost equidistant from either Trinity College or St. Stephen's Green. It is also within a block of the various government buildings, so it attracts a mixed crowd of politicians, professors, and professionals who seek lively food and atmosphere. The eclectic menu ranges from roast suckling pig or paella with saffron rice; to confit of duck with angel hair; roast leg of spring lamb with black olives and garlic; poached sea bass; roast filet of red tuna; chargrilled whole quail; and médaillons of beef with black truffles and Madeira wine sauce.

SOUP BOWL, 2 Molesworth Place, off Molesworth St., Dublin 2. Tel. 618918.

Cuisine: IRISH/CONTINENTAL. **Reservations:** Required. **Transportation:** DART to Pearse Station or bus no. 10, 11A, 11B, 13, or 20B.

$ Prices: Appetizers Ł3–Ł7.95 ($4.95–$13.15); lunch main courses Ł7–Ł10 ($11.55–$16.50); dinner main courses Ł12.95–Ł17.95 ($21.40–$29.65). AE, DC, MC, V.

Open: Lunch Mon–Sat 12:30–2:30pm; dinner Mon–Sat 6:30–11:30pm.

Although fairly new to the Dublin scene, this restaurant has made waves by reviving the name of an earlier eatery that enjoyed great stature in the 1960s and 70s. With seating for just 35 people, the "new" Soup Bowl seeks to impart exclusivity and a clubby atmosphere, nestled in an ideal setting near the government buildings, museums, and fashionable shopping streets. The menu leans heavily toward fish choices, such as poached turbot with wine and lobster sauce; filet of plaice with prawns in Mornay sauce; poached or grilled salmon with tartar or béarnaise sauce; the "house special" of prawns, crab, and other fish in lobster sauce topped with cheese; and grilled lamb with mint sauce. For nonfish eaters, there are always vegetarian choices as well as a half duckling in brandy sauce, chicken Kiev, or steak with Madeira sauce.

IMPRESSIONS

The most hospitable city I ever passed through.
—MARY WOLLSTONECRAFT, 1796

'Enjoy yourself now!' everybody says in Dublin, and they mean enjoy yourself notwithstanding.
—JAN MORRIS, TRAVELS, 1976

The most instantly talkative city in Europe.
—V. S. PRITCHETT, 1978

IMPRESSIONS

This is the royal city and seat of Ireland, a famous town for merchandise, the chief court of Justice, in munition strong, in buildings gorgeous, in citizens populous. . . . Seated it is in a right delectable and wholesome place: for to the south yee have hills mounting up aloft, westward an open champion ground, and on the east the sea at hand and in sight: The River Liffey running down at north-east affordeth a safe road and harbor for ships. By the river side, are certain wharves or quays, as we term them, whereby the violent force of the water might be restrained.
—WILLIAM CAMDEN, 1610

A handsomer town, with fewer people in it, it is impossible to see on a summer's day.
—W. M. THACKERAY, 1843

GALLERY 22, 22 St. Stephen's Green, Dublin 2. Tel. 616669.
Cuisine: FRENCH. **Reservations:** Recommended. **Transportation:** DART to Pearse Station or bus no. 10, 11A, 11B, 13, or 20B.
$ Prices: Appetizers Ł3.25–Ł5.95 ($5.40–$9.85), lunch main courses Ł6–Ł10 ($9.90–$16.50); dinner main courses Ł10.95–Ł14.95 ($18.10–$24.70). AE, DC, MC, V.
Open: Lunch Mon–Fri 12:15–2:30pm; dinner Tues–Sat 6:15–10:45pm.

Just five doors from the Shelbourne Hotel on the north side of St. Stephen's Green, this 50-seat basement restaurant is a convenient in-town dining venue, with a gardenlike setting. The menu offers choices such as rack of lamb; sole meunière; poached breast of chicken with smoked salmon cream [sauce] and spinach filling with prawn sauce; salmon en croûte with mushrooms and herb-dill sauce; julienne of chicken and prawns with lemon-garlic sauce; and duck with orange and Cointreau sauce.

MODERATE

CAFE CARUSO, 47 S. William St., Dublin 2. Tel. 770708.
Cuisine: ITALIAN/INTERNATIONAL. **Reservations:** Recommended. **Bus:** No. 16A, 19A, 22A, 55, or 83.
$ Prices: Appetizers Ł2.75–Ł4.50 ($4.55–$7.45); lunch main courses Ł5.50–Ł11.50 ($9.10–$19); dinner main courses Ł7.40–Ł12.50 ($12.25–$20.65). AE, MC, V.
Open: Lunch Mon–Fri 12:30–2:30pm; dinner Mon–Sat 6pm–12:15am, Sun 6–11:15pm.

Skylit and plant filled, this festive and airy eatery is just 2 blocks from St. Stephen's Green or Grafton Street. As its name implies, it brings a touch of Italy and beyond to this corner of the city. The menu features a variety of freshly made pastas as well as such dishes as pork marsala and osso buco. In addition, the choices often include steaks, seafood, lamb kidneys; chicken Kiev, rack of lamb; and traditional Irish stew. A resident pianist supplies background music.

LA GRENOUILLE, 64 S. William St., Dublin 2. Tel. 779157.
   Cuisine: FRENCH. **Reservations:** Recommended. **Transportation:** DART to Tara Street Station or bus no. 16A, 19A, 22A, 55, or 83.
$ Prices: Appetizers ŧ1.50–ŧ4.50 ($2.50–$7.45); main courses ŧ6–ŧ10.50 ($9.90–$17.35). AE, DC, MC, V.
   Open: Dinner daily 6–11pm.

Ⓢ Situated within a block of the Westbury Hotel and the Powerscourt Town House complex, this basement restaurant is small and intimate, like a Parisian bistro, with a creative menu offering dishes such as rack of lamb; filet of sole in pastry with basil coulis; rainbow trout amandine with tomato sauce; brace of deboned quail with Cumberland sauce; lamb kidney in Dijon sauce; chicken stuffed with smoked salmon and veal mousse; or filet of beef with a choice of sauces.

RAJDOOT TANDOORI, 26/28 Clarendon St., Dublin 2. Tel. 679-4274 or 679-4280.
   Cuisine: NORTH INDIAN. **Reservations:** Recommended. **Transportation:** DART to Tara Street Station or bus no. 16A, 19A, 22A, 55, or 83.
$ Prices: Set lunch from ŧ6.95 ($11.50); dinner appetizers ŧ3.45–ŧ4.95 ($6–$8.20); dinner main courses ŧ6.95–ŧ10.95 ($11.50–$18.10). AE, DC, MC, V.
   Open: Lunch Mon–Sat noon–2:30pm; dinner Mon–Sat 6:30–11:30pm.

Chefs from India and Nepal combine their talents to produce meals of impeccable quality at this richly decorated outpost of Eastern cuisine located next to the Westbury Hotel. Tandoori cooking in a charcoal clay oven is featured here for barbecued beef, chicken, prawns, and lamb. Other main dishes range from spicy quail to pheasant and lobster, as well as chicken and prawn curries, shish kebabs, and vegetarian dishes.

MODERATE/INEXPENSIVE

MITCHELL'S CELLARS, 21 Kildare St., Dublin 2. Tel. 680367.
   Cuisine: IRISH/CONTINENTAL. **Reservations:** Not accepted. **Transportation:** DART to Pearse Station or bus no. 10, 11A, 11B, 13, or 20B.
$ Prices: Appetizers ŧ1.50–ŧ2 ($2.50–$3.30); main courses ŧ4.75–ŧ6.50 ($7.85–$10.75). AE, DC, MC, V.
   Open: Oct–May, lunch Mon–Sat 12:15–2:30pm; June–Sept, lunch Mon–Fri 12:15–2:30pm.

Originally a wine cellar, this trendy 60-seat luncheon spot has lots of atmosphere, with barrel-shaped tables, tiled floors, a beamed ceiling, and red-and-white lights. A favorite with Dubliners, it's located close to Grafton Street, Trinity College, St. Stephen's Green, and the Irish government buildings. The ever-changing menu often includes seafood salads, country pâtés, vegetable quiches, sweet-and-sour pork, beef braised in Guinness, chicken à la Suisse, or fricassee of veal. It's very popular, so get here early.

UNICORN, 12B Merrion Court, off Merrion Row, Dublin 2. Tel. 688552 or 762182.

Cuisine: ITALIAN. **Reservations:** Recommended. **Transportation:** DART to Pearse Station or bus no. 10.

$ Prices: Appetizers Ł1.50–Ł5.80 ($2.50–$9.60); lunch main courses Ł3.50–Ł5 ($5.80–$8.25); dinner main courses Ł4.60–Ł9.80 ($7.60–$16.20). MC, V.

Open: Lunch Mon–Sat noon–3pm; dinner Mon–Sat 6–10pm.

Ever since 1939, this has been a favorite place to go in Dublin for Italian food. Renato and Nina Sidoli combine the freshest of Irish ingredients with old family recipes from their homeland. Menu choices include whole-meal smoked salmon pizza; pizza pescatore with prawns and mussels; vitello alla casalinga (veal with capers, garlic, anchovies, parsley, and white wine); and veal Valdostana (with cheese sauce, tomatoes, and asparagus tips), as well as a variety of freshly made pastas and seafood. Situated close to St. Stephen's Green, this 76-seat Irish trattoria is a favorite with local TV personalities, university professors, and politicians.

INEXPENSIVE

PASTA FRESCA, 3/4 Chatham St., Dublin 2. Tel. 679-2402.

Cuisine: ITALIAN. **Reservations:** Recommended. **Bus:** No. 10, 11A, 11B, 13, or 20B.

$ Prices: Appetizers Ł1.95–Ł3.95 ($3.25–$6.55); main courses Ł4.95–Ł8.95 ($8.20–$14.80). MC, V.

Open: Lunch Mon–Sat 11:30am–6pm; dinner Tues–Sat 6–11:30pm.

Situated just a block from Grafton Street and St. Stephen's Green and around the corner from the Gaiety Theatre, this trattoria-style eatery is popular with shoppers and for pre- and post-theater dinners. The menu features a variety of pastas, from fettuccine or tagliatelle to lasagne, spaghetti, and ravioli. Most pasta main courses entitle you to helpings from the well-stocked salad bar.

PERIWINKLE SEAFOOD BAR, 59 S. William St., Dublin 2. Tel. 679-4203.

Cuisine: SEAFOOD. **Reservations:** Not required. **Transportation:** DART to Tara Street Station or bus no. 16A, 19A, 22A, 55, or 83.

$ Prices: Appetizers Ł1.75–Ł4 ($2.90–$6.60); main courses Ł4–Ł9 ($6.60–$14.85). No credit cards.

Open: Mon–Fri 10:30am–5pm, Sat 11:30am–5pm.

Situated on the ground floor of the Powerscourt Town House Centre, this small and informal eatery is an Irish version of an oyster bar. The ever-changing menu features the freshest of the local Irish catch, from Dublin prawns to smoked salmon platters, toasted crab toes in garlic butter, and monkfish kebabs, as well as salmon and mackerel pâtés, and a house chowder, made of smoked fish filets, tomato, and potato, served piping hot in an Irish-made pottery bowl.

BUDGET

BEWLEY'S CAFE, 78/79 Grafton St., Dublin 2. Tel. **776761.**
   Cuisine: IRISH. **Reservations:** Not required. **Transportation:** DART to Pearse Station or bus no. 15A, 15B, 15C, 46, 55, 63, or 83.
$ **Prices:** All items £1–£5 ($1.65–$8.25). AE, DC, MC, V.
   Open: Mon–Fri 7:30am–10pm, Sat 8am–10pm, Sun 9:30am–7pm.

To experience the real flavor of Dublin, you have to sip a cup of coffee or tea at Bewley's, a three-story landmark founded in 1840 by a Quaker named Joshua Bewley. With a traditional decor of high ceilings, stained-glass windows, and dark woods, this busy coffee shop–cum–restaurant serves breakfast and light meals, but is best known for its dozens of different types of freshly brewed coffees and teas, accompanied by home-baked scones, pastries, or sticky buns. Other items on the menu range from soups and salads to sandwiches and quiches. There's a choice of self-service or waitress/waiter service, depending on which floor or room you choose. There are several branches throughout Dublin, including 11/12 Westmoreland St., Dublin 2 (tel. 776761), and 13 S. Great George's St., Dublin 2 (tel. 679-2078).

ST. TERESA'S COURTYARD, Clarendon St., Dublin 2. Tel. **718466** or 718127.
   Cuisine: IRISH/SELF-SERVICE. **Reservations:** Not required.
   Transportation: DART to Tara Street Station or bus no. 16, 16A, 19, 19A, 22A, 55, or 83.
$ **Prices:** All items 50p–£1.90 (85¢–$3.15). No credit cards.
   Open: Mon–Sat 10:30am–4pm.

Situated in the cobbled courtyard of early-19th-century St. Teresa's Church (see "More Attractions" in Chapter 6), this serene little dining room is one of a handful of new eateries inconspicuously springing up in historic or ecclesiastical surroundings. With high ceilings and an old-world decor, it offers a welcome contrast to the bustle of Grafton Street a block away or Powerscourt Town House Centre across the street. The menu changes daily but usually includes homemade soups, sandwiches, salads, quiches, lasagnes, sausage rolls, hot scones, and other baked goods.

4. FITZWILLIAM/MERRION SQUARES

VERY EXPENSIVE

PATRICK GUILBAUD, 46 James Place, off Lower Baggot St., Dublin 2. Tel. 764192.
   Cuisine: FRENCH NOUVELLE. **Reservations:** Required.
   Transportation: DART to Pearse Station or bus no. 10.

$ Prices: Set lunch Ł16 ($26.40); dinner appetizers Ł4–Ł10 ($6.60–$16.50); dinner main courses Ł14–Ł18 ($23.10–$29.70). AE, DC, MC, V.

Open: Lunch Tues–Sat 12:30–2pm; dinner Tues–Sat 7:30–10:15pm.

Tucked in an laneway behind the Bank of Ireland building between Fitzwilliam Street and the Grand Canal, this modern skylight restaurant could be easily overlooked except for its glowing reputation for fine food and artful service. The menu features such dishes as casserole of black sole and prawns; steamed salmon with orange and grapefruit sauce; breast of pheasant on warm cabbage and bacon salad; filet of beef served with red wine and marrow bone sauce; roast duck with honey; and breast of guinea fowl with cloves and bacon cream.

EXPENSIVE

DOBBINS WINE BISTRO, 15 Stephen's Lane, off Upper Mount St., Dublin 2. Tel. 764679 or 764670.

    Cuisine: IRISH/CONTINENTAL. **Reservations:** Recommended. **Transportation:** DART to Pearse Station or bus no. 5, 7A, 8, 46, or 84.

$ Prices: Set lunch Ł14.50 ($23.95); dinner appetizers Ł3.95–Ł7.95 ($6.55–$13.15); dinner main courses Ł13.50–Ł15 ($22.30–$24.75). AE, DC, MC, V.

Open: Lunch Mon–Fri 12:30–3pm; dinner Tues–Sat 8pm–midnight.

Tucked in a laneway between Upper and Lower Mount Streets 1 block east of fashionable Merrion Square, this friendly enclave is a haven for inventive cuisine. The menu changes often, but usually includes such items as duckling with orange-and-port sauce; steamed paupiette of black sole with salmon, crab, and prawn filling; fresh prawns in garlic butter; breast of chicken stuffed with potato and mushrooms wrapped in smoked bacon; brace of quail with caramelized red cabbage and port sauce, and filet of beef topped with crispy herb breadcrumbs with a shallot and Madeira sauce. You'll have a choice of sitting in the main bistro-style restaurant with checkered tablecloths and sawdust on the floor or in the leafy tropical patio area with an all-weather sliding glass roof.

GREY DOOR, 23 Upper Pembroke St., Dublin 2. Tel. 763286.

    Cuisine: RUSSIAN/SCANDINAVIAN. **Reservations:** Required. **Bus:** No. 46A, 46B, or 86.

$ Prices: Set lunch Ł15 ($24.75); appetizers Ł4–Ł8 ($6.60–$13.20); main courses Ł11–Ł21 ($18.15–$34.65). AE, DC, MC, V.

Open: Lunch Mon–Fri 12:30–2:30pm; dinner Mon–Sat 7–11pm.

Housed in a fine old Georgian town house with a gray front door, this 35-seat restaurant is known for its eastern and northern European delicacies. Specialties include seafood Zakuski in puff pastry; Kotlety

Kiev, a variation of chicken Kiev stuffed with vodka butter; Galupsti Maskova, minced lamb wrapped in cabbage; and Scandinavian seafood combinations. For a more informal setting and some of the same menu items, there is a basement-level wine bar and bistro, Blushes, with more moderate prices. It is located less than a block southwest of Fitzwilliam Square near the junction of Leeson Street.

MODERATE

ANTE ROOM, 20 Lower Baggot St., Dublin 2. Tel. 604716 or 618832.
   Cuisine: SEAFOOD. **Reservations:** Recommended. **Transportation:** DART to Pearse Station or bus no. 10.
$ **Prices:** Appetizers Ł2.80–Ł6.50 ($4.65–$10.75); lunch main courses Ł3.95–Ł6.95 ($6.55–$11.50); dinner main courses Ł6.90–Ł14.50 ($11.40–$23.95). AE, DC, MC, V.
   Open: Lunch Mon–Fri noon–3pm; dinner daily 6–11pm.

Housed in the basement of Georgian House Guesthouse at the juncture of Pembroke Street in between Merrion and Fitzwilliam Squares, this cozy bistro-style eatery specializes in seafood. The menu focuses on several variations of salmon, trout, sole, lobster, scallops, and crab claws, as well as such landlubber dishes as filet of beef in pastry, stir-fry chicken, vegetable and bean sprout casseroles, and an assortment of steaks.

CELTIC MEWS BISTRO, 109A Lower Baggot St., Dublin 2. Tel. 760796 or 682327.
   Cuisine: NEW IRISH/INTERNATIONAL. **Reservations:** Recommended. **Transportation:** DART to Pearse Station or bus no. 10.
$ **Prices:** Set lunch Ł12 ($19.80); dinner appetizers Ł2.65–Ł5.75 ($4.40–$9.50); dinner main courses Ł8.95–Ł12.95 ($14.80–$21.40). AE, MC, V.
   Open: Lunch Mon–Fri 12:30–2pm; dinner Mon–Sat 6:30–11pm.

As its name implies, this is a cozy Georgian-style mews in the heart of the city, just off Fitzwilliam Street. It was converted into a restaurant by the Gray family more than 20 years ago. The atmosphere here is warm and welcoming, with restful tones of salmon pink and blue, banquette seating, and original copper wall hangings, with skylight by day or candlelight in the evening. The menu ranges from Celtic steak flambé and filet of spring lamb with batons of vegetables to traditional Irish lamb stew, sautéed chicken with egg noodles and bean sprouts, or vegetarian risotto with tomato-and-cheese sauce. Low-calorie dishes are also a specialty.

THE LANE GALLERY, 55 Pembroke Lane, off Pembroke St., Dublin 2. Tel. 611829.
   Cuisine: FRENCH. **Reservations:** Recommended. **Transportation:** DART to Pearse Station or bus no. 10.
$ **Prices:** Set lunch Ł7.50–Ł12.50 ($12.40–$20.65); dinner appe-

tizers Ł1.90–Ł7 ($3.15–$11.55); dinner main courses Ł9.50–Ł12 ($15.70–$19.80). MC, V.
Open: Lunch Mon–Fri 12:30–2:30pm; dinner Tues–Sat 7:30–11pm.

An ever-changing display of paintings and works by local artists is the focal point of this restaurant, tucked in a laneway between Baggot Street and Fitzwilliam Square near the Focus Theatre. The decor compliments the art, with skylight or candlelight, whitewashed brick walls, and pastel linens. The menu is equally artistic, with choices such as filet of beef with smoked bacon and black-pepper sauce; rack of lamb with tomato coulis and mint jus; prawns in chive and ginger sauce; salmon on a bed of leeks with spinach-butter sauce; roast brace of quail with white and black pudding and whiskey sauce; Barbary duck; or breast of chicken stuffed with walnut mousse. There is live piano music most evenings from 9pm.

McGRATTAN'S IN THE LANE, 76 Fitzwilliam Lane, Dublin 2. Tel. 618808.
   Cuisine: IRISH/FRENCH. **Reservations:** Recommended.
   Transportation: DART to Pearse Station or bus no. 10.
$ **Prices:** Appetizers Ł3.75–Ł8.95 ($6.20–$14.80); lunch main courses Ł4–Ł8 ($6.60–$13.20); dinner main courses Ł10.50–Ł13.95 ($17.35–$23). AE, MC, V.
   Open: Lunch Sun–Fri noon–3pm; dinner Mon–Sun 6–11pm.

Out of view from the general flow of traffic, this restaurant is tucked in a laneway between Baggot Street and Merrion Square. There is a lovely Georgian doorway at the entrance, and inside the decor ranges from a homey fireside lounge with "oldies" background music to a bright skylit and plant-filled dining room. The creative menu includes main dishes such as paupiettes of sole florentine; baked salmon in pastry with ginger and lettuce sauce; mille-feuilles of seafood with Provençal sauce; mousse of plaice and red caviar in a smoked-salmon jacket; breast of free-range chicken stuffed with Parma ham and cheese in cèpes sauce; breast of Barbary duck served with beer and raspberry sauce; escalope of veal in mushroom and apple sauce; and charcoal-grilled steaks.

MODERATE/INEXPENSIVE

SHEARES, 31 Lower Baggot St., Dublin 2. Tel. 768103.
   Cuisine: FRENCH/ITALIAN. **Reservations:** Recommended.
   Transportation: DART to Pearse Station or bus no. 10.
$ **Prices:** Appetizers Ł1.95–Ł4.95 ($3.25–$8.20); lunch main courses Ł3.95–Ł7.95 ($6.50–$13.15); dinner main courses Ł7–Ł9.95 ($11.55–$16.45). MC, V.
   Open: Lunch Mon–Sat noon–2:30pm; dinner Mon–Sat 6–11pm.

Steaks cooked to order—enhanced by various sauces and marinades, are the specialty of this small 30-seat candlelit restaurant, nestled in the basement of a Georgian town house. In addition, the menu offers rack of lamb with rosemary and garlic breadcrumbs in a concassé sauce; chicken prepared à la Kiev, florentine, or lemon-style; fresh jumbo prawns in garlic sauce or cooked to order; fresh salmon in sorel sauce, and sole bonne femme.

INEXPENSIVE

GRAYS, 109D Lower Baggot St., Dublin 2. Tel. 760676.
 Cuisine: INTERNATIONAL. **Reservations:** Not required at lunch; recommended for dinner. **Transportation:** DART to Pearse Station or bus no. 10.
$ Prices: Lunch items Ŀ1.50–Ŀ4.95 ($2.50–$8.20); dinner appetizers 95p–Ŀ2.95 ($1.60–$4.90); dinner main courses Ŀ4.50–Ŀ9.50 ($7.45–$15.70). MC, V.
 Open: Breakfast and lunch Mon–Fri 7:30am–5pm; dinner Tues–Sat 5–11pm.

A self-service eatery by day (until 5pm), this cozy converted mews becomes a full-fledged restaurant at night. The decor is eclectic, with choir benches, caned chairs, and lots of hanging plants, and seating is offered on ground and upstairs levels, including an outdoor courtyard for dining in fine weather. For lunch, the choices concentrate on sandwiches and salads made to order, while the dinner main courses range from simple fare of burgers, steaks, pastas, and pizzas, to more creative cooking—poached salmon with dill sauce, chicken Kiev, and médaillons of pork with mustard sauce. If you arrive between 5pm and 7pm, there is usually an early-bird menu, with most main courses under Ŀ5 ($8.25).

5. BALLSBRIDGE/EMBASSY ROW

VERY EXPENSIVE

KISH, Pembroke Rd., Ballsbridge, Dublin 4. Tel. 605000.
 Cuisine: SEAFOOD. **Reservations:** Required. **Transportation:** DART to Lansdowne Road Station or bus no. 5, 7, 7A, 8, 46, 63, or 84.
$ Prices: Appetizers Ŀ5.75–Ŀ10.65 ($9.50–$17.60); main courses Ŀ13.85–Ŀ29.95 ($22.85–$49.45). AE, CB, DC, MC, V.
 Open: Dinner only Mon–Sat 6:30–10:45pm.

Fish and crustacean lovers, take note. Overlooking the skylit Pavilion of Jurys Hotel, this award-winning restaurant has set the standard for creatively prepared Irish seafood. Ideal for a special occasion or for that big splurge, this elegant two-tiered dining room is named after a landmark lighthouse off the Irish coast. The extensive menu offers all types of piscine delights from nearby seas, rivers, lakes, brooks, and bays, all cooked to order or prepared in a variety of memorable ways.

Signature dishes include sole Waleska, filets garnished with lobster, prawns, truffles, and coated with cheese sauce; filet of salmon in phyllo pastry, filled with a prawn parfait on a yellow pepper and scallop coral sauce; lightly steamed smoked haddock wrapped in lettuce leaves and garnished with anchovy filets on a tomato and ginger sauce; lobster in cognac sauce with pilaf rice or served à la crème, Newburg, or thermidor style; scallops and prawns with julienne of leek, flamed with cognac and finished with lobster sauce. In addition to the more than two dozen seafood dishes regularly featured, there are nightly seasonal specials, several low-calorie and vegetarian dishes, and a token landlubber main course (strips of beef and prawns in paprika, flamed in Irish whiskey and finished with lemon sauce).

LE COQ HARDI, 35 Pembroke Rd., Ballsbridge, Dublin 4. Tel. 684130 or 689070.

Cuisine: FRENCH. **Reservations:** Required. **Transportation:** DART to Lansdowne Road Station or bus no. 18, 46, 63, or 84.

$ Prices: Set lunch Ł16.50 ($27.25); dinner appetizers Ł5–Ł15 ($8.25–$24.75); dinner main courses Ł20–Ł30 ($33–$49.50). AE, DC, MC, V.

Open: Lunch Mon–Fri 12:30–3pm; dinner Mon–Sat 7–11pm.

They say that this is the only place in Dublin where Rolls-Royces vie nightly for parking places. Located on the corner of Wellington Road in a Georgian town house setting close to the American embassy and leading hotels such as Jurys and the Berkeley Court, this plush 50-seat restaurant has no trouble drawing a well-heeled local and international business clientele. Chef John Howard has garnered many an award by offering such specialties as Dover sole stuffed with prawns; turbot with beef marrow; filet of prime beef in red wine sauce with wild mushrooms; pot au feu; caneton à l'orange; and steaks flamed in Irish whiskey. Eight or nine-course *dégustation* menus are also offered for those who want to sample the best of everything. The 600-bin wine cellar boasts a complete collection of Château Mouton Rothschild, dating from 1945 to the present.

EXPENSIVE

EMBASSY GARDEN, Pembroke Rd., Ballsbridge, Dublin 4. Tel. 605000.

Cuisine: INTERNATIONAL. **Reservations:** Recommended. **Transportation:** DART to Lansdowne Road Station or bus no. 5, 7, 7A, 8, 46, 63, or 84.

$ Prices: Set lunch Ł13–Ł15.50 ($21.45–$25.60); dinner appetizers Ł2–Ł8 ($3.30–$13.20); dinner main courses Ł11–Ł19 ($18.15–$31.35). AE, CB, DC, MC, V.

Open: Lunch daily 12:30–2:15pm; dinner daily 6:15–10:45pm.

As the main dining room of Jurys Hotel, this restaurant has wide-windowed views of the hotel's central palm tree–lined gardens, waterfall, and swimming pool. It's a relaxing setting, with ambience and service that stand out among the city's hotel dining rooms. Main courses include free-range breast of duck with apricot and cassis sauce; seared calves' liver and smoked bacon with toasted mushrooms; wild suprême of salmon; filet of sole garnished with lobster, prawns, and truffles in buttered cheese sauce; chateaubriand with a bouquet of vegetables; filets of baby beef filled with cream cheese and wild mushrooms; trio of beef, lamb, and veal in three sauces; rack of mountain lamb with garlic sauce; and roast beef cut to order from the trolley. In addition, there are several low-calorie and vegetarian choices such as roast crispy avocado in phyllo pastry with vegetable mousse on cauliflower purée sauce.

KITES, 17 Ballsbridge Terrace, Ballsbridge, Dublin 4. Tel. 607415.

Cuisine: CHINESE. **Reservations:** Recommended. **Transportation:** DART to Lansdowne Road Station or bus no. 5, 7, 7A, 8, 46, 63, or 84.

$ Prices: Appetizers Ł3.50–Ł9 ($5.80–$14.85); lunch main courses Ł6.50–Ł12 ($10.75–$19.80); dinner main courses Ł8.50–Ł16 ($14–$26.40). AE, DC, MC, V.

Open: Lunch Mon–Fri 12:30–2pm; dinner daily 6:30–11:30pm.

Handily located between the American embassy and the Royal Dublin Society Showgrounds, this Asian-themed restaurant is housed in a Georgian town house just off Pembroke Road and diagonally across the street from Jurys Hotel. The menu features the usual chow meins, curries, and sweet-and-sour dishes, as well as a host of creative main courses such as king prawns with Chinese leaves in oyster sauce, stuffed crab claws, Singapore fried noodles, and birds' nests of fried potatoes.

LOBSTER POT, 9 Ballsbridge Terrace, Ballsbridge, Dublin 4. Tel. 680025.

Cuisine: SEAFOOD. **Reservations:** Required. **Transportation:** DART to Lansdowne Road Station or bus no. 5, 7, 7A, 8, 46, 63, or 84.

$ Prices: Appetizers Ł2–Ł5.25 ($3.30–$8.70); lunch main courses Ł7–Ł10 ($11.55–$16.50); dinner main courses Ł9.95–Ł16.25 ($16.45–$26.85). AE, DC, MC, V.

Open: Lunch Mon–Fri 12:30–2:30pm; dinner Mon–Sat 6:30–10:30pm.

Positioned between the American embassy and the Royal Dublin Society Showgrounds, almost opposite Jurys Hotel, this upstairs restaurant is known for its lobster dishes, as its name implies. Other entrees on the menu range from sole on the bone and coquilles St-Jacques, prawns Mornay, and monkfish thermidor, to tableside preparations of steak Diane, prawns sautéed in garlic butter, pepper steak, and steak tartare.

MODERATE

KILMARTINS, 19 Upper Baggot St., Dublin 4. Tel. 686674.

Cuisine: CONTINENTAL. **Reservations:** Recommended. **Transportation:** DART to Lansdowne Road or bus no. 10.

$ Prices: Set lunch Ł10.50 ($17.35); dinner appetizers Ł1.75–Ł4.50 ($2.90–$7.45); dinner main courses Ł6.85–Ł9.95 ($11.30–$16.45). AE, DC, MC, V.

Open: Lunch Mon–Fri 12:30–2:30pm; dinner Mon–Sat 6–11:30pm, Sun 6–11pm.

S Housed in a shopfront building that was originally a turf account's office (bookie), this small homey wine bar restaurant has an old-world atmosphere, with a decor of antiques, globe lights, lace curtains, red, white, and blue table settings, and leafy plants. The menu features a diversity of European fare ranging from cannelloni and other pastas to steak-and-venison pie; seafood in pastry; breast of chicken stuffed with Stilton cheese, wrapped in bacon, and cooked in red wine and herbs; crispy duck in apple cider sauce; spinach and Cashel Blue cheese pancake; and sirloin steak with black-pepper cream sauce.

THE OSPREY, 41-42 Shelbourne Rd., Ballsbridge, Dublin 4. Tel. 608087.
   Cuisine: CONTINENTAL. **Reservations:** Recommended.
   Transportation: DART to Lansdowne Road Station or bus no. 5, 7, 7A, 8, 18, 46, 63, or 84.
$ Prices: Set lunch Ł10.50 ($17.35); dinner appetizers Ł2–Ł4.90 ($3.30–$8); dinner main courses Ł9–Ł12.50 ($14.85–$20.65). AE, DC, MC, V.
   Open: Lunch Mon–Fri 12:30–2:30pm; dinner Mon–Sat 6:45–10:15pm.

A small homey place with open fireplaces, this restaurant is located within walking distance of the Royal Dublin Society, American embassy, and Jurys Hotel. Owned by the Oppermann family, long associated with fine cuisine in the Dublin area, it features a menu with French, German, and Austrian influences, offering main courses such as sole Véronique; sea trout amandine; coquilles St-Germaine (king scallops poached in chablis and lobster sauce au gratin); roulade of salmon and sole wrapped in puff pastry and baked in saffron sauce; breast of duckling in port wine sauce; rack of lamb; veal Irlandaise (with fresh prawns and whiskey sauce); and weinerschnitzel. "Early bird" dinner specials are often featured—ask in advance; lunch in the summer months sometimes takes the format of a buffet.

SENOR SASSI'S, 146 Upper Leeson St., Dublin 4. Tel. 684544.
   Cuisine: MEDITERRANEAN. **Reservations:** Recommended.
   Bus: No. 10, 11A, 11B, 13, 46A, or 46B.
$ Prices: Appetizers Ł1.50–Ł6.50 ($2.50–$10.75); lunch main courses Ł4.50–Ł8.50 ($7.45–$14); dinner main courses Ł6.50–Ł11.75 ($10.75–$19.40). AE, MC, V.
   Open: Lunch Mon–Fri 12:30–2:30pm; dinner Mon–Sat 6–11:30pm.

New and innovative, this restaurant blends the simple and spicy flavors of Spain, Italy, southern France, and the Middle East, in a busy shopfront location at the juncture of Sussex and Mespil Roads within a block of the Burlington Hotel. The contemporary and casual setting includes slate floors, marble-topped tables, and walls painted a sunny shade of yellow; seating is also available in a conservatory extension overlooking a courtyard garden. The menu includes items such as Morroccan-style couscous; paella; tagliatelle; prawns in whiskey Spanish-style; charcoal steaks; duck with honey and thyme sauce; kebabs of beef with peppers, onions, and mushrooms in avocado sauce; and all-vegetarian dishes. Be sure to try the olive bread, somewhat unique for Dublin. *Note:* This restaurant may open on Sunday by presstime; call in advance.

INEXPENSIVE

COFFEE DOCK, Pembroke Rd., Ballsbridge, Dublin 4. Tel. 605000.
> **Cuisine:** INTERNATIONAL. **Reservations:** Not required. **Transportation:** DART to Lansdowne Road or bus no. 5, 7, 7A, 8, 46, 63, or 84.
>
> **$ Prices:** Appetizers Ł2–Ł5.25 ($3.30–$8.70); main courses Ł2.30–Ł10.95 ($3.80–$18). AE, CB, DC, MC, V.
>
> **Open:** Daily breakfast 6am–11:30am; lunch and dinner menu 11:30am–10:45pm; late-night menu 10:45pm–4:30am.

Located on the ground floor of Jurys Hotel, this spot is unique—open almost around the clock, 22½ hours a day. It's handy to know for off-hours snacks, a late or very early breakfast, after-theater suppers, or after-nightclub nourishment. At almost any time of day or night, you can find a top class selection of salads, sandwiches, soups, pastas, seafood, steaks, mixed grills, and burgers, served either counter-style or with waitress service.

DAVINCENZO, 133 Upper Leeson St., Dublin 4. Tel. 609906.
> **Cuisine:** ITALIAN. **Reservations:** Recommended. **Bus:** No. 10, 11A, 11B, 13, 46A, or 46B.
>
> **$ Prices:** Set lunch Ł5.95 ($9.80); dinner appetizers Ł1.95–Ł2.95 ($3.20–$4.90); dinner main courses Ł4.95–Ł10.50 ($8.20–$17.35). AE, MC, V.
>
> **Open:** Mon–Fri 12:30pm–midnight, Sat 1pm–midnight, Sun 1–10pm.

Occupying a shopfront location within a block of the Hotel Burlington, this informal Italian bistro offers ground-level and upstairs seating, amid a casual decor of glowing brick fireplaces, pine walls, vases and wreaths of dried flowers, modern art posters, blue-and-white pottery, and a busy open kitchen. Pizza with a light pita-style dough is a specialty here, cooked in wood-burning oven. Other main courses range from pastas such as tagliatelle, lasagne, cannelloni, spaghetti, and fettuccine, to veal and beef dishes.

6. O'CONNELL STREET

EXPENSIVE

ABERDEEN ROOM, 23 Upper O'Connell St., Dublin 1. Tel. 746881.
> **Cuisine:** CONTINENTAL. **Reservations:** Recommended. **Transportation:** DART to Connolly Station or bus no. 40A, 40B, 40C, or 51A.
>
> **$ Prices:** Set lunch Ł11 ($18); dinner appetizers Ł2–Ł6 ($3.30–

$9.90); dinner main courses Ł15–Ł20 ($24.75–$33). AE, CB, DC, MC, V.

Open: Lunch daily noon–2:30pm; dinner daily 6–11:30pm.

Housed on the ground floor of the Gresham Hotel, at the back of the lobby/lounge area, this stately dining room has hosted many an international celebrity and star. It has a bi-level format, a huge central chandelier, original Irish art spotlit on the walls, and furnishings of white and pastel tones. The menu includes the standard Irish hotel fare from prime ribs and steaks to fish of the day and various chicken and veal dishes. Save room for the dessert trolley.

EXPENSIVE/MODERATE

CHAPTER ONE, 18/19 Parnell Sq., Dublin 1. Tel. 732266 or 732281.

Cuisine: IRISH. **Reservations:** Recommended. **Transportation:** DART to Connolly Station or bus no. 10, 11, 11A, 11B, 12, 13, 14, 16, 16A, 19, 19A, 22, 22A, or 36.

$ Prices: Set lunch Ł10 ($16.50); dinner appetizers Ł2.50–Ł5 ($4.15–$8.25); dinner main courses Ł9–Ł15 ($14.85–$24.75). AE, MC, V.

Open: Lunch Mon–Fri noon–2:30pm; dinner Fri–Sat 6–11pm.

In both setting and menu, a literary theme prevails at this new relatively new restaurant, housed in the basement of the Dublin Writers Museum (see "The Top Attractions" in Chapter 6), just north of Parnell Square and the Garden of Remembrance. The layout is spread over three rooms and alcoves, all accentuated by stained-glass windows, paintings, sculptures, and literary memorabilia. The menu is based on the favorite foods of Irish writers and the description of each dish is backed up by quotations from various scribes.

Main courses include filet of beef stuffed with Roscahill oysters, wrapped in bacon, brandy-butter sauce, and watercress; breast of Silver Hill duckling with peppered pineapple, wild rice, pine nuts, and walnut stuffing; breast of chicken filled with spinach and cream cheese, wrapped in a lattice of puff pastry on a white wine sauce; trio of Wicklow lamb cutlets topped with kidney, with a rosemary and thyme sauce; pan-fried plaice on the bone topped with cockles and mussels and lemon butter; and black sole topped with chopped tomatoes, mushrooms, asparagus, and lobster sauce. Traditional items ranging from Irish stew to Dublin coddle are also offered, as are vegetarian dishes such as creamed mushroom Stroganoff or curried peanut loaf. Live piano music usually is on tap in the evenings. *Note:* This restaurant will probably be open almost every night of the week by presstime, so call in advance.

MODERATE

CAFE ROYALE BRASSERIE, 40 Upper O'Connell St., Dublin 1. Tel. 733666.

Cuisine: IRISH/CONTINENTAL. **Reservations:** Recommended. **Transportation:** DART to Connolly Station or bus no. 36A, 40A, 40B, 40C, or 51A.

$ Prices: Appetizers Ł1.40–Ł3.50 ($2.35–$5.80); lunch main

courses Ł1.50–Ł5.75 ($2.50–$9.50); dinner main courses Ł6–Ł11 ($9.90–$18.15). AE, CB, DC, MC, V.
Open: Lunch daily 12:30–2:15pm; dinner daily 6–10pm.

One of the best new dining spots along Dublin's main thoroughfare, this lively restaurant offers an informal brasserie setting, with skylights, lots of hanging plants, brass fixtures, and stained-glass windows. The menu is an enticing blend of Irish and European choices, from filet of salmon in court bouillon or traditional Gaelic stew to vegetable tagliatelle with prawns; suprême of chicken in red wine sauce; Barbary duck with kumquat sauce; médaillons of pork with mushrooms in cream; or filet of lemon sole in a tomato with white wine sauce.

MODERATE/INEXPENSIVE

101 TALBOT, 101 Talbot St., Dublin 1. Tel. 745011.
   Cuisine: INTERNATIONAL/VEGETARIAN. **Reservations:** Recommended. **Transportation:** DART to Connolly Station or bus no. 27A, 31A, 31B, 32A, 32B, 42B, 42C, 43, or 44A.
$ Prices: Appetizers Ł1.50–Ł2.50 ($2.50–$4.15); lunch main courses Ł3–Ł6 ($4.95–$9.90); dinner main courses Ł6.50–Ł7.50 ($10.75–$12.40). MC, V.
   Open: Mon noon–4pm, Tues–Sat noon–4pm and 6:30–11pm.

Opened in 1991, this second-floor shopfront restaurant features light and healthy foods, with an emphasis on vegetables. The setting is bright and casual, with contemporary Irish art on display, big windows, yellow rag-rolled walls, ash-topped tables, and newspapers to read. Main courses include chicken breast with spinach mousse; plaice with lemon beurre blanc; médaillons of pork with brandy and mustard sauce; spanikopita (Greek spinach and feta cheese pie); parsnip stuffed with brazil nuts and vegetables in red pepper sauce; and various pastas. Espresso and cappuccino are always available for sipping. It's located at Talbot Lane near Marlborough Street, convenient to the Abbey Theatre.

P.O.E.T.S., 5 Beresford Place, Dublin 1. Tel. 363209.
   Cuisine: INTERNATIONAL/VEGETARIAN. **Reservations:** Not required. **Transportation:** DART to Connolly Station or bus no. 27A, 27B, or 53B.
$ Prices: Appetizers Ł1.50–Ł2.50 ($2.50–$4.15); lunch main courses Ł3.75–Ł4 ($6.20–$6.60); dinner main courses Ł4.50–Ł10 ($7.45–$16.50). MC, V.
   Open: Mon–Fri 8am–midnight, Sat–Sun noon–midnight.

Situated across the street from Busaras (Central Bus Station), behind the Custom House, and within a block of the new Custom House Quay development, this is a lively and fun restaurant in an area that is burgeoning. Surprisingly, the name has nothing to do with literary associations, but stands for a local acronym, with a roughly translated meaning of "Thank God it's Friday." The menu blends local and European influences, with menu items such as Rösti potatoes, chicken Kiev, shepherd's pie, traditional Irish fry (liver, bacon, sausage), Dublin Bay prawn fry, baked sole and salmon en croûte, veal Holstein, Greek kebabs, Viennese steaks, chicken teriyaki, burgers, steaks, sandwiches, and vegetarian dishes such as nut roasts, spinach roulade, and vegetarian lasagne. For something different, try the P.O.E.T.S. special land, air, and sea platter (ribs, chicken wings, and crab cakes).

INEXPENSIVE

TODDY'S, 23 Upper O'Connell St., Dublin 1. Tel. 746881.
   Cuisine: INTERNATIONAL. **Reservations:** Not required. **Transportation:** DART to Connolly Station or bus no. 40A, 40B, 40C, or 51A.
$ **Prices:** Appetizers Ł1–Ł2.50 ($1.65–$4.15); main courses Ł4.50–Ł9.50 ($7.45–$15.70).
   Open: Mon–Sat noon–10:30pm.

This is the newest innovation of the landmark Gresham Hotel, named after Toddy O'Sullivan, one of the hotel's legendary managers. Designed in the format of a modern art deco pub with light woods, contemporary art prints, and lots of leafy plants and palms, it offers a casual and upbeat setting for a light meal in the north end of the city. The menu ranges from oysters on the half shell to crab, smoked salmon, club sandwiches, vegetable platters, soups, steaks, lamb chops, and carved roast of the day.

7. SUBURBS — SOUTH

EXPENSIVE

GUINEA PIG, 17 Railway Rd., Dalkey, Co. Dublin. Tel. 285-9055.
   Cuisine: SEAFOOD. **Reservations:** Required. **Transportation:** DART to Dalkey Station or bus no. 8.
$ **Prices:** Set lunch Ł12.95 ($21.40); dinner appetizers Ł3–Ł8 ($4.95–$13.20); dinner main courses Ł11–Ł21 ($18.15–$34.65). AE, DC, MC, V.
   Open: Lunch Sun noon–3pm; dinner Mon–Sat 6–11:30pm.

⭐ Don't worry about the name of this restaurant; there is absolutely nothing experimental about the way guests are treated here. Emphasizing whatever is freshest and in season, the menu often includes a signature dish called "symphony de la mer" (a potpourri of fish and crustaceans), lobster Newburg, crab au gratin, steak au poivre, roast stuffed pork, and rack of lamb. The culinary domain of chef-owner Mervyn Stewart, former Dalkey mayor, it is decorated in a stylish Irish country motif with Victorian touches.

NA MARA, 1 Harbour Rd., Dun Laoghaire, Co. Dublin. Tel. 280-6767.
   Cuisine: SEAFOOD. **Reservations:** Recommended. **Transportation:** DART to Dun Laoghaire Station or bus no. 7, 7A, or 8.
$ **Prices:** Set lunch Ł15 ($24.75); dinner appetizers Ł2–Ł8 ($3.30–$13.20); dinner main courses Ł12–Ł22 ($19.80–$36.30). AE, DC, MC, V.

Open: Lunch Mon–Sat 12:30–2:30pm; dinner Mon–Sat 7–10:30pm.

Housed in a former Victorian railway station, this elegant eatery is located next to the ferry dock overlooking Dublin Bay and the Irish Sea. As its name (which means "of the sea") implies, it has a mostly seafood menu, with such dishes as lobster thermidor, oysters Mornay, sole bonne femme, salmon steak, prawns flamed in Pernod, or a hearty fisherman's platter. For those who prefer meat, there is always prime filet of beef or steaks.

TRUFFLES, Killiney Hill Rd., Killiney, Co. Dublin. Tel. 284-0700.

Cuisine: INTERNATIONAL. **Reservations:** Recommended. **Transportation:** DART to Dalkey or Killiney Station or bus no. 59.

$ Prices: Appetizers £1.95–£6.95 ($3.25–$11.50); lunch main courses £6.95–£14.95 ($11.50–$24.70); dinner main courses £9.95–£16.95 ($16.45–$28). AE, CB, DC, MC, V.

Open: Lunch daily 12:30–2:30pm; dinner Mon–Sat 7–10:30pm, Sun 7–9:30pm.

As the signature restaurant of Fitzpatrick's Castle Hotel, this posh dining room has all the trappings of a regal Victorian palace, with rich red tones, original oil paintings, brass fixtures, sparkling crystal, and suits of armor at the entrance.

The menu is a fitting match to the surroundings—offering such choices as chateaubriand; steak Diane flambé; filet mignon stuffed with foie gras and wrapped in smoked ham; chicken truffles (with smoked salmon resting on a creamy mushroom sauce); veal Rösti; médaillons of venison in a rich red wine and light pepper sauce with Spätzle; sole Véronique; and, for vegetarians, a fruit and vegetable kebab on saffron rice, or a mozzarella and whole-meal fritter. In addition, house specials include three Irish traditional special occasion dishes—roast stuffed pork steak, sole bonne femme, and "roast stuffed chicken on the hour"—every hour a new chicken is turned out of the castle oven, with home-style stuffing and all the trimmings.

MODERATE

SOUTH BANK, 1 Martello Terrace at Islington Ave., Dun Laoghaire, Co. Dublin. Tel. 280-8788.

Cuisine: IRISH/CONTINENTAL. **Reservations:** Recommended. **Transportation:** DART to Sandycove Station or bus no. 8.

$ Prices: Appetizers £1.75–£6.95 ($2.90–$11.50); main courses £9–£12 ($14.85–$19.80). MC, V.

Open: Dinner Tues–Sat 6–10:30pm.

On the seafront across from the waterside promenade, this cozy 50-seat candlelit restaurant is one of the few Dublin eateries that offers glimpses of the sea. A relaxing ambience also pervades as chamber music plays in the background. The eclectic menu changes often, but usually includes such dishes as maple chicken with grapefruit and watercress; breast of turkey with bourbon and peaches; pork steak with cider, nutmeg, and apple; roast duck with Cointreau and kumquat sauce; escalope of veal with mushrooms and mustard; strips of beef with mango, chili, and ginger; and fresh salmon in a dill and light lemon sauce. Situated within walking distance of the James Joyce Tower, this place is also noted for its annual Bloomsday breakfast every June 16th.

WRIGHT'S BRASSERIE, Monkstown Crescent, Monkstown. Co. Dublin. Tel. 280-5174.
    Cuisine: INTERNATIONAL. **Reservations:** Recommended. **Transportation:** DART to Salthill Station or bus no. 7, 7A, or 8.
$ Prices: Lunch bar menu £2.95–£5.95 ($4.90–$9.90); dinner appetizers £2.25–£3.95 ($3.75–$6.55); dinner main courses £6.95–£9.95 ($11.50–$16.45). MC, V.
    Open: Mon–Sat noon–11pm.

Situated 6 miles south of Dublin City, this skylit Irish brasserie invites guests to order to suit their mood and appetite, from snacks to four-course meals, throughout the day, in the main dining room or in the stylish wine bar area. The menu ranges from salads, pastas, and smoked-fish platters, to imaginative main courses such as king prawn and saké stir-fry; trellis of sea trout and lemon sole with prawn sauce; coquille of seafood with Mornay sauce; crab claws in garlic butter; chicken in pastry; and duck in sweet-and-sour ginger sauce; as well as rack of lamb and steaks.

MODERATE/INEXPENSIVE

LA ROMANA, Castle St., Dalkey, Co. Dublin. Tel. 285-4569.
    Cuisine: ITALIAN. **Reservations:** Not required. **Transportation:** DART to Dalkey Station or bus no. 8.
$ Prices: Appetizers £1–£3 ($1.65–$4.95); lunch main courses £3.95–£5.95 ($6.55–$9.85); dinner main courses £3.95–£7.95 ($6.55–$13.15); snack menu £2.25–£4.95 ($3.75–$8.20). MC, V.
    Open: Lunch Mon–Fri 12:30–2:30pm; dinner Mon–Fri 5:30–11:30pm, Sat–Sun 12:30–11pm.

Housed in the front section of the historic Queens Pub in the center of town, this informal trattoria has its own open kitchen, offering a contrast to the usual pub grub. The menu concentrates on pastas and pizzas, but also offers meat dishes such as chicken breast stuffed with cream cheese and chives or pork escalope in Italian sherry with cream and mushroom sauce. In addition, there are daily specials and an interesting selection of antipasti. To maintain an ambience separate to the pub surroundings, Pavarotti music usually plays in the background.

8. SUBURBS — NORTH

VERY EXPENSIVE/EXPENSIVE

KING SITRIC, East Pier, Howth, Co. Dublin. Tel. 325235.
    Cuisine: SEAFOOD. **Reservations:** Required. **Transportation:** DART to Howth Station or bus no. 31.

$ Prices: Appetizers Ł2.50–Ł11 ($4.15–$18.15); main courses Ł14–Ł20 ($23.10–$33). AE, DC, MC, V.
Open: Dinner Mon–Sat 6:30–11pm.

⭐ Situated right on the bay 10 miles north of Dublin, this long established 70-seat restaurant is housed in a 150-year-old former harbormaster's building. On a fine summer's evening, it is well worth a trip out here to savor the finest of local fish and crustaceans, prepared and presented in a creative way. Award-winning main courses range from filet of sole with Cashel Blue cheese on a bed of spinach with butter sauce, and filet of brill Deauvillaise (in a cream and wine sauce), to grilled monkfish on a bed of aubergines (eggplant) topped with tomato coulis; lobster from the tank; lobster thermidor; and Howth fish ragoût, a signature combination of the best of the day's catch. For those who prefer meat, there is always a prime sirloin steak with red wine sauce. Game fishes are also featured in season.

EXPENSIVE/MODERATE

ABBEY TAVERN, Abbey St., Howth, Co. Dublin. Tel. 390307.
    Cuisine: SEAFOOD/INTERNATIONAL. **Reservations:** Recommended. **Transportation:** DART to Howth Station or bus no. 31.
$ Prices: Appetizers Ł2.75–Ł8.25 ($4.55–$13.65); main courses Ł11.50–Ł14.75 ($19–$24.35). AE, DC, MC, V.
    Open: Dinner Mon–Sat 7–11pm.

⭐ Although this old-world tavern has achieved its greatest fame for nightly traditional music ballad sessions (see "The Performing Arts" in Chapter 9), the premises also holds a very fine à la carte candlelit restaurant upstairs, just the spot for a relaxing meal in this seaside suburb. Although the menu changes depending on the season, main courses often include such dishes as scallops Ty Ar Mor (with mushrooms, prawns, and cream sauce); filet of sole with prawns; crêpes fruits de mer; poached salmon; sole on the bone; duck with orange and Curaçao sauce; steak au poivre; and veal à la crème. After a meal, diners are welcome to descend to the lower level and join in the audience for some lively Irish music.

MODERATE

HYLAND'S, Harbour Rd., Howth, Co. Dublin. Tel. 391193 or 392318.
    Cuisine: IRISH/SEAFOOD. **Reservations:** Recommended.
    Transportation: DART to Howth Station or bus no. 31.
$ Prices: Appetizers Ł1.95–Ł5.95 ($3.25–$9.85); lunch main courses Ł3.95–Ł5.95 ($6.55–$9.85); dinner main courses Ł5.95–Ł12.95 ($9.85–$21.40). AE, MC, V.
    Open: Daily noon–11pm.

Overlooking Dublin Bay along the harbor at Howth and across from the local yacht club, this informal restaurant is housed in an old stone building, with lots of atmosphere and a nautical decor. Taking advantage of the daily catch brought in each day, the menu relies heavily on fresh fish choices, but also features Irish stew, Dublin coddle, chicken Kiev, duck, prime rib, pastas, vegetarian choices such as spinach pancakes, and a signature dish known as "chicken beside the sea" (stuffed with smoked salmon).

9. SPECIALTY DINING

Local Favorites/Pubs   In Dublin, pubs are a focal point for eating as well as drinking. Many pubs serve inexpensive fare (known locally as pub grub), particularly at lunchtime, ranging from soups and sandwiches to seafood platters and salads as well as hearty stews and meat pies. A good pub lunch will cost around £5 ($8.25) including beverage.

A complete description of Dublin's pubs is given in "The Pubs" in Chapter 9. Among those recommended for good pub grub downtown are the **Brazen Head,** 20 Lower Bridge St., Dublin 8 (tel. 679-5186); **Davy Byrnes,** 21 Duke St., Dublin 2 (tel. 775217); **Kitty O'Shea's,** 23/25 Upper Grand Canal St., Dublin 4 (tel. 609965); **Old Stand,** 37 Exchequer St., Dublin 2 (tel. 777220); and the **Stag's Head,** 1 Dame Court, Dublin 2 (tel. 679-3701).

In the suburbs, try **P. McCormack & Sons,** 67 Lower Mounttown Rd., Dun Laoghaire (tel. 280-5519), and **The Queens',** 12/13 Castle St., Dalkey, Co. Dublin (tel. 285-4569).

Museum/Art Gallery Coffee Shops   Many of Dublin's museums and art galleries operate excellent coffee shops and snack bars, offering good value, convenience, and an atmospheric setting.

The menus, usually on chalkboards, feature homemade soups, salads, sandwiches, and daily hot plates. These eateries are normally open during the same hours as the attractions in which they are housed (consult Chapter 6). Prices average £3 to £5 ($4.95 to $8.25) for a complete meal or £1 to £2 ($1.65 to $3.30) for snacks.

Among the best are the **Dublin Writers Museum Coffee Shop,** 18/19 Parnell Sq. North, Dublin 1 (tel. 722077); **Hugh Lane Municipal Gallery of Modern Art Coffee Shop,** Parnell Square, Dublin 1 (tel. 741903); **National Gallery Restaurant,** Merrion Square West, Dublin 2 (tel. 686481); and **Royal Hospital/ Museum of Modern Art Coffee Shop,** Kilmainham, Dublin 8 (tel. 718666).

Afternoon Tea   As in Britain, afternoon tea is a time-revered tradition in Ireland, especially in the grand hotels of Dublin. Afternoon tea in its fullest form is a sit-down event and a relaxing experience, not just a quick hot beverage taken on the run.

Properly presented, afternoon tea is also almost a complete meal—with a pot of freshly brewed tea accompanied by finger sandwiches, pastries, hot scones, cream-filled cakes, and other sweets arrayed on a silver tray. To enhance the ambience, there is a little live background music, usually piano or harp. Best of all, this sumptuous mid-afternoon pick-me-up is priced to please—averaging £5 to £6 ($8.25 to $9.90) per head even in the lobby lounges of the city's best hotels.

Afternoon tea hours are usually 3 to 4:30pm. Among the hotels offering this repast are the Berkeley Court, Gresham, Royal Dublin, Shelbourne, and Westbury (see Chapter 4 for full address and phone numbers of each hotel).

Late-night/24 Hour   There is really only one restaurant in Dublin that approaches the 24-hour category—the **Coffee Dock** at Jurys Hotel, Ballsbridge (see above in this chapter). It is open 22½ hours a day, from 6am until 4:30am.

Picnic Fare   The many parks of Dublin offer sylvan and relaxed settings for a picnic lunch. Most of the parks have plentiful benches or you can pick a grassy patch and spread open a blanket. In particular, try St. Stephen's Green at lunchtime (in the summer there are open-air band concerts), Phoenix Park, and Merrion Square (all of these parks are described in "More Attractions" in Chapter 6). You can also take a ride on the DART to the suburbs of Dun Laoghaire (to the south) or Howth (to the north) and set up a picnic along a bayfront pier or promenade.

In recent years, Dublin has fostered some fine delicatessens and gourmet food shops, ideal for picnic fare. For the best selection of good picnic fixings, we recommend: **Dunn's,** 6 Upper Baggot St., Dublin 4 (tel. 602688), for take-out for sandwiches, soup, salad, soft drinks; **Gallic Kitchen,** Back Lane, Dublin 8 (tel. 544912), for gourmet prepared food-to-go, from salmon en croûte to pastries filled with meats or vegetables, pâtés, quiches, sausage rolls, and homemade pies, breads, and cakes; **La-Potiniere,** Powerscourt Town House Centre, 59 S. William St., Dublin 2 (tel. 711300), for salads, sandwiches, nuts, mustards, teas, sodas, Irish cheeses, honey, sodas, and champagne; **Magills Delicatessen,** 14 Clarendon St., Dublin 2 (tel. 713830), for Asian and continental delicacies, meats, cheeses, spices, and salads; and **T. Mulloy,** 12 Lower Baggot St., Dublin 2 (tel. 762137), for smoked salmon and other seafoods.

CHAPTER 6

WHAT TO SEE & DO IN DUBLIN

- **SUGGESTED ITINERARIES**
- **DID YOU KNOW...?**
1. **THE TOP ATTRACTIONS**
2. **MORE ATTRACTIONS**
- **FROMMER'S FAVORITE DUBLIN EXPERIENCES**
3. **COOL FOR KIDS**
4. **SPECIAL-INTEREST SIGHTSEEING**
5. **ORGANIZED TOURS**
6. **SPORTS & RECREATION**

Dublin is a city of many parts—from medieval churches and majestic castles, to graceful Georgian squares and lantern-lit lanes, broad boulevards and busy bridges, picturesque parks and pedestrian walkways, intriguing museums and marketplaces, glorious gardens and galleries, and so much more.

To inhale the ambience of Ireland's number one city, you should walk up Grafton Street, sip a cup of coffee at Bewley's, stroll through St. Stephen's Green, browse along the quays, step into a few pubs, and, above all, chat with the Dubliners. And that's just for starters.

You could devote a week, a month, or a lifetime to Dublin and still not see all the sights and savor all the experiences. But, by planning wisely, taking note of the suggestions on the following pages, and using a good map, you can spend a few days in Dublin and thoroughly relish the major highlights of this Fair City.

SUGGESTED ITINERARIES

IF YOU HAVE 1 DAY

Day 1: Start at the beginning—Dublin's medieval quarter, the area around Christ Church and St. Patrick's Cathedrals. Tour these great churches and then walk the cobblestone streets and inspect the nearby old city walls at High Street. From Old Dublin, take a turn eastward and stroll eastward to see Dublin Castle and then to Trinity College with the famous Book of Kells. Cross over the River Liffey to O'Connell Street, Dublin's main thoroughfare. Walk up this wide street, flanked by such landmarks as the General Post Office (GPO) and the Gresham Hotel, to Parnell Square and the picturesque Garden of Remembrance. If time permits, visit the Dublin Writers Museum, and then hop on a double-decker bus heading to the south bank of the Liffey for some shopping along Grafton Street and finally

2 DID YOU KNOW . . . ?

- Dublin is the only European city to be the birthplace of three writers who received the Nobel Prize for literature in the 20th century—Yeats, Shaw, and Beckett.
- Phoenix Park is the largest enclosed park in Europe.
- The Brazen Head Pub (1198) is the oldest tavern in Ireland.
- The American embassy in Ballsbridge is designed to reflect the circular shape of a Celtic fortress with its own moat.
- The Viking excavation at Dublin's Wood Quay is considered to be the most important of its kind outside of Scandinavia.
- Dublin's botanic gardens were designed as a smaller version of the great gardens at Kew in England.
- In 1759 Arthur Guinness established the Guinness Brewery at St. James's Gate in Dublin and took a 9,000-year lease on the property.
- The word "donnybrook" takes its origins from the raucous 19th-century Donnybrook Fair, held in a Dublin suburb of the same name.

a visit to St. Stephen's Green for a relaxing stroll amid the greenery or to sit on a bench and chat with the Dubliners. Cap the day with a show at the Abbey Theatre and maybe a drink or two at a nearby pub.

IF YOU HAVE 2 DAYS

Day 1: Spend Day 1 as above.

Day 2: In the morning, take a Dublin Bus city sightseeing tour to give you an overview of the city—you'll see all of the local downtown landmarks, plus the major buildings along the River Liffey, and some of the leading sites on the edge of the city such as the Guinness Brewery, the Royal Hospital, the Irish Museum of Modern Art, and Phoenix Park. In the afternoon, head for Grafton Street for some shopping, with a slight detour to Powerscourt Town House Centre, a four-story midcity complex of shops, eateries, and art galleries. If time allows, stroll Merrion or Fitzwilliam Squares to give you a sampling of the best of Dublin's Georgian architecture.

IF YOU HAVE 3 DAYS

Days 1 and 2: Spend Days 1 and 2 as above.

Day 3: Make this a day for Dublin's artistic and cultural attractions—visit some of the top museums and art galleries—from the National Museum and National Gallery, Natural History Museum, Heraldic Museum, Dublin Civic Museum, National Wax Museum, and the Chester Beatty Museum, to the Guinness Hop Store or the Irish Whiskey Corner, or a special-interest museum, such as the Irish Jewish Museum, the Kilmainham jail museum, the Museum of Childhood, or the Irish Traditional Music Archive. Consider purchasing a Heritage Tour ticket—a continuous bus tour that allows you to visit many of these museums and galleries, with boarding and reboarding privileges throughout the day (easier on the feet than walking from place to place!). Save time for a walk around Temple Bar, the city's "Left Bank" district, lined with art galleries and film studios, interesting secondhand shops, and casual eateries.

IF YOU HAVE 5 DAYS OR MORE

Days 1–3: Spend Days 1 to 3 as above.

Day 4: Take a ride aboard DART, Dublin's rapid transit system, to the suburbs, either southward to Dun Laoghaire or Dalkey, or northward to Howth. The DART routes follow the rim of Dublin Bay in both directions, so you'll enjoy a scenic ride and get to spend some time in an Irish coastal village.

Day 5: Fan out a little farther by taking a sightseeing bus tour southward to County Wicklow, known as the "Garden of Ireland," or northward to the Boyne River Valley, known for its historic sites such as prehistoric Newgrange and the Hill of Tara, once the royal and ecclesiastical capital of Ireland.

Or More: Rent a car or take a train to more far-flung parts of Ireland—it's less than 100 miles to Kilkenny, Waterford, and Wexford, and just a little farther to Limerick, Galway, Sligo, or Shannon; and in less than 200 miles, you can be in Killarney or Cork.

---

1. THE TOP ATTRACTIONS

CHRIST CHURCH CATHEDRAL, Christchurch Place, Dublin 8. Tel. 778099.

⭐ Standing on high ground in the oldest part of the city, this cathedral is one of Dublin's finest historic buildings. It dates back to 1038 when Sitric, the then-Danish king of Dublin, built the first wooden Christ Church here. In 1171 the original simple foundation was extended into a cruciform and rebuilt in stone by Strongbow, although the present structure dates mainly from 1871 to 1878 when a huge restoration was undertaken. Only the transepts, the crypt, and a few other portions date from medieval times.

Highlights of the interior include magnificent stonework and graceful pointed arches, with delicately chiseled supporting columns. Strongbow himself is among the historic figures buried in the church, as is Archbishop Browne, the first Protestant to occupy the see of Dublin, during the reign of Henry VIII. It is the mother church for the diocese of Dublin and Glendalough of the Church of Ireland.

Admission: 50p (85¢) adults; free for children under 12.

Open: Daily 10am–5pm. **Closed:** Dec 26. **Bus:** No. 21A, 50, 50A, 78, 78A, or 78B.

DUBLIN CASTLE, Palace St., off Dame St., Dublin 2. Tel. 679-3713.

⭐ Built between 1208 and 1220, this complex represents some of the oldest surviving architecture in the city, and was the center of British power in Ireland for over seven centuries until it was taken over by the new Irish government in 1922. Highlights include the 13th-century Record Tower, the largest visible fragment of the original Norman castle; the State Apartments, once the residence of

English viceroys and now the focal point for government ceremonial functions, including the inauguration of Ireland's presidents; and the Chapel Royal, formerly the Church of the Holy Trinity, a 19th-century early Gothic building with particularly fine plaster decoration and carved oak gallery fronts and fittings.

The newest development is the opening to view for visitors of the Undercroft, an excavated site on the grounds where an early Viking fortress stood. As we go to press, restoration of the Treasury is in progress; built between 1712 and 1715, it is believed to be the oldest surviving purpose-built office building in Ireland. It will house a new visitor center in its vaulted basement, which will also serve as an entrance to the medieval undercroft.

Admission: £1 ($1.65) adults; 50p (85¢) for seniors, students, and children under 12.

Open: Mon–Fri 10am–12:15pm and 2–5pm, Sat–Sun 2–5pm. Guided tours are conducted every 20–25 minutes. **Bus:** No. 50, 50A, 54, 56A, or 77.

DUBLINIA, Christchurch Place, at the corner of Winetavern St. and High St., Dublin 8. Tel. 758137.

What was Dublin like in medieval times? Here is a historically accurate presentation of the Old City from 1170 to 1540, re-created through a series of themed exhibits, spectacles, and experiences. Sponsored by Ireland's Medieval Trust and housed at the Synod Hall of Christ Church Cathedral, this is one of Dublin's newest attractions, slated to open in March 1993. A historic landmark itself, the three-story Synod Hall was built in the mid-1870s, and is joined by an archway (bridge) to Christ Church Cathedral.

Visitors enter Dublinia through a courtyard which features authentic medieval games in progress, and then through a glazed pavilion that illustrates Dublin's early history. Next is an illuminated Medieval Maze, complete with visual effects, background sounds, and aromas, that lead you on a journey through time from the first arrival of the Anglo-Normans in 1170 to the closure of the monasteries in the 1530s. The next segment depicts everyday life in medieval Dublin with a diorama, as well as a prototype of a 13th-century quay along the banks of the Liffey. You can roam among craftsmen and guildsmen at work, learn what they were paid, visit a typical merchant's house of the 15th century, and enter a medieval parish church. The final segment takes you to The Great Hall for a 360° wrap-up portrait of medieval Dublin via a 12-minute cyclorama-style audiovisual. Facilities include a medievally themed restaurant and gift shop.

Admission: £4 ($6.60) adults, £2 ($3.30) children under 12.

Open: Daily 9am–5pm. **Bus:** No. 21A, 50, 50A, 78, 78A, or 78B.

DUBLIN WRITERS MUSEUM, 18/19 Parnell Sq. North, Dublin 1. Tel. 722077.

As a city known for its literary contributions to the world, Dublin has embraced this new museum with open arms. Housed in two restored 18th-century buildings, it is situated

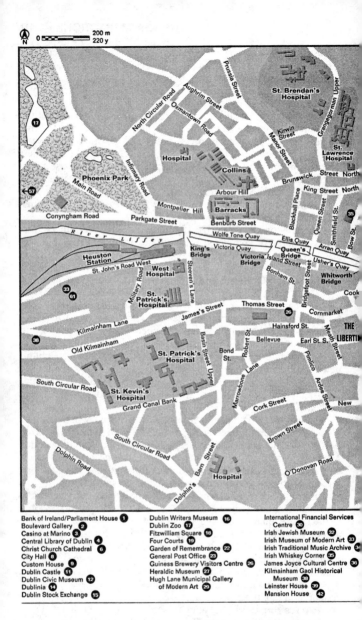

on the north side of Parnell Square, within a stone's throw of other literary landmarks, such as the Gate and Abbey Theatres. The exhibits focus on Ireland's many great writers, including Dublin's three Nobel Prize winners for literature—George Bernard Shaw, William Butler Yeats, and Samuel Beckett, and a host of others from Jonathan Swift and Oscar Wilde to Sean O'Casey, James Joyce, and Brendan Behan. Besides focusing on well-known names, there is good coverage of the history of Irish literature with a collection of

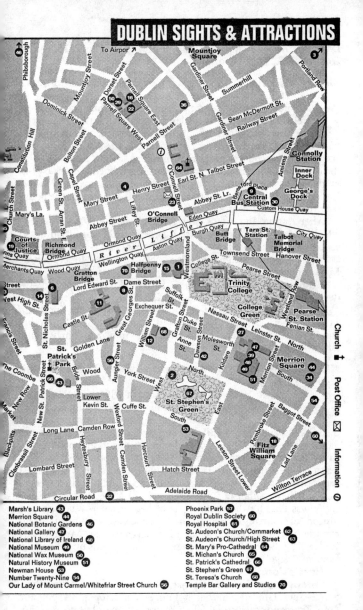

DUBLIN SIGHTS & ATTRACTIONS

rare editions, manuscript items, and memorabilia. In addition, there is a library, gallery of portraits and busts, bookshop, restaurant, coffee shop, and areas for lectures and readings. The museum also houses the Irish Writers Centre, a meeting place for contemporary scribes.

Admission: Ł2 ($3.30) adults, Ł1 ($1.65) seniors and students, 50p (85¢) children under 12.

Open: Mon–Sat 10am–5pm, Sun 2–6pm. **Transportation:**

DART to Conolly Station or bus no. 10, 11, 11A, 11B, 12, 13, 14, 16, 16A, 19, 19A, 22, 22A, or 36.

MALAHIDE CASTLE, Malahide, Co. Dublin. Tel. 845-2337 or 845-2655.

Situated about 10 miles north of Dublin, Malahide is one of Ireland's most historic castles, founded in the 12th century by Richard Talbot and occupied by his descendants until 1976. Fully restored, the interior of the building is the setting for a very comprehensive collection of Irish furniture, dating from the 17th through the 19th centuries, and the walls are lined with one-of-a-kind Irish historical portraits and tableaux on loan from the National Gallery. The furnishings and the art reflect life in and near the house over the past eight centuries.

After touring the house, you can explore the 270-acre estate, which includes 20 acres of prized gardens with more than 5,000 species of plants and flowers (see "Gardens, Parks, and Squares," below). The Malahide grounds also contain the Fry Model Railway Museum (see "Cool for Kids," below).

Admission: £2.45 ($4) adults, £1.85 ($3.05) seniors and students, £1.25 ($2.05) children under 12.

Open: May–Sept, Mon–Fri 10am–5pm, Sat 11am–6pm, Sun 11:30am–6pm; Apr and Oct, Mon–Fri 10am–5pm, Sat 11am–6pm, Sun 2–6pm; Nov–Mar, Mon–Fri 10am–5pm, Sat–Sun 2–5pm. **Bus:** No. 42.

NATIONAL GALLERY, Merrion Sq. West, Dublin 2. Tel. 615133.

Established by an act of Parliament in 1854, this gallery first opened its doors in 1864, with just over 100 paintings. Today the collection is considered one of Europe's finest, with more than 2,400 paintings; 15,200 drawings, watercolors, and miniatures; 3,000 prints; and 300 pieces of sculpture, vestments and objets d'art. Every major European school of painting is represented, as is an extensive grouping of Irish work. Among the gallery's staunchest supporters over the years was celebrated Dublin writer George Bernard Shaw, author of *Pygmalion* (on which the musical *My Fair Lady* was based), who spent many of his early days studying here instead of formal schooling. Shaw bequeathed one-third of his royalties to the gallery and hence it is often called the "My Fair Lady Gallery" by the locals. Small wonder his statue stands on the lawn in front of the gallery!

Admission: Free.

Open: Mon–Wed and Fri–Sat 10am–6pm, Thurs 10am–9pm, Sun 2–5pm. Guided tours Sat at 3pm, Sun at 2:30pm, 3:15pm, and 4pm. **Transportation:** DART to Pearse Station or bus no. 5, 7, 7A, 8, 10, 44, 47, 48A, or 62.

NATIONAL MUSEUM, Kildare St. and Merrion Row, Dublin 2. Tel. 618811.

Opened in 1890, this museum is a reflection of Ireland's heritage from 2,000 B.C. to the present. It is the home of many of the country's greatest historical finds including "The Treasury" exhibit that toured the U.S. and Europe in the 1970s and comprises the Ardagh Chalice, Tara Brooch, and Cross of Cong. Other highlights range from the artifacts from the Wood Quay excavations of the "Old Dublin" settlements to "Or," an extensive exhibition of Irish Bronze Age gold ornaments, dating from 2200 to 700 B.C. In addition, there is a Ceramics Room, Japanese Decorative Arts Room, and a Music Room that features classical and traditional instruments including the Irish harp.

Admission: Free.

Open: Tues–Sat 10am–5pm, Sun 2–5pm. **Transportation:** DART to Pearse Station or bus no. 7, 7A, 8, 10, 11, or 13.

PHOENIX PARK, Parkgate St., Dublin 7. Tel. 213021 or 771425.

✪ This is Dublin's playground—the largest urban enclosed park in Europe, with a circumference of 7 miles and a total area of 1,760 acres. Opened in 1747, it is also the home of the Irish president and the U.S. ambassador to Ireland and assorted wildlife. Situated 2 miles west of the city center, it is traversed by a network of roads and quiet pedestrian walkways, and informally landscaped with ornamental gardens, nature trails, and broad expanses of grassland, separated by avenues of trees, including oak, beech, pine, chestnut, and lime. Livestock graze peacefully on pasturelands, deer roam the forested areas, and horses romp on polo fields. Landmarks in the park range from the Phoenix Column, erected in 1747 beside the natural spring that gives the park its name ("Fionn Usice"—pronounced "phoenix" in English and meaning "clear water") and the Wellington Monument, a 205-foot obelisk said to be the highest of its kind in the world, to a giant white cross commemorating the papal visit of 1979. The grounds also include a 30-acre zoo (see "Cool for Kids," below).

Admission: Free.

Open: Daily 24 hours. **Bus:** No. 10, 25, or 26.

ROYAL HOSPITAL, Military Rd., Kilmainham, Dublin 8. Tel. 718666.

✪ Built in 1680, this is the oldest surviving fully classical building in Ireland, and is the largest structure, other than a monastery or castle, existing from before 1700. It was built by James Butler, the duke of Ormonde, who obtained a charter from King Charles II to create a hospice for retired soldiers. Patterned after Les Invalides in Paris, it is in the form of a quadrangle, with two stories and dormer windows.

Fully restored by the Irish government in 1986 at a cost of £21 ($35) million, the building today houses various temporary exhibits and is the permanent home, since 1991, of the Irish Museum of Modern Art (IMMA). Other highlights include a chapel with a baroque ceiling, stained glass, and intricate wood carvings, a sculpture park, and an 18th-century formal garden. The main building and grounds are also used for concerts and other major cultural events.

Admission: Free.

Open: Tues–Sun 10am–5:30pm, Sun noon–5:30pm. **Bus:** No. 24, 79, or 90.

ST. PATRICK'S CATHEDRAL, Patrick's Close, Patrick St., Dublin 8. Tel. 754817.

⭐ It is said that St. Patrick baptized converts on this site and consequently a church has stood here since 450 A.D., making it the oldest Christian site in Dublin. The present cathedral dates from 1190, but because of a fire and a rebuilding in the 14th century, not much remains from the cathedral's foundation days. It is mainly Early English in style, with a square medieval tower that houses the largest ringing peal bells in Ireland, an 18th-century spire, and a 300-foot-long interior, making it the longest church in Ireland. The building's history is as colorful as Dublin itself. In 1320 it was the headquarters for a great university that flourished for over 100 years until it was suppressed by Henry VIII. During the 17th century, Cromwelliam troopers stabled horses in the aisles, leaving the building in a forlorn state. Fortunately, a complete restoration followed in the 1860s.

St. Patrick's is closely associated with Jonathan Swift, who was dean here from 1713 to 1745. You can not only see his tomb in the south aisle, but also the pulpit from which he preached, and the epitaph he wrote for himself: "He lies where furious indignation can no longer rend his heart." Nearby is the grave of Esther Johnson, otherwise known as Stella, one of his two great loves. Other famous Irishmen who are memorialized within the cathedral include Turlough O'Carolan, a blind harper and composer and the last of the great Irish bards; Michael William Balfe, the composer; and Douglas Hyde, the first president of Ireland. St. Patrick's is the national cathedral of the Church of Ireland.

Admission: Suggested donations 90p ($1.50) adults, 30p (50¢) students and children under 12.

Open: Apr–Oct, Mon–Fri 9am–6:15pm, Sat 9am–5pm, Sun 10am–4:30pm; Nov–Mar, Mon–Fri 9am–6:15pm, Sat 9am–4pm, Sun 10:30am–4:30pm. **Bus:** No. 50, 50A, 54, 54A, or 56A.

TRINITY COLLEGE AND THE BOOK OF KELLS, College Green, Dublin 2. Tel. 772941.

⭐ The oldest university in Ireland, Trinity was founded in 1592 by Queen Elizabeth I. It sits in the heart of the city on a 40-acre site just south of the River Liffey, with cobbled squares, gardens, a picturesque quadrangle, and a varied layout of buildings dating from the 17th to the 20th centuries, ranging from the Chapel (1798), Public Theatre and Examination Hall (1791), to the Dining Hall (1761), the Old Library (1732), and the New Library (1967).

Although there have been many famous graduates of Trinity, the college is most celebrated as the custodian of the Book of Kells, an 8th-century version of the four Gospels with elaborate scripting and illumination. This famous treasure and other early Christian manuscripts are on permanent view for the public in The Colonnades, a new exhibition area located on the ground floor of the Old Library. The complete Trinity College Library contains over a half-million volumes, a figure that is always growing, thanks to a copyright law of 1801 specifying that a copy of every book published in Britain or Ireland must be sent here. Trinity is also the home of the Dublin Experience, a multimedia show (see "Sight-and-Sound Shows," below) and the Douglas Hyde Art Gallery (see "Art Galleries," below).

Admission: Ł2.50 ($4.15) adults, Ł2 ($3.30) students and seniors, free for children under 12.

Open: Mon–Sat 9:30am–5:30pm, Sun noon–5pm. **Transportation:** DART to Tara Street Station or bus no. 5, 7A, 8, 15A, 15B, 15C, 46, 55, 62, 63, 83, or 84.

2. MORE ATTRACTIONS

ART GALLERIES

BOULEVARD GALLERY, Merrion Sq. West, Dublin 2.

The fence around Merrion Square (see "Parks, Gardens, and Squares," below) doubles as a display railing on summer weekends in an outdoor display of local art similar to New York's Greenwich Village or Paris' Montmartre. Permits are given to local artists only to sell their own work, so this is a chance to "meet-an-artist" as well as to browse or buy.

Admission: Free.

Open: May–Sept, Sat–Sun 10:30am–6pm. **Transportation:** DART to Pearse Station or bus no. 5, 7A, 8, 46, or 62.

CITY ARTS CENTER, 23 Moss St., Dublin 2. Tel. 770643.

Situated along the south bank of the River Liffey on City Quay opposite the new Custom House Quay development, the galleries at this exhibition center are part of an overall four-story arts complex that is geared toward Ireland's young adults and is backed by such stars as U2. The emphasis is on contemporary art produced by local groups and individuals although works by international artists are also featured. The facilities also include a coffee shop overlooking the river.

Admission: Free.

Open: Mon–Fri 10:30am–5:30pm, Sat 11:30am–5pm. **Transportation:** DART to Tara Street Station or bus no. 1, 3, 44B, 45, 47A, 47B, 48A, or 62.

DOUGLAS HYDE GALLERY, Nassau St., Dublin 2. Tel. 772941, ext. 1116.

Housed in a modern building on the Trinity College campus and named after Ireland's first president, this two-story gallery focuses on contemporary Irish and international avant-garde art, bringing in works from Berlin, Tokyo, and New York as well as London and Paris. There is also a regular program of lectures, performances, and events related to the artistic works on display.

Admission: Free.

Open: Mon–Wed and Fri 11am–6pm, Thurs 11am–7pm, Sat 11am–5pm. **Bus:** No. 5, 7A, 8, 15A, 15B, 15C, 46, 55, 63, 83, or 84.

GALLERY OF PHOTOGRAPHY, 37-39 Wellington Quay, Dublin 2. Tel. 714654.

Situated between the River Liffey and the Temple Bar district, this is Dublin's only photographic gallery with exhibitions of international and Irish contemporary photographs, posters, and books on photography. It is a great spot to view photos of old Dublin as well as the contemporary scene.

Admission: Free.

Open: Mon–Sat 11am–6pm, Sun noon–6pm. **Bus:** No. 51B, 51C, 68, 69, or 79.

GRAPHIC STUDIO GALLERY, off Cope St., Dublin 2. Tel. 679-8021.

In the heart of the Temple Bar district, this modern and skylit gallery concentrates solely on Ireland's graphic arts. It is best reached through the arch behind the Central Bank.

Admission: Free.

Open: Mon–Sat 10:30am–6pm. **Bus:** No. 21A, 46A, 46B, 51B, 51C, 68, 69, or 86.

GUINNESS HOP STORE, Crane St., off Thomas St., Dublin 8. Tel. 536700.

Housed in a converted brewery building, this second- and third-floor gallery hosts a variety of contemporary art exhibitions, primarily of paintings and posters. The Guinness Brewery Visitor Centre (see below) is also housed here.

Admission: £2 ($3.30) adults, 50p (85¢) children under 12.

Open: Mon–Wed and Fri 10am–5pm, Thurs 10am–7pm. **Bus:** No. 21A, 78, or 78A.

HUGH LANE MUNICIPAL GALLERY OF MODERN ART, Parnell Sq., Dublin 1. Tel. 741903 or 788761.

Housed in a finely restored 18th-century building known as Charlemont House, this gallery is situated next to the Dublin Writers Museum and across the street from the Garden of Remembrance. It is named after Hugh Lane, an Irish art connoisseur who was killed in the sinking of the *Lusitania* in 1915 and who willed his collection (including works by Courbet, Manet, Monet, and Corot) to be shared between the government of Ireland and the National Gallery of London. With the Lane collection as its nucleus, this gallery also contains paintings from the impressionist and postimpressionist traditions, sculptures by Rodin, stained glass, and works by modern Irish artists, with emphasis on the first half of the 20th century. In April through June, a summer concert series takes place, free of charge, at the gallery, on Sunday at noon.

Admission: Free; donations accepted.

Open: Tues–Fri 9:30am–6pm, Sat 9:30am–5pm, Sun 11am–5pm. **Transportation:** DART to Connolly Station or bus no. 10, 11, 11A, 11B, 12, 13, 14, 16, 16A, 19, 19A, 22, 22A, or 36.

IRISH MUSEUM OF MODERN ART (IMMA), Military Rd., Kilmainham, Dublin 8. Tel. 718666.

Housed in the splendidly restored 17th-century edifice known as the Royal Hospital (see "The Top Attractions," above), IMMA is a showcase of Irish and international art from the latter half of the 20th century. The buildings and grounds also provide a venue for theatrical and musical events, with particular emphasis on the overlap between the visual and performing arts.

Admission: Free.

Open: Tues–Sat 10am–5:30pm, Sun noon–5:30pm. **Bus:** No. 24, 79, or 90.

ORIEL GALLERY, 17 Clare St., Dublin 2. Tel. 763410.

This gallery specializes in the paintings of 19th- and early 20th-century Irish artists, ranging from Paul Henry to Jerome O'Connor and Jack Yeats, as well as contemporary work.

Admission: Free.

Open: Mon–Fri 10am–5:30pm, Sat 10am–1pm. **Transportation:** DART to Pearse Station or bus no. 5, 7A, 8, or 62.

PROJECT ARTS CENTRE, 39 East Essex St., Dublin 2. Tel. 712321.

Situated in the Temple Bar district, this building, which doubles as a theater at night, serves as a showcase for avant-garde painting, free-expression sculpture, and other modern trends in the visual arts.

Admission: Free.

Open: Mon–Sat 11:30am–8pm. **Bus:** No. 51B, 51C, 68, 69, or 79.

RIVERRUN GALLERY, 82 Dame St., Dublin 2. Tel. 679-8606.

Situated opposite City Hall at the corner of Parliament Street and on the edge of the Temple Bar district, this modern gallery showcases all forms of contemporary Irish art.

Admission: Free.

Open: Mon–Fri 10:30am–5:30pm, Sat 11am–4pm. **Bus:** No. 51B, 51C, 68, 69, or 79.

SOLOMON GALLERY, 59 S. William St., Dublin 2. Tel. 679-4237.

Housed on the top floor of the Powerscourt Town House Centre, this gallery specializes in the highly decorative works of contemporary Irish artists, from paintings and sculptures to screen prints.

Admission: Free.

Open: Mon–Sat 10am–5:30pm. **Bus:** No. 10, 11A, 11B, 13, 16A, 19A, 20B, 22A, 55, or 83.

TEMPLE BAR GALLERY AND STUDIOS, 4-8 Temple Bar, Dublin 2. Tel. 679-9259.

Founded in 1983 in the heart of Dublin's "Left Bank," this is one of the largest studio/gallery complexes in Europe. More than 30 Irish artists work here at a variety of contemporary visual arts, from sculpture and painting to printing and photography. Only the gallery section is open to the public, but, with advance notice, appointments can be made to view individual artists at work.

Admission: Free.

FROMMER'S FAVORITE DUBLIN EXPERIENCES

"Dublin must be heaven, with coffee at 11." This is the way Dubliners sing the praises of their mid-morning break. And no place is better for that cup of coffee or tea than Bewley's, the city's landmark coffee emporium.

Afternoon Tea in one of the Old-World Hotels. With piano or harp music in the background, and a silver tray full of finger sandwiches, pastries, and a huge pot of tea, sink into a comfortable chair and enjoy a proper "afternoon tea."

A Stroll Through St. Stephen's Green. Smell the flowers, watch the birds soar overhead and the swans glide along the pond, or just stop and smile at the passersby in this bucolic oasis in the middle of the city.

A Walk Along High Street. In the heart of the Old City, you can listen to the carillon of bells singing in the air at Christ Church Cathedral at 11am on a Sunday morning.

Hop Aboard a Double Decker. Take a bus and survey the city sights from the upper deck.

An Evening at the Theatre. Be part of the audience at a performance of the Abbey Theatre or one of the city's other great show places.

Do a Pub Crawl. Join in a session of traditional Irish music or just sit back and enjoy the conversation at one of Dublin's pubs.

DART Around Dublin's Coast. Ride the city's high-speed rail system along the wide sweep of Dublin Bay from Ballsbridge to Dun Laoghaire Harbor.

Stand on the Pier at Howth Harbor. Watch the yachts glide by and the fishing boats bring in the day's catch.

Explore Dublin's "Left Bank." Walk the cobblestone streets of Temple Bar with its parade of colorful shops, art galleries, theaters, and music studios.

Amble up or down Grafton Street, Dublin's "Fifth Avenue." Look into the windows of the trendy shops, listen to the music of the buskers (street musicians), or watch the sidewalk artists chalk up a masterpiece at your feet.

Climb Aboard a Horse-Drawn Carriage. Clip-clop along the wide Georgian streets and squares in the gentle style of yesteryear.

Open: Mon–Fri 11am–5:30pm, Sat noon–4pm. **Bus:** No. 21A, 46A, 46B, 51B, 51C, 68, 69, or 86.

BREWERIES/DISTILLERIES

GUINNESS BREWERY VISITOR CENTRE, Crane St., off Thomas St., Dublin 8. Tel. 536700, ext. 5155.

Founded in 1759, the Guinness Brewery is one of the world's largest breweries, producing the distinctive dark beer called stout, famous for its thick creamy head. Although tours of the brewery itself are no longer allowed, visitors are welcome to explore the adjacent Guinness Hop Store, a converted 19th-century four-story building. It houses the World of Guinness Exhibition, an audiovisual showing how the stout is made, plus a museum and a bar that dispenses free samples of the famous brew. The two top floors of the building also serve as a venue for a variety of art exhibits.

Admission: £2 ($3.30) adults, 50p (85¢) children under 12.

Open: Mon–Fri 10am–4:30pm. **Bus:** No. 21A, 78, or 78A.

IRISH WHISKEY CORNER, Irish Distillers, Bow St., Dublin 7. Tel. 725566.

This museum illustrates the history of Irish whiskey, known as *uisce beatha* (the water of life) in Gaelic. Housed in a former distillery warehouse, it presents a short introductory audiovisual, an exhibition area, and a whiskey-making demonstration. At the end of the tour, the products can be sampled at an in-house pub. Since there is only one tour a day, it's wise to make a reservation in advance.

Admission: £2.50 ($4.15) per person.

Open: Mon–Fri tours at 3:30pm. **Bus:** No. 34, 70, or 80.

PLACES OF BUSINESS

BANK OF IRELAND/PARLIAMENT HOUSE, 2 College Green, Dublin 2. Tel. 776801.

Although now it is a busy bank, this building was erected in 1729 to house the Irish Parliament, but it became superfluous when the British and Irish Parliaments were merged in London. In fact, the Irish Parliament voted itself out of existence—the only recorded parliament in history to do so. Highlights include the windowless front portico, built to avoid distractions from the outside when the parliament was in session, and the unique House of Lords chamber—famed for its woodwork in Irish oak, 18th-century tapestries, golden mace, and a sparkling Irish crystal chandelier of 1,233 pieces, dating from 1765. It is conveniently situated opposite Trinity College.

Admission: Free.

Open: Mon–Wed and Fri 10am–3pm, Thurs 10am–5pm (except holidays); guided 45-minute tours of the House of Lords chamber on Tues at 10:30am, 11:30am, and 1:45pm. **Transportation:** DART to Tara Street Station or bus no. 15A, 15B, 15C, 21A, 46, 46A, 46B, 46C, 51B, 51C, 55, 63, 68, 69, 86, 78A, 78B, or 83.

DUBLIN STOCK EXCHANGE, 28 Anglesea St., Dublin 2. Tel. 778808.

Like its counterparts all over the world, this is a busy place of bells ringing and stockbrokers rushing around to keep in touch with the rise and fall of stocks around the globe. Stockbroking was first established in Dublin in 1799 and the present exchange dates from 1878. For visitors, there is a spectators gallery on the third floor, giving a sweeping view of all the activity. Call in advance to arrange for an admission ticket.

Admission: Free.

Open: Mon–Fri 9:30–10am and 2:15–3pm. **Transportation:** DART to Tara Street Station or bus no. 21A, 46A, 46B, 51B, 51C, 68, 69, or 86.

GENERAL POST OFFICE [GPO], O'Connell St., Dublin 1. Tel. 728888.

This post office is the symbol of Irish freedom. Built in 1815–18, it was the main stronghold of the Irish Volunteers in 1916, led by Padraic Pearse and James Connolly. Set afire by shelling, the building was gutted and abandoned after the surrender and execution of many of the Irish rebel leaders. It was reopened as a post office in 1929 after the formation of the Irish Free State. In memory of the building's dramatic role in Irish history, today there is an impressive bronze statue of Cuchulainn, the legendary Irish hero, on display in the central hall. Architecturally, it is a gem, with a 200-foot-long and 56-foot-high facade of Ionic columns and pilasters in the Greco-Roman style.

Admission: Free.

Open: Mon–Sat 8am–8pm, Sun 10–6pm. **Transportation:** DART to Connolly Station or bus no. 25, 26, 34, 37, 38A, 39A, 39B, 66A, or 67A.

INTERNATIONAL FINANCIAL SERVICES CENTRE, Custom House Quay, Dublin 1. Tel. 363122.

This is a government-inspired purpose-built center for international banking and finance, aiming to make Dublin a link between the New Europe, the U.S., and the rest of the world. First conceived in 1985 and still in the building stages, it has turned a 27-acre portion of the neglected north quays area of the city into a vibrant hub of activity. The green-tinted glass facades of the new buildings stand out along the River Liffey skyline as tangible reminders that this development is not only the most important urban renewal project in Dublin in the 20th century, but also the largest single project to be carried out in the inner city since the 18th century. At the moment, the center consists mainly of bank offices, but plans call for a cultural complex, theaters, restaurants, a hotel, and residential housing by 1995.

Admission: Free.

Open: Mon–Wed and Fri 10am–12:30pm and 1:30–3pm, Thurs 10am–12:30pm and 1:30–5pm. **Transportation:** DART to Tara Street Station or bus no. 27A, 27B, 53A, or 53B.

CATHEDRALS & CHURCHES

OUR LADY OF MOUNT CARMEL/WHITEFRIAR STREET CARMELITE CHURCH, 57 Aungier St., Dublin 2. Tel. 758821.

One of the city's largest churches, it was built in 1825–27 on the site of pre-Reformation Carmelite priory (1539) and an earlier Carmelite abbey (13th century). It has since been extended, with a new entrance from Aungier Street. This is a favorite place of pilgrimage on February 14th because the body of St. Valentine is enshrined here, presented to the church by Pope Gregory XVI in 1836. The other highlight is the 15th-century black oak Madonna, *Our Lady of Dublin.*

Admission: Free.

Open: Mon and Wed–Thurs 8am–6:30pm, Tues 8am–9:30pm, Sat 8am–7pm, Sun 8am–7:30pm. **Bus:** No. 16, 16A, 19, 19A, 22, 22A, 55, or 83.

ST. AUDEON'S CHURCH, Cornmarket, off High St., Dublin 8. Tel. 778714.

This is the smallest and oldest of Dublin's two St. Audeon's churches—both are named for St. Ouen of Rouen, patron saint of the Normans, and both are situated side by side next to the only remaining gate of the Old City walls (1214). This Norman edifice, belonging to the Church of Ireland, is said to be the only surviving medieval parish church in Dublin. Although it is partly in ruins, significant parts have survived, including the west doorway, which dates from 1190, and the nave from the 13th century. In addition, the 17th-century bell tower houses three bells that were cast in 1423, making them the oldest in Ireland; the other bells were added in 1658 and 1694. The grounds also include an early Christian gravestone, dating from the 8th century, an indication that there may have been an even earlier Christian foundation on the site.

Admission: Free.

Open: Fri–Wed 11:30am–1:30pm. **Bus:** No. 21A, 78A, or 78B.

ST. AUDEON'S CHURCH, High St., Dublin 8. Tel. 679-1855 or 679-1018.

Built in 1841–46, this St. Audeon's is considerably younger and larger than the edifice described above. This church, belonging to the Roman Catholic denomination, maintains a commanding presence, with a dark stone exterior and a Corinthian portico, sitting next to the old city walls in Dublin's oldest neighborhood. But unlike its neighbor, this church is fully operational, with some added commercial enterprises including a coffee shop and an audiovisual show, open to the public (see "Sight-and-Sound Shows," below).

Admission: Free.

Open: Daily 9am–6pm. **Bus:** No. 21A, 78A, or 78B.

ST. MARY'S PRO-CATHEDRAL, Cathedral and Marlborough Sts., Dublin 1. Tel. 745441.

Since Dublin's two main cathedrals (Christ Church and St. Patrick's—see "The Top Attractions," above) belong to the Protestant Church of Ireland denomination, St. Mary's is the closest that the Catholics get to having a cathedral of their own. Tucked into a corner of a rather unimpressive back street, it is situated in the heart of the city's north side and is considered the main Catholic parish church of the city center. Built between 1815 and 1825, it is of the Greek Revival Doric style, providing a distinct contrast to the Gothic Revival look of most other churches of the period. The exterior portico is modeled on the Temple of Theseus in Athens, with six Doric columns, while the Renaissance-style interior is patterned after the church of St. Phillippe-le-Roule of Paris. The church is noted for its Palestrina Choir, which sings the mass every Sunday at 11am.

Admission: Free.

Open: Mon–Sat 8am–6pm, Sat 8am–9pm, Sun 8am–8pm.

Transportation: DART to Connolly Station or bus no. 28, 29A, 30, 31A, 31B, 32A, 32B, or 44A.

ST. MICHAN'S CHURCH, Church St., Dublin 8. Tel. 724154.

Built on the site of an early Danish chapel (1095), this 17th-century edifice claims to be the only parish church on the north side of the Liffey surviving from a Viking foundation. Now under the Church of Ireland banner, it has some very fine interior woodwork and an organ (dated 1724) on which Handel is said to have played his *Messiah*. The most unique—and, in some ways, macabre—feature of this church, however, is the underground burial vault. Because of the dry atmosphere, bodies have laid for centuries without showing signs of decomposition. If you touch the skin of these corpses, you'll find it to be soft even though it is brown and leatherlike in appearance. If you "shake hands" with the figure known as The Crusader, it is said you will always have good luck.

Admission: ₤1.20 ($2) adults, ₤1 ($1.65) seniors, 50p (85¢) children under 12.

Open: Mon–Fri 10am–12:45pm and 2–5pm, Sat 10am–12:45pm. **Bus:** No. 34, 70, or 80.

ST. TERESA'S CHURCH, Clarendon St., Dublin 2. Tel. 718466 or 718127.

Opened in 1810 by the Discalced Carmelite Fathers, this church has been continuously enlarged until it reached its present form in 1876. This was the first post–Penal Law church to be legally and openly erected in Dublin following the Catholic Relief Act of 1793. Over the years, it has given a peaceful respite to many Irish notables, from Daniel O'Connell, the Pearses, Kevin Barry, and Matt Talbot, to Mother Catherine McAuley. Because of its location, tucked between Grafton Street and the Powerscourt Town House Center, today it is a favorite haven for shoppers and tourists.

Among the artistic highlights are John Hogan's *Dead Christ,* a sculpture displayed beneath the altar, and Phyllis Burke's seven beautiful stained-glass windows. Under the current enlightened prior, Fr. Michael Coen, this church has also launched a number of innovations for the inner-city community and visitors including an informal coffee shop on the premises. (*Note:* Since St. Teresa's foundation stone was laid in 1793, the church is celebrating its 200th anniversary in 1993).

Admission: Free; donations welcome.

Open: Daily 8am–8pm or later. **Bus:** No. 16, 16A, 19, 19A, 22, 22A, 55, or 83.

HISTORIC BUILDINGS

CASINO AT MARINO, Malahide Rd., Marino, Dublin 3. Tel. 331618.

Standing on a gentle rise 3 miles north of the city center, this 18th-century building is considered to be one of the finest garden temples in Europe. Designed in the Franco-Roman style of neoclassicism by the Scottish architect Sir William Chambers, it was constructed in the garden of Lord Charlemont's house by the Italian sculptor Simon Vierpyl. Work commenced in 1762 and it took 15 years to build. It is particularly noteworthy for its elaborate stone carvings and compact structure which makes it appear to be a single story from the outside when it is actually two stories tall.

Admission: £1 ($1.65) adults, 70p ($1.15) seniors, 40p (65¢) students and children under 12.

Open: Mid-June to mid-Sept, daily 10am–6:30pm. **Bus:** No. 20A, 20B, 27, 27A, 32A, 42, or 42B.

CITY HALL, Lord Edward St., Dublin 8. Tel. 776811.

Built in 1769–79 as the Royal Exchange by the Dublin Guild of Merchants, this Corinthian-style structure was originally a focal point of city commerce. Since 1852, however, it has been the center of municipal government, housing the offices of the Dublin Corporation and other city departments. The building is distinguished by its Corinthian portico facing Parliament Street and by its interior rotunda, designed as a circle within a square, with a central mosaic depicting the city arms and a dozen colorful frescoes showing the heraldic arms of the Four Provinces of Ireland and various aspects of Dublin. The City Archives are also housed here, including the mace and sword of Dublin plus 102 royal charters.

Admission: Free.

Open: Mon–Fri 10am–1pm and 2:15–5pm. **Bus:** No. 21A, 78A, or 78B.

CUSTOM HOUSE, Custom House Quay, Dublin 1. Tel. 742961.

No view of the Dublin skyline is complete without a tableau of the Custom House, one of Dublin's finest Georgian buildings. Designed by James Gandon and completed in 1791, it is beautifully proportioned, with a long classical facade of graceful pavilions, arcades, columns, and a central dome topped by a 16-foot statue of *Commerce*, and 14 keystones over the doors and windows, known as the *Riverine Heads* because they represent the Atlantic Ocean and the 13 principal rivers of Ireland. Although burned to a shell in 1921, this building has been masterfully restored and its bright Portland stone recently cleaned.

Admission/Open: Not open to the public, but worth looking at the exterior. **Bus:** No. 27A, 27B, 53A.

FOUR COURTS, Inns Quay, Dublin 8. Tel. 725555.

The home of the Irish law courts since 1796, this fine 18th-century building overlooks the north bank of the River Liffey on the west side of Dublin. With a sprawling 440-foot facade, it was designed by James Gandon and is distinguished by its graceful Corinthian columns, massive dome (64 feet in diameter), and exterior statues of *Justice, Mercy, Wisdom,* and *Moses* (sculpted by Edward Smyth). The building was severely burned during the Irish Civil War of 1922, but has been artfully restored. The public is admitted only when court is in session, so it is best to phone in advance.

Admission: Free.

Open: Mon–Fri 11am–1pm and 2–4pm. **Bus:** No. 34, 70, or 80.

LEINSTER HOUSE, Kildare St. and Merrion Sq., Dubline 2. Tel. 789911.

Dating back to 1745 and originally known as Kildare House, this building was once considered the largest Georgian house in Dublin, because of its 11-bay and 140-foot facade. With an impressive central pediment and Corinthian columns, it is also said to have been the model from which the White House in Washington, D.C., was later designed by Irish-born architect James Hoban. It was sold in 1815 to the Royal Dublin Society, which developed it as a cultural center, with the National Museum, Library, and Gallery all surrounding it. In 1924, however, it took on a new role when it was acquired by the Irish Free State government as a parliament house. Since then, it has been the meeting place for Ireland's Dail Eireann (House of Representatives) and Seanad Eireann (Senate), which together constitute the Oireachtas (National Parliament). Tickets for admission when the Dail is in session must be arranged by writing in advance, or by contacting a member of Parliament directly.

Admission: Free.

Open: Oct–May, Tues–Thurs; hours vary. **Transportation:** DART to Pearse Station or bus no. 5, 7A, or 8.

MANSION HOUSE, Dawson St., Dublin 2. Tel. 762852.

Built by Joshua Dawson, this Queen Anne–style building is the official residence of Dublin's lord mayors since 1715. It was here that the first Dail Eireann (Irish Parliament) assembled in 1919 to adopt Ireland's Declaration of Independence and ratify the proclamation of the Irish Republic by the insurgents of 1916.

Admission/Open: Not open to the public, but worth looking at the exterior. **Transportation:** DART to Pearse Station or bus no. 10, 11A, 11B, 13, or 20B.

NEWMAN HOUSE, 85/86 St. Stephen's Green, Dublin 2. Tel. 757255 or 751752.

Situated in the heart of Dublin on the south side of St. Stephen's Green, this is the historic seat of the Catholic University of Ireland, named for Cardinal John Henry Newman, the 19th-century writer and theologian, and first rector of the university. It is comprised of two 18th-century town houses, dating back to 1740, that are decorated with outstanding Palladian and rococo plasterwork, marble-tiled floors, and wainscot paneling. Other highlights include an early Georgian entrance hall, two splendid reception rooms overlooking the green, and an impressive Bishop's Room that evokes the spirit of the 19th-century university ambience. The site also contains a basement restaurant known as The Commons, an outdoor terrace, and a "secret garden."

Admission: Ł1 ($1.65) adults; 75p ($1.15) seniors, students, and children under 12.

Open: May–Oct, Tues–Fri 10am–4pm, Sat 2–4pm, Sun 11am–2pm. **Bus:** No. 14, 14A, 15A, or 15B.

INSTITUTES

IRISH FILM CENTRE, 6 Eustace St., Dublin 2. Tel. 679-5744 or 778788.

As a city with great dramatic and theatrical traditions and as a setting for many recent movies, Dublin is a natural location for a film center. Scheduled to open as we go to press, this new center is appropriately located right in the heart of Dublin's burgeoning Temple Bar arts district, incorporating the historic Friends Meeting House as part of its layout.

A long-awaited development for the Irish film industry and for filmgoers, it houses seven film components under one roof, including two movie theaters, the National Film Archive, a film and television museum, film information office, and film and video libraries. Plans call for Film Trail tours (visiting local Dublin sites that were featured in major movies) to depart from the site regularly.

Admission/Open: Details not final at presstime. **Bus:** No. 21A, 46A, 46B, 51B, 51C, 68, 69, or 86.

ROYAL DUBLIN SOCIETY [RDS], Merrion Rd., Balls-bridge, Dublin 4. Tel. 680645.

One of the great institutions of Dublin, the RDS was formed in 1731 to foster industry, the arts, and sciences. To this end, in the past 260 years, it has been responsible for the establishment of Ireland's botanic gardens, National Gallery, National Library, and National College of Art and Design. The RDS is most noted, however, as the driving force behind Dublin's two prime agricultural shows, the Spring Show (May) and the Dublin Horse Show (July or August). The RDS buildings, show jumping arena, and grounds in Ballsbridge serve as a setting for both shows, as well as a variety of other events and concerts throughout the year. The RDS complex is only open to the public when an event is scheduled.

Admission: Ł2–Ł25 ($3.30–$41.25), depending on event.

Open: Hours vary according to events. **Transportation:** DART to Lansdowne Road Station or bus no. 5, 7, 7A, or 45.

LIBRARIES

CENTRAL LIBRARY OF DUBLIN, Henry St., Dublin 1. Tel. 734333.

Housed on the upper floor of the ILAC shopping complex, this is the keystone of Dublin's library system, with a variety of cultural and leisure services as well as books of all descriptions. Some of the facilities offered include Irish and foreign newspapers, journals, and magazines; trade and telephone directories from around the world; children's library; language center; video viewing room; and business information services. Concerts and lectures are also scheduled on a regular basis.

Admission: Free.

Open: Mon–Thurs 10am–8pm, Fri–Sat 10am–5pm. **Transportation:** DART to Connolly Station or bus no. 25, 26, 34, 37, 38A, 39A, 39B, 66A, or 67A.

CHESTER BEATTY LIBRARY AND GALLERY OF ORIENTAL ART, 20 Shrewsbury Rd., Ballsbridge, Dublin 4. Tel. 269-2386.

Bequeathed to the Irish nation in 1956 by Sir Alfred Chester Beatty, this collection contains approximately 22,000 manuscripts, rare books, miniature paintings, and objects from Western, Middle Eastern, and Far Eastern cultures. Highlights include copies of the Koran, Turkish manuscripts and biblical papyruses dating from the early 2nd to the 4th century A.D., as well as Japanese and Chinese collections of paintings, prints, snuff bottles, jade books, and rhinoceros-horn cups. In addition, there are Burmese, Siamese, Tibetan, and Mongolian collections including parabatiks, books painted on mulberry-leaf paper and on coarse linen cloth. There is also a reference library and a bookshop.

Admission: Free.

Open: Tues–Fri 10am–5pm, Sat 2–5pm; free guided tours on Wed and Sat at 2:30pm. **Transportation:** DART to Sandymount Station or bus no. 5, 6, 6A, 7A, 8, 10, or 46A.

MARSH'S LIBRARY, St. Patrick's Close, Upper Kevin St., Dublin 8. Tel. 543511.

Housed in a building adjoining St. Patrick's Cathedral, this is Ireland's oldest public library, founded in 1701 by Narcisus Marsh, archbishop of Dublin. It is a repository for more than 25,000 scholarly volumes, chiefly on theology, medicine, ancient history, maps, Hebrew, Syriac, Greek, Latin, and French literature. If you are a fan of Jonathan Swift, you can see a copy of Clarendon's *History of the Great Rebellion,* with Swift's penciled notes still on the page edges. Also on view are the library's original carved dark oak bookcases and three wired alcoves or "cages" into which readers were locked to prevent the stealing of rare books. The premises also contains the Delmas Conservations Bindery which artfully restores and repairs rare books and manuscripts.

Admission: Free, but a donation of £1 ($1.65) expected.

Open: Mon and Wed–Fri 10am–12:45pm and 2–5pm, Sat 10:30am–12:45pm. **Bus:** No. 50, 50A, 54, 54A, or 56A.

NATIONAL LIBRARY OF IRELAND, Kildare St., Dublin 2. Tel. 765521.

For visitors who come to Ireland to research their roots, this library is often the first point of reference, with thousands of volumes and records yielding ancestral information. Opened at this location in 1890, this is the largest public library in Ireland, and is particularly noted for its collection of first editions and the works of Irish authors, such as Goldsmith, Swift, Yeats, Shaw, and Joyce, as well as modern-day volumes. For Joyce fans, it is of interest to know that this building was the scene of the great literary debate in *Ulysses*. The library also has an unrivaled collection of maps of Ireland, plus an extensive accumulation of Irish newspapers.

Admission: Free.

Open: July–Aug, Mon–Fri 10am–5pm, Sat 10am–1pm; Sept–June, Mon–Thurs 10am–9pm, Fri 10am–5pm, Sat 10am–1pm.

Transportation: DART to Pearse Station or bus no. 10, 11A, 11B, 13, or 20B.

MUSEUMS

DUBLIN CIVIC MUSEUM, 58 S. William St., Dublin 2. Tel. 679-4260.

Located in the old City Assembly House, next to the Powerscourt Town House Centre, this museum focuses on the history of the Dublin area from medieval to modern times. In addition to old street signs, maps, and prints, you can see Viking artifacts, wooden water mains, coal covers, and even the head from the statue of Lord Nelson, which stood in O'Connell Street until it was blown up 1965.

Admission: Free.

Open: Tues–Sat 10am–6pm, Sun 11am–2pm. **Bus:** No. 10, 11, and 13.

IRISH JEWISH MUSEUM, 3/4 Walworth Rd., off Victoria St., S. Circular Rd., Dublin 8. Tel. 974252.

Housed in a former synagogue, this is a museum of Irish-Jewish documents, photographs, and memorabilia, tracing the history of the Jews in Ireland over the last 500 years.

Admission: Free; donations welcome.

Open: Oct–Apr, Sun 10:30am–2:30pm; May–Sept, Tues, Thurs, and Sun 11am–3pm. **Bus:** No. 15A, 15B, 47, or 47B.

KILMAINHAM GAOL HISTORICAL MUSEUM, Kilmainham, Dublin 8. Tel. 535984.

Dating back to 1795, the gaol (jail) at Kilmainham was once the prime place of imprisonment for Irish freedom fighters. Leaders of the rebellions of 1798, 1803, 1848, 1867, and 1916, were all detained here, including Robert Emmet, Thomas Francis Meagher, Charles Stewart Parnell, and Eamonn De Valera. Closed as a jail in 1924, the site now offers a look at what confinement was like within these walls, via a guided tour, audiovisual presentation, and an exhibition.

Admission: £1.50 ($2.50) adults, £1 ($1.65) seniors, 60p ($1) children under 12.

Open: June–Sept, daily 11am–6pm; Oct–May, Wed and Sun 2–6pm. **Bus:** No. 23, 51, 51A, 78, or 79.

NATURAL HISTORY MUSEUM, Merrion St., Dublin 2. Tel. 618811.

A division of the National Museum of Ireland, this complex

focuses on the zoological aspect of Irish history, with collections illustrating wildlife, both vertebrate and invertebrate, ranging from Irish mammals and birds, to butterflies and insects. In addition, there is a World Collection, and an African and Asian exhibition.

Admission: Free.

Open: Tues–Sat 10am–5pm, Sun 2–5pm. **Bus:** No. 7, 7A, or 8.

NUMBER TWENTY-NINE, 29 Lower Fitzwilliam St., Dublin 2. Tel. 765831.

✪ Situated in the heart of one of Dublin's fashionable Georgian streets, this is a unique museum—a restored four-story town house that reflects the lifestyle of a Dublin middle-class family during the period 1790 to 1820. The accoutrements range from artifacts and works of art of the time, to carpets, curtains, floor coverings, decorations, paintwork, plasterwork, and bellpulls. The nursery also includes dolls and toys of the era.

Admission: Free.

Open: Tues–Sat 10am–5pm, Sun 2–5pm. **Transportation:** DART to Pearse Station or bus no. 6, 7, 8, 10, or 45.

PARKS, GARDENS & SQUARES

GARDEN OF REMEMBRANCE, Parnell Sq., Dublin 1.

Built in 1966 in Parnell Square, it is dedicated to all those who died in the cause of Irish freedom. The central feature of the garden is a large crucifix-shaped pool dominated by a sculpture depicting the legendary Children of Lir.

Admission: Free.

Open: May–Sept, daily 9:30am–8pm; Mar–Apr and Oct, daily 11am–7pm; Nov–Feb, daily 11am–4pm. **Transportation:** DART to Connolly Station or bus no. 10, 11, 11A, 12, 13, 14, 16, 16A, 19, 19A, 22, 22A, or 36.

HOWTH CASTLE GARDENS, Howth, Co. Dublin. Tel. 322624.

Set on a steep slope about 8 miles north of downtown, this 30-acre garden was first planted in 1875 and is best known for its 2,000 varieties of rhododendron. Peak bloom time is in May and June. *Note:* The castle on the grounds is not open to the public.

Admission: Free.

Open: Daily 8am–sunset. **Transportation:** DART to Howth Station or bus no. 31.

MALAHIDE DEMESNE GARDENS, Malahide, Co. Dublin. Tel. 450940.

On the grounds of Malahide Castle (see "The Top Attractions," above), this botanic garden is planted with more than 5,000 species of plants from around the world.

Admission: Free.

Open: May–Sept, daily 10am–6pm. **Bus:** No. 42.

MERRION AND FITZWILLIAM SQUARES, Dublin 2.

✪ These two Georgian squares, within 2 blocks of each other on Dublin's south side, are known for their beautiful town houses with colorful doorways and decorations. Visitors stroll along these two squares, cameras in hand, to take pictures of some of Dublin's best Georgian architecture.

Merrion Square, laid out in 1762, is the larger of the two specimens and has always been a very distinguished address for Dubliners—residents have ranged from Daniel O'Connell, W. B. Yeats, and the duke of Wellington to Sir William and Lady Wilde (parents of Oscar). The park in the center of the square, opened to the public in 1974, contains flowers, shrubs, trees, and benches, as well as the Rutland Fountain of 1791, one of the few Georgian drinking fountains left in the city. In contrast, Fitzwilliam Square, developed in the 1820s, is Dublin's smallest and best preserved Georgian square; it is also the only one in the city whose central park is open to residents only.

Admission: Free.

Open: Both squares always open. The park in Merrion Square open during daylight hours; the park in Fitzwilliam Square is not open to the public. **Transportation:** DART to Pearse Station or bus no. 5, 7A, or 8 for Merrion Square; bus no. 46A, 46B, or 86 for Fitzwilliam Square.

NATIONAL BOTANIC GARDENS, Botanic Rd., Glasnevin, Dublin 9. Tel. 377596 or 374388.

Established by the Royal Dublin Society in 1795 on a rolling 50-acre expanse of land north of the city center, this garden was intended to be a smaller version of London's great Kew Gardens. Today, with more than 20,000 different plants and cultivars, it has become Ireland's prime horticultural attraction. The complex includes a Great Yew Walk, a bog garden, water garden, rose garden, student garden, herb garden, and a variety of Victorian-style glasshouses built to house tropical plants and exotic species.

Admission: Free.

Open: May–Sept, Mon–Sat 9am–6pm, Sun 11am–6pm; Oct–Apr, Mon–Sat 10am–4:30pm, Sun 11am–4:30pm. **Bus:** 13, 19, 34, 34A.

ST. STEPHEN'S GREEN, top of Grafton St., Dublin 2.

The oldest of the Dublin squares, this 22-acre oasis of greenery in the heart of the city dates back to medieval times but was first enclosed in 1670. It was formally laid out as a public park in 1880, thanks to Lord Ardilaun (Sir Arthur Edward Guinness of brewery fame). It contains flowers, trees, and shrubs of all descriptions, statuary, gazebos, an ornamental lake with waterfowl, and a garden for the blind, with the names of plants written in braille on tags. In the summer months, a Victorian bandshell serves as the setting for free lunchtime concerts.

IMPRESSIONS

The trees in St. Stephen's Green were fragrant of rain and the rainsodden earth gave forth its mortal odor, a faint incense rising upward through the mould of many hearts.
—JAMES JOYCE (1882–1941), *PORTRAIT OF THE ARTIST AS A YOUNG MAN*

The buildings that surround the park, using the green as an address, are also worthy of note, from the landmark Shelbourne Hotel and the Royal College of Surgeons, to Iveagh House, the headquarters of Ireland's Department of Foreign Affairs, and Newman House (see "Historic Buildings," above), as well as an assortment of international banks and fine shops.

Admission: Free.

Open: Mon–Sat 8am–dark, Sun 10am–dark. **Transportation:** DART to Pearse Station or bus no. 10, 11A, 11B, 13, 14, 14A, 20B, or 62.

SIGHT-&-SOUND SHOWS

DUBLIN EXPERIENCE, Trinity College, Davis Theatre, Dublin 2. Tel. 772941.

An ideal orientation for first-time visitors to the Irish capital, this 45-minute multimedia sound-and-light show traces the history of Dublin from the earliest times to the present. It is presented in the Davis Theatre of Trinity College on Nassau Street.

Admission: ₤2.75 ($4.40) adults, ₤2.25 ($3.70) seniors and students, ₤1.50 ($2.50) children under 12.

Open: Mid-May to early Oct, daily 10am–5pm, continuous showings on the hour. **Transportation:** DART to Tara Street Station or bus no. 5, 7A, 8, 15A, 15B, 15C, 46, 55, 62, 63, 83, or 84.

THE FLAME ON THE HILL, St. Audeon's Church, High St., Dublin 8. Tel. 679-1855 or 679-1018.

Presented by the St. Audeon Heritage Foundation of the Dublin Diocese, this 35-foot-screen audiovisual focuses on Ireland before the Vikings—the Celtic gods and Druids, high kings and legendary folk heroes, St. Patrick and monastic life, and the influence of the Irish saints and scholars on Europe.

Admission: ₤1.50 ($2.50) adults; ₤1 ($1.65) seniors, students, and children under 12.

Open: Mon–Sat showings at 11:30am, 2pm, 3pm, and 4pm. **Transportation:** DART to Tara Street Station or bus no. 21A, 78, 78A, or 78B.

3. COOL FOR KIDS

DUBLIN ZOO, Phoenix Park, Dublin 8. Tel. 771425.

Established in 1830, this is the third-oldest zoo in the world (after London and Paris), nestled in the midst of the city's largest playground, Phoenix Park, about 2 miles west of the city center. This 30-acre zoo provides a naturally landscaped habitat for more than 235 species of wild animals and tropical birds. Highlights for youngsters include the Children's Pets' Corner and a train ride around the zoo. Other facilities include a restaurant, coffee shop, and gift shop.

Admission: Ł4.20 ($6.95) adults, Ł1.80 ($3) children under 12 and seniors.

Open: Mon–Sat 9:30am–6pm, Sun 11am–6pm. **Bus:** No. 10, 25, or 26.

THE FRY MODEL RAILWAY MUSEUM, Malahide, Co. Dublin. Tel. 452758.

Housed on the grounds of Malahide Castle, this is an exhibit of rare handmade models of more than 300 Irish trains from the introduction of rail to the present. The trains were built in the 1920s and 1930s by Cyril Fry, a railway engineer and draftsman. The complex includes items of Irish railway history dating back 1834, and models of stations, bridges, trams, buses, barges, boats, the River Liffey, and the Hill of Howth.

Admission: Ł2 ($3.30) adults, Ł1.45 ($2.40) seniors and students, Ł1.15 ($1.90) children under 12.

Open: Apr–Oct, Mon–Thurs 10am–1pm and 2–5pm, Sat 11am–1pm and 2–6pm, Sun 2–6pm; Jul–Aug, also Fri 10am–1pm and 2–5pm; Nov–Mar, Sat–Sun 2–5pm. **Bus:** No. 42.

MUSEUM OF CHILDHOOD, The Palms, 20 Palmerstown Park, Rathmines, Dublin 6. Tel. 973223.

Part of a large suburban house on the south side of Dublin, this museum specializes in dolls and dollhouses of all nationalities, from 1730 to 1940. Among the unique items on display are dollhouses that belonged to Empress Elizabeth of Austria and Daphne du Maurier. In addition, there are some antique toys, rocking horses, and doll carriages.

Admission: Ł1 ($1.65) adults, 75p ($1.25) children under 12.

Open: July–Aug, Wed and Sun 2–5:30pm, Sept and Nov–June, Sun 2–5:30pm. **Bus:** No. 13 or 14.

NATIONAL WAX MUSEUM, Granby Row, at Upper Dorset St., off Parnell Sq., Dublin 1. Tel. 726340.

For an overall life-size view of Irish history and culture, this museum presents wax figures of Irish people of historical, political, literary, theatrical, and sporting fame. A push-button narration gives the background on each character as you walk from section to section. In addition to the Irish men and women of note, there is also a wide range of international tableaux featuring everything from the Last Supper and Pope John Paul II, to world leaders, as well as music stars like Michael Jackson, Madonna, and Elvis Presley. For younger children, there is also a Children's World that depicts characters from fairy tales such as "Jack and the Beanstalk," "Robin Hood," "Sleeping Beauty," and "Snow White."

Admission: Ł2.50 ($4.15) adults, Ł1.50 ($2.50) children under 12.

Open: Mon–Sat 10am–5:30pm, Sun 1–5:30pm. **Bus:** No. 11, 13, 16, 22, or 22A.

NEWBRIDGE HOUSE AND PARK, Donabate, Co. Dublin. Tel. 436534.

Situated about 12 miles north of Dublin, this country mansion dates back to 1740 and was once the home of Dr. Charles Cobbe, an archbishop of Dublin. Occupied by the Cobbe family until 1984, this house is a showcase of family memorabilia including hand-carved furniture, portraits, daybooks, and dolls, as well as a museum of world travels. The Great Drawing Room, in its original state, is reputed to be one of the finest Georgian interiors in Ireland.

In the downstairs quarters originally occupied by servants and staff, a mid-18th-century kitchen and laundry room can be seen complete with utensils and implements of long ago. In the adjacent courtyard, there is a coachhouse and various workshops belonging to the estate. There are 350 acres of grounds, laid out with picnic areas and walking trails. The grounds also include a 20-acre working Victorian farm, stocked with farmyard animals.

Admission: Ł2.20 ($3.65) adults, Ł1.80 ($3) seniors and students, Ł1.20 ($2) children under 12.

Open: Apr–Oct, Tues–Fri 10am–1pm and 2–5pm, Sat 11am–6pm, Sun 2–6pm; Nov–Mar, Sat–Sun 2–6pm. **Bus:** No. 33B.

4. SPECIAL-INTEREST SIGHTSEEING

ANCESTOR-TRACING CENTERS

HERALDIC MUSEUM/GENEALOGICAL OFFICE, 2 Kildare St., Dublin 2. Tel. 608670 or 618811.

The only one of its kind in the world, this museum focuses on the uses of heraldry. Exhibits include shields, banners, coins, paintings, porcelain, and stamps depicting coats-of-arms. The office of Ireland's chief herald also offers a consulting service (from Ł10, or $16.50, basic fee) on the premises, so this is the ideal place to start researching your own roots.

Admission: Free.

Open: Mon–Fri 10am–12:45pm and 2–4:30pm. **Transportation:** DART to Pearse Station or bus no. 5, 7A, or 8.

NATIONAL LIBRARY OF IRELAND (see "Libraries," above).

LITERARY & MUSIC CENTERS

IRISH TRADITIONAL MUSIC ARCHIVE, 63 Merrion Sq., Dublin 2. Tel. 619699.

Housed in a Georgian town house, this archive is an information and research center for the traditional song, music, and dance of Ireland. Set up by the Irish Arts Council in 1987 and also supported by the Arts Council of Northern Ireland, it is the first center of its kind to be concerned exclusively with the making and maintaining of a comprehensive reference collection of materials for the appreciation and study of Irish traditional music. The resources include sound recordings, manuscripts, books, periodicals, pamphlets, photographs, films, videos, musical instruments, posters, and newspaper clippings.

Admission: Free.

Open: Mon–Fri 10am–1pm and 2–5pm. **Transportation:** DART to Pearse Station or bus no. 5, 7A, or 8.

JAMES JOYCE CULTURAL CENTER, 35 N. Great George's St., Dublin 1. Tel. 731984.

Located near Parnell Square and the Dublin Writers Museum, this new attraction gives literary enthusiasts one more reason to visit Dublin's north side. Still in the process of restoration as we go to press, it is a 1784 Georgian mansion that is being converted into a museum, archive, and study center devoted to Ireland's great 20th-century novelist, James Joyce. The project is being spearheaded by Ken Monaghan, Joyce's nephew, who also gives tours covering Joycean connections in the area.

Admission/Open: Details have not yet been set; check with the Dublin Tourism office, just 2 blocks away, at the time of your visit. **Transportation:** DART to Connolly Street or bus no. 1, 40A, 40B, or 40C.

JOYCE TOWER, Sandycove, Co. Dublin. Tel. 280-9265 or 280-8571.

✪ Sitting on the edge of Dublin Bay about 6 miles south of the city center, this 40-foot granite monument is one of a series of martello towers built in 1804 to withstand a threatened invasion by Napoléon. Its greatest claim to fame, however, is that it was inhabited in 1904 by James Joyce, staying as the guest of Oliver Gogarty, who had rented the tower from the army for an annual fee of Ł8 ($13). Joyce, in turn, made the tower the setting for the first chapter of his famous novel, *Ulysses,* and it's been known as "Joyce's Tower" ever since. It contains a collection of Joycean memorabilia including letters, documents, first and rare editions, personal possessions, and photographs.

Admission: Ł1.60 ($2.65) adults, Ł1.30 ($2.15) seniors and students, 90p ($1.50) children.

Open: May–Sept, Mon–Fri 10am–1pm and 2–5pm, Sat 10am–5pm, Sun 2–6pm. **Transportation:** DART to Sandycove Station or bus no. 8.

NATIONAL CEMETERY

GLASNEVIN CEMETERY, Finglas Rd., Dublin 11. Tel. 301133.

Situated north of the city center, this is the Irish National Cemetery, founded in 1832 and covering over 124 acres. The majority of the people buried here are ordinary citizens, but there are also many famous names to be found on the headstones, from former Irish presidents, such as Sean T. O'Kelly and Eamonn De Valera, to other political heroes such as Daniel O'Connell, Roger Casement, Michael Collins, and Charles Stewart Parnell. Literary figures are also commemorated here, from poet Gerard Manley Hopkins to writers Christy Brown and Brendan Behan. Although open to all, it is a largely Catholic burial ground, with a large proportion of Celtic crosses used as monuments. A *Heritage Map,* on sale in most bookshops, serves as a guide as to who is buried where.

Admission: Free.

Open: Daily 8am–4pm. **Bus:** No. 34 or 38A.

---

5. ORGANIZED TOURS

BY BUS

DUBLIN BUS, 59 Upper O'Connell St., Dublin 1. Tel. 720000, ext. 3028.

Dublin Bus, the city's official transport company, operates several different tours. Seats can be booked in advance at the Dublin Bus office or through a hotel porter or concierge desk. All tours depart from the Dublin Bus office, but free pickup from many Dublin hotels is available for morning tours.

Dublin City Tour: For a good overview of the capital, hop on board this 3-hour sightseeing tour. It goes to Trinity College, St. Patrick's Cathedral, Christ Church Cathedral, the Royal Hospital, Kilmainham, Phoenix Park, and many other sights. Depending on the weather, the tours are conducted via a unique double-decker bus, with either an open-air or glass-enclosed upper level. It's a great vantage point for picture-taking. In the summer months, this tour is also available at night. The price is £7 ($11.55) adults, £3.50 ($5.80) children under 16 years. The tour operates Jan–Feb, Tues and Fri–Sat at 10:15am; Mar to mid-Dec, daily at 10:15am and 2:15pm (also at 6:15pm June to mid-Sept).

Heritage Tour: For those who enjoy flexibility, this is a continuous guided bus service connecting 10 major points of interest including museums, art galleries, churches and cathedrals, libraries, and historic sites. For one flat fare that is valid throughout the day, you can get off the bus when you wish, take as much time as you require at each site, and then reboard another bus to continue the circuit at your own pace; you can also take the complete tour first and then get off when you wish. The price is £5 ($8.25) adults, £2.50 ($4.15) children under 16. Departures are mid-April to Sept daily 10am–5pm.

North Coast Tour: Operated via a double-decker bus, this 3-hour morning tour covers all the major sights on Dublin's north side, from the National Botanic Gardens and the Casino at Marino to the seaside town of Malahide and the fishing village of Howth. The price is £7 ($11.55) adults, £3.50 ($5.80) children under 16. The tour is offered mid-May to mid-Sept daily at 10:30am.

South Coast Tour: The scenic suburbs of Dublin's south side are the focus of this 4-hour afternoon tour, aboard the upper deck of a double-decker bus. The itinerary includes the seaside towns of Dun Laoghaire, Dalkey, and Bray, the famous James Joyce Tower at Sandycove, and a panoramic trip through the Wicklow and Dublin Mountains. The price is £7 ($11.55) adults, children £3.50 ($5.80) under 16. The tour operates mid-May to mid-Sept, daily at 2pm.

"Ceol agus Craic": Roughly translated from the Gaelic or Irish, the name of this tour means "music and fun." It's an evening of traditional Irish music and dance at the Irish Culture and Music Centre (Culturlann na hEireann) at Monkstown, a southern coastal suburb of Dublin. The tour price includes pickup and return to the Shelbourne, Burlington, Berkeley Court, or Jurys Hotels; a scenic tour to Monkstown; admission to the live stage show; and a cup of tea or coffee with a homemade Irish scone. The price is Ł10 ($16.50) adults, Ł6 ($9.90) children under 16. Departures are end-June–early Sept, Tues–Thurs at 6:30pm.

BUS EIREANN, Travel Centre, Busaras, Store St., Dublin 1. Tel. 366111.

This is the official bus company of Ireland, running scheduled services to all major cities and towns and sightseeing tours within and from Dublin to many parts of Ireland. All tours depart from the Travel Centre at Busaras (Dublin's main bus terminal) where bookings can also be made. Reservations can also be made at the Bus Eireann Desks at the Dublin Bus office (address above) and the Dublin Tourism office, 14 Upper O'Connell St. The following tour of the city is offered:

Dublin City Sightseeing Tour: This is a 4-hour basic overview of the city with admissions to major sights. The itinerary provides an opportunity to view the Georgian squares of Merrion and Fitzwilliam, and to visit St. Patrick's Cathedral, Trinity College, and the Book of Kells. The price also includes a stop at the Tower Design Centre, to see Irish craftspeople at work. The price is Ł9 ($14.85) adults, Ł4.50 ($7.45) children under 16. Departures are May–Sept, Mon–Sat at 11:15am.

In addition, Bus Eireann operates a dozen other tours, ranging from 7 to 12 hours in duration, from Dublin into surrounding areas both near and far. The selection includes scenic places such as Glendalough and Wicklow, the Boyne Valley, Powerscourt Gardens, and a Shannon River cruise, and cities such as Kilkenny and Waterford. Prices range from Ł10 to Ł23 ($16.50 to $37.95) adults and from Ł5 to Ł16 ($8.25 to $26.40) for children.

GRAY LINE TOURS IRELAND, 3 Clanwilliam Terrace, Grand Canal Quay, Dublin 2. Tel. 619666 or 744466.

A branch of the world's largest sightseeing organization, this company offers a range of full-day and half-day sightseeing tours of Dublin City and its environs, in the tourist season. All tours depart from the Gray Line Desk at the Dublin Tourism office, 14 Upper O'Connell St. Pickups are also made from the following hotels: Gresham, Shelbourne, Conrad, Burlington, Jurys, Berkeley Court, and Mont Clare. Reservations can be made through hotel porters and concierges, travel agents, or at the Gray Line desk in the Dublin Tourism office. The selection of tours includes:

Morning Dublin City Tour: A 3-hour guided bus tour of Georgian Dublin including historic squares and streets. Admission is provided into the National Museum or Art Gallery and Trinity College to view the Book of Kells. The price is Ł13 ($21.45) per person, with departures May–Oct, Mon–Sat at 10am, Sun at 10:30am.

Afternoon Dublin City Tour: The historic section of Dublin is the focus of this 3-hour tour, providing admission into St. Patrick's Cathedral and Dublin Castle. The tour also takes in the Liberties, the heart of Old Dublin, and visits Phoenix Park, the largest enclose park in Europe. The price is £13 ($21.45) per person. The tour operates May–Oct, daily at 2:30pm.

Full-Day Dublin City Tour: A combination of the morning and afternoon tour described above, making a 7-hour exploration of Dublin's highlights. The price is £25 ($41.25) per person. Departures are scheduled May–Oct, Mon–Sat at 10am, Sun at 10:30am.

Malahide Castle & Coastal Drive: This 3-hour tour travels past the famous Abbey Theatre and heads northward for a visit inside the famous 12th-century Malahide Castle, about 10 miles north of the city. The return trip follows the coastal route along Dublin Bay. The price is £13 ($21.45) per person, with departures May–Oct, Mon and Fri at 2:30pm.

Newbridge House & Coastal Drive: Travel approximately 12 miles via the city's northern suburbs to Newbridge House, a magnificent 18th-century home with its own parklands and working Victorian farm. Return via the coastal route including a stop at the seaside village of Howth. Tour lasts approximately 4 hours. The price is £13 ($21.45) per person. The tour is offered May–Oct, Sat at 10am.

Dublin Night-Life Tours: This trip takes you to Jurys Irish Cabaret at Jurys Hotel or Doyle's Irish Cabaret at the Burlington Hotel, for a festive evening with a 3-hour show and dinner, or show with two drinks. Either cabaret provides a magical program of music, song, dance, and good humor. Prices are: Jurys £29.50 ($48.70) show/dinner, £17.50 ($28.90) show/drinks; Doyle's £27.90 ($46) show/dinner, £17.50 ($28.90) show/drinks. The tour operates May–Oct, Tues–Sun at Jurys and Mon–Sat at Doyle's. (Call 619666 for departure times.)

In addition, Gray Line provides a choice of tours to areas outside Dublin including Powerscourt Gardens, Newgrange, Glendalough and County Wicklow, the Boyne Valley, and various combinations of each, priced from £13 ($21.45) for a half-day and £25 ($41.25) for a full-day trip per person.

ON FOOT

Small and compact, Dublin lends itself to walking tours. You can set out with a map on your own, but, in order not to miss anything, we recommend that you consider one of the following self-guided or escorted group tours.

Self-Guided Walking Tours

TOURIST TRAILS The Dublin Tourism office, 14 Upper O'Connell St., Dublin 1 (tel. 747733), has pioneered in the development of self-guided walking tours around Dublin. To date, there are four different "tourist trails" that have been mapped out and signposted throughout the city. For each trail, the tourist office has also produced a handy booklet that maps out the route and provides a commentary about each place along the trail. The booklets covering the Old City, Georgian and Cultural Tours each cost £1 ($1.65), and the *Rock 'n' Stroll* booklet costs £1.95 ($3.20).

The four tourist trails cover the following:

Old City Heritage Trail—Starting at Trinity College, this walking route covers the Dublin of Viking and medieval times—from

Christ Church and St. Patrick's Cathedrals to Dublin Castle and City Hall. The trail wends its way along High Street, where parts of the Old City walls can be seen, and Francis Street, Dublin's "antiques row," as well as through the ancient Liberties section and ends in the Temple Bar district, an area of narrow cobbled 18th-century streets that have recently been rejuvenated and pedestrianized into a "Left Bank" enclave.

Georgian Heritage Trail—This walking route, which commences at Trinity College, follows some of the most attractive Georgian streets in the city south of the River Liffey including Merrion and Fitzwilliam Squares, St. Stephen's Green, and Dawson, Kildare, Leeson, and Upper Mount Streets. The commentary points out the architectural features of the period as well as buildings and events of note dating from other times.

Cultural Heritage Trail—Although this tour starts and finishes at Trinity College, its primary focus is on the great architectural and cultural landmarks on the north side of the River Liffey, including the Four Courts, the Custom House, the Abbey and Gate Theatres, the Hugh Lane art gallery, and the Dublin Writers Museum. Aiming to bring to life the Dublin of Joyce, O'Casey, and Gogarty, it also takes in parks and quays, churches and markets, fine houses and ancient ruins.

Rock 'n' Stroll Trail—This trail is designed to take visitors to the principal places in Dublin associated with the contemporary music scene. The stops along the route, all of which are marked with a plaque, include buildings and places associated with U2, Sinead O'Connor, Bob Geldof, the Chieftains, and other leading musical artists. In addition, the guide booklet for this trail also lists milestones in Irish rock music history and provides a roundup of leading music venues in Dublin, from rock concerts to jazz sessions.

Guided Group Walking Tours

DUBLIN FOOTSTEPS, c/o Tour Guides Ireland, 12 Parliament St., Dublin 2. Tel. 679-4291 or 679-4345.
This company offers a variety of themed tours including a Medieval Walk, Literary Walk, and Georgian Walk. Each walk lasts about 2 hours and departs from Bewley's Café, Grafton Street.
Price: £4–£5 ($6.60–$8.25) per person.
Schedule: June–Sept, daily; usually at 10:30am and 3pm, but hours vary, depending on tour; call in advance for schedule.

DUBLIN LITERARY PUB CRAWL. Tel. 540228.
Walking in the footsteps of Joyce, Behan, Beckett, Shaw, Kavanagh, and other Irish literary greats, this walking tour rambles from pub to pub, with appropriate commentary in between stops. Tour assembles at the Bailey pub on Duke Street, but it can be booked at the Dublin Tourism office, 14 Upper O'Connell St. (tel. 747733).
Price: £5 ($8.25) plus the cost of drinks.
Schedule: June–Aug, Tues–Thurs at 7:30pm.

FILM TRAIL TOURS, Irish Film Centre, 6 Eustace St., Dublin 2. Tel. 679-5744 or 778788.

Places in Dublin associated with films and filmmaking are the focus of a new series of walking tours to be operated by the Irish Film Institute, slated to open by early 1993. Details of price and schedule not final at presstime.

OLD DUBLIN TOURS, 90 Meath St., Dublin 8. Tel. 01/ 532407, 533423, or 556970.

This company conducts guided walks in and around Old Dublin, amid the city's medieval and Viking remains. Conducted by native Dubliners, these 2-hour tours give visitors the opportunity to soak up the ambience and meet the people of the area. Tours assemble at the gate of Christ Church Cathedral.

Price: Ł3 ($4.95) per person.

Schedule: May–Sept, daily at 10:30am and 2pm, Oct–Apr, Fri–Sat at 10:30am, Sun at 2pm.

TRINITY TOURS, c/o Tour Guides Ireland, 12 Parliament St., Dublin 2. Tel. 679-4291 or 679-4345.

This firm operates walking tours around Trinity College including admission to the Old Library and the new Colonnades Gallery to see the Book of Kells. Tours assemble and depart every 15 minutes from Front Square. Reservations not necessary, but appreciated.

Price: Ł3 ($4.95) per person.

Schedule: May–Oct, Mon–Sat 9:30am–4:30pm, Sun noon–4pm.

VIA HANSOM CABS

DUBLIN HORSE-DRAWN CARRIAGE TOURS, St. Stephen's Green, Dublin 2. Tel. 726968 or 613111.

Tour Dublin in style via a handsomely outfitted horse-drawn carriage. The driver commentates on the sights as you travel around the streets and squares of this Fair City. To arrange a ride, consult with one of the drivers stationed with carriages at the Grafton Street side of St. Stephen's Green. Rides range from a short swing around the green to an extensive half-hour Georgian tour or an hour-long Old City Tour. Rides are available on a first-come basis, but can also be booked by phone in advance.

Price: Ł5–Ł30 ($8.25–$49.50) for two to five passengers, depending on the duration of ride.

Schedule: Apr–Oct, daily and nightly, depending on weather.

6. SPORTS & RECREATION

It is no secret that sporting events dominate the Irish national calendar and character—Ireland is indeed a sports-loving land—and Dublin is the hub. And if there's one thing that the Dubliners love more than participating, watching, wagering, and talking about their own athletic pursuits, it is sharing their sporting passion with visitors. Here are a few ways you can join in the fun.

SPECTATOR SPORTS

GAELIC GAMES   If your schedule permits, don't miss attending one of Ireland's national games, hurling and Gaelic football. Hurling, one of the world's fastest field sports, is played by two teams of 15, using wooden sticks and a small leather ball. Gaelic football, also played by two teams of 15, is a field game similar to rugby or soccer except that the ball is round and it can be played with the hands. These two amateur sports are played every weekend throughout the summer at various local fields, culminating in September with the All-Ireland Finals, an Irish version of the Super Bowl. For schedules and admission charges, phone the **Gaelic Athletic Association,** Croke Park, Jones Road, Dublin 3 (tel. 363222).

GREYHOUND RACING   Watching these lean and swift canines is one of the leading spectator sports in the Dublin area. Racing is held throughout the year at **Shelbourne Park Stadium,** Bridge Town Road, Dublin 4 (tel. 683502), and **Harold's Cross Stadium,** 151 Harold's Cross Rd., Dublin 6 (tel. 971081). For a complete schedule and details, contact Bord na gCon (The Greyhound Board), Shelbourne Park, Bridge Town Road, Dublin 4 (tel. 683502).

HORSE RACING   In legend and lifestyle, Ireland has always been synonymous with the horse. Where else but in this horse-happy country would you find horse racing scheduled over 250 days a year. Once considered the sport of kings, horse racing in the Emerald Isle is truly the sport of the people. Admission to any track averages Ł4 to Ł7 ($6.60 to $11.55). There is computerized betting at the windows (minimum bet: Ł1 or $1.65), but the most fun is in watching the fast-fingered bookmakers chalking up the odds on their boards in the "betting ring" and then placing a bet with these bookies (minimum bet: Ł5 or $8.25).

In the Dublin area, there are two racetracks within easy reach.

Leopardstown Racecourse, off the Stillorgan Road (N11), Foxrock, Dublin 18 (tel. 289-3607), is located 6 miles south of the city center. This is a modern facility with all-weather glass-enclosed spectator stands. Races are scheduled throughout the year, two or three times a month, on weekdays or weekends. You can take a taxi or bus no. 86.

The Curragh, Dublin-Limerick road (N7), Co. Kildare (tel. 045/41205), often referred to as "the Churchill Downs of Ireland," is the country's best-known racetrack, located 30 miles west of Dublin in neighboring County Kildare. Majestically sitting on the edge of Ireland's central plain, it is the home of the Irish Derby, held each

---

IMPRESSIONS

The most important week in Ireland is the week of the Dublin Horse Show. The best hunters, the best draught horses, and the nippiest harness ponies in the world are on show. Grafton Street becomes a garden of girls.
—DONN BYRNE (1889–1928), "DESTINY BAY"

year on the last Saturday of June. Racing at the Curragh also normally occurs on at least one Saturday a month during March through October. Special buses run from the Central Bus Station on racing days.

In addition, there is hurdle racing at two tracks within an hour's drive of the city at **Fairyhouse,** County Meath (tel. 256167) and **Punchestown** in County Kildare (tel. 045/97704). For a copy of the Irish Racing Calendar, contact the Irish Racing Board, Leopardstown Racecourse, Foxrock, Dublin 18 (tel. 289-2888).

POLO With the Dublin Mountains as a backdrop, polo is played during the May to mid-September period on the green fields of Phoenix Park, on Dublin's west side. Matches take place on Wednesday evenings, and on Saturday and Sunday afternoons. Any of these games can be attended free of charge. For full details, contact the **All Ireland Polo Club,** Phoenix Park, Dublin 8 (tel. 776248), or check the sports pages of the newspapers.

RECREATION

BEACHES The following beaches on the outskirts of Dublin offer safe swimming and sandy strands and can all be reached via city buses heading northward: **Dollymount,** 3½ miles away; **Sutton,** 7 miles away; Howth, 9 miles away; and **Portmarnock** and **Malahide,** each 10 miles away. In addition, the southern suburb of Dun Laoghaire, 7 miles away, offers a beach (at **Sandycove**) and a long bayfront promenade, ideal for strolling in the sea air. For more details, inquire at the Dublin Tourism office.

GOLF As a country known for its 40 shades of green, Ireland also has an abundance of golfing greens, with 200 courses throughout the country and at least 30 within easy distance of Dublin.

Dublin's courses welcome visitors on weekdays, but getting starting time on weekends can be difficult. Greens fees range from £10 to £25 ($16.50 to $41.25). Electric carts are not readily available, but caddie cars (pull carts) can be rented for about £2 ($3.30) per round. Some of the leading courses in the Dublin area are described below.

Portmarnock Golf Club, Portmarnock, Co. Dublin (tel. 323082), located 10 miles from the city center on Dublin's north side, sits on a spit of land between the Irish Sea and a tidal inlet. First opened in 1894, this 18-hole championship links has been the scene of leading tournaments during the years—from the Dunlop Masters (1959, 1965), Canada Cup (1960), Alcan (1970), and St. Andrews Trophy (1968), to many an "Irish Open." Many experts consider this course as the benchmark of Irish golf.

IMPRESSIONS

*Along Dublin Bay, on a sunny July morning, the public
gardens . . . look bright as a series of parasols.*
—ELIZABETH BOWEN (1899–1973), "UNWELCOME IDEA"

Royal Dublin Golf Club, Bull Island, Dollymount, Dublin 3 (tel. 337153), often compared to St. Andrews in layout, is a century-old 18-hole seaside links situated on an island in Dublin Bay, 3½ miles north of the city center. Like Portmarnock, it has been rated among the top courses of the world and has also hosted several "Irish Open" tournaments. The home base of Ireland's legendary champion, Christy O'Connor, Sr., the Royal Dublin is well known for its fine bunkers, close lies, and subtle trappings.

Elm Park Golf Club, Nutley Lane, Dublin 4 (tel. 693014), lies on the south side of Dublin. This 18-hole inland course is very popular with visitors because it is located within 3½ miles of the city center and close to Jurys, Berkeley Court, and Burlington Hotels.

For more information on golf courses, contact the Irish Tourist Board and ask for the *Golfing Ireland/Only the Best* brochure.

HORSEBACK RIDING: For equestrian enthusiasts, Dublin offers opportunities to both experienced and novice riders, with almost a dozen riding stables within easy reach. Prices average about £10 ($16.50) an hour, with or without instruction. Many stables offer guided trail-riding as well as courses in show jumping, dressage, prehunting, eventing, and cross-country riding. Among the riding centers nearest to downtown are **Calliaghstown Riding Centre,** Calliaghstown, Rathcoole, Co. Dublin (tel. 589236); **Carrickmines Equestrian Centre,** Glenamuck Road, Foxrock, Dublin 18 (tel. 955990); **Kilternan Country Club,** Kilternan, Co. Dublin (tel. 957136); and **Malahide Riding School,** Ivy Grange, Malahide, Co. Dublin (tel. 463622).

For a list of all riding establishments in Dublin and throughout Ireland, contact the **Association of Irish Riding Establishments,** Daffodil Lodge, Eadestown, Naas, Co. Kildare (tel. 01/ 955990).

TENNIS Some hotels, such as the Berkeley Court, Burlington, and Westbury, offer their guests playing privileges at the **Riverview Racquet and Fitness Club,** Beech Hill, Clonskeagh, Dublin 14 (tel. 283-0322).

For the use of public courts, one of Dublin's most centrally located facilities is at **Herbert Park,** Herbert Park Road, Ballsbridge, Dublin 4 (tel. 684364). Situated near the American embassy and the Royal Dublin Society Show Grounds, it welcomes visitors, if arrangements are made in advance. The fee for hourly games is around £2 ($3.30).

In addition, there are about a dozen other courts in suburban parts of the city; for a full list, contact **Tennis Ireland,** 54 Wellington Rd., Dublin 4 (tel. 681841).

CHAPTER 7

STROLLING AROUND DUBLIN

1. THE OLD CITY
2. THE GEORGIAN DISTRICT
3. THE NORTH SIDE

The best way to discover and to savor Dublin is on foot. Ramble along the quays of the River Liffey, duck down tiny thoroughfares with descriptive names like Bull or Crown Alley, Cuckoo or Fumbally Lane, Fishamble or Winetavern Street, The Coombe or Stoneybatter, cross under Merchant's Arch or over Ha'penny Bridge. Only on foot can you experience all of the features of the incomparable face of Dublin's Fair City.

WALKING TOUR — The Old City

Start: Westmoreland Street.
Finish: St. Stephen's Green or Trinity College.
Time: Allow at least 3 hours, not including interior visits or tours of major buildings.
Best Times: Mid-morning, mid-afternoon, or weekends.
Worst Times: Weekday rush hours.

With emphasis on Dublin's glorious past, this walk covers the principal historic sites south of the River Liffey. Begin your exploration on Westmoreland Street, just south of the river's expansive O'Connell Bridge. Walk around the corner to College Green and you will be standing in front of:

1. **The Parliament House** (now the Bank of Ireland), regarded as one of Dublin's finest specimens of 18th-century architecture. Begun in 1729 from the designs of Sir Edward Lovett Pearce, the surveyor-general of Ireland, the building was also enhanced by the later work of James Gandon (1785). It is unique because it has a windowless facade. Even though it is now the home of the Bank of Ireland, if you time your visit to be on a Tuesday, you can tour the original House of Lords room, with its elaborate coffered ceiling, heirloom tapestries, and a Waterford glass chandelier dating back to 1765 (tours at 10:30am, 11:30am, and 1:45pm).

   Across the street from the old Parliament House is one of Dublin's best-known landmarks:

2. **Trinity College,** founded in 1592, although the earliest surviving portions of buildings date from 1722. As you enter the main gates, note the great 300-foot Palladian facade, erected from 1752 to 1759; statues at the entrance commemorate two

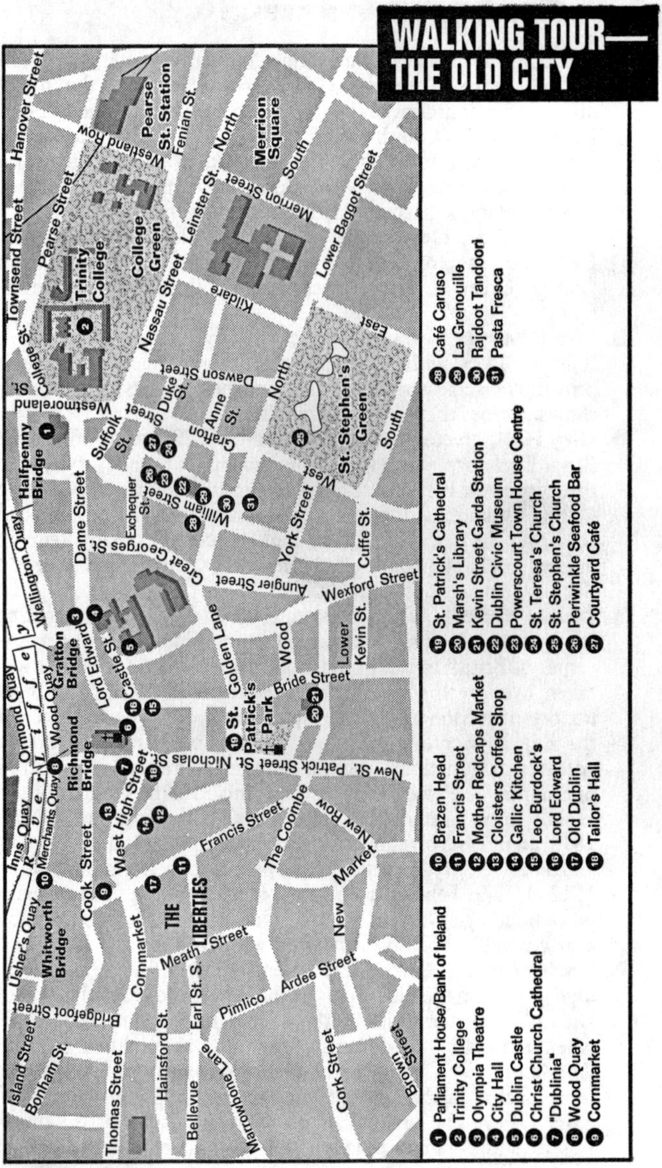
WALKING TOUR—
THE OLD CITY
1 Parliament House/Bank of Ireland
2 Trinity College
3 Olympia Theatre
4 City Hall
5 Dublin Castle
6 Christ Church Cathedral
7 "Dublinia"
8 Wood Quay
9 Cornmarket
10 Brazen Head
11 Francis Street
12 Mother Redcaps Market
13 Cloisters Coffee Shop
14 Gallic Kitchen
15 Leo Burdock's
16 Lord Edward
17 Old Dublin
18 Tailor's Hall
19 St. Patrick's Cathedral
20 Marsh's Library
21 Kevin Street Garda Station
22 Dublin Civic Museum
23 Powerscourt Town House Centre
24 St. Teresa's Church
25 St. Stephen's Church
26 Periwinkle Seafood Bar
27 Courtyard Café
28 Café Caruso
29 La Grenouille
30 Rajdoot Tandoori
31 Pasta Fresca
River Liffey
Trinity College
College Green
Merrion Square
St. Stephen's Green
St. Patrick's Park
THE LIBERTIES
Pearse St. Station

distinguished 18th-century alumni, Oliver Goldsmith, the poet and dramatist, and Edmund Burke, political philosopher and orator. Inside this 7,000-student enclave you will find a cobbled walkway and a series of buildings which include the chapel (1798), public theater or examination hall (1791), dining hall (1761), the old library (1732) and the new library (1967).

The pièce de résistance of the old library is its Long Room, 210 feet long, 41 feet wide, and 40 feet high. It houses a large collection of medieval manuscripts and early printed books. In the adjacent Colonnades Gallery you can view the hand-illustrated manuscript of the four Gospels known as the Book of Kells, dating back to the 9th century or earlier. Each day a new page is turned for visitor viewing. Other ancient items on permanent exhibit include the Books of Armagh and Durrow, and the elaborately carved ancient musical instrument considered to be the 11th-century harp of Irish chieftain Brian Boru. Exit from the front of the Trinity complex and walk from College Green to Dame Street and continue westward passing:

3. **The Olympia Theatre,** one of the city's leading showplaces, built in 1879 with an elaborate Victorian facade. Today it provides a stage for musicals, comedies, mimes, and variety shows. Across the street is Dublin's:

4. **City Hall,** erected between 1769 and 1779, and formerly the Royal Exchange. It is a square building in Corinthian style, with three fronts of Portland stone. The interior is designed as a circle within a square, with fluted columns supporting a dome-shaped roof over the central hall. The building contains many items of interest, including 102 royal charters and the mace and sword of the city. Adjacent to City Hall is:

5. **Dublin Castle,** built between 1208 and 1220. Representing some of the oldest surviving architecture in the city, this was the center of British power in Ireland for seven centuries until it was taken over by the new Irish government in 1922. The most important section is the State Apartments, once the residence of the English viceroys and now the focal point for government ceremonial functions, such as the inauguration of Ireland's presidents. The castle complex also includes the Church of the Holy Trinity, formerly the Chapel Royal, built between 1807 and 1814; an undercroft showcasing recent archeological excavations and The Treasury, presently in the process of restoration, built in 1712–15 and believed to be the oldest surviving purpose-built office building in Ireland. At this point, Dame Street has taken on a new name, Lord Edward Street, and leads to:

6. **Christ Church Cathedral** at Christchurch Place. Standing on high ground in the oldest part of the city, this cathedral is one of Dublin's finest historic buildings. It dates back to 1038 A.D. when Sitric, the then-Danish king of Dublin, built the first wooden Christ Church here. The original city of Dublin was then located in the 2-block area between the church and the River Liffey. The original simple foundation of Christ Church was extended into a cruciform design and rebuilt in stone in 1171, although the present structure dates mostly from 1871–78 when a huge restoration was undertaken. Across the street, in the former Synod Hall of the cathedral, you can visit:

7. **Dublinia,** a tri-level re-creation of Dublin in medieval times. This new attraction is slated to debut in early 1993. For a slight detour, take a turn on Winetavern Street toward the River Liffey in front of Dublinia, and you will come to:

8. **Wood Quay,** hugging the south bank of the River Liffey. Although today you will see a modern office complex, the home

of the Dublin Corporation Civic Offices, this was the site of the original Viking city in Dublin. During recent excavations, before the offices were built, archeological digs revealed the layout, houses, walls, and quays of Dublin as they existed in the 9th to 11th centuries. Returning back up Winetavern Street, turn right and the continuation of the same thoroughfare is now known as High Street. On the right hand side are the two St. Audoen's Churches, one Protestant and one Catholic, dating back to the 13th and 19th centuries respectively, and both sitting beside a portion of the old city walls. Next is the:

9. Cornmarket, dating from the 13th century when it was an important trade and open market site on the west end of the old city. Nothing remains of the original cornmarket except the name. As a slight detour, turn right and walk down Bridge Street toward the river. At the lower end of Bridge Street you will see the:

10. Brazen Head, dating back to 1198 and reputed to be the city's oldest pub. Stroll back up Bridge Street to the Cornmarket. A detour across the main thoroughfare will bring you to:

11. Francis Street, known as Dublin's "antiques row" because of its abundance of fine antiques shops and indoor markets. Returning to High Street, walk along the opposite side of the street in an eastward direction. Take the cutoff for Back Lane and arrive at:

12. Mother Redcaps Market, a bargain-filled indoor market, and:

REFUELING STOPS For light lunches or snacks, there are many good choices in this area including the **(13) Cloisters Coffee Shop** at St. Audoen's Church, High Street; the **Brazen Head,** (see 10 above) at 20 Lower Bridge St.; or the **(14) Gallic Kitchen** at Mother Redcaps Market, Back Lane. If you have a craving for authentic fish-and-chips, try **(15) Leo Burdock's,** off Christchurch Place. For a more formal lunch or full dinner, reserve a table at the **(16) Lord Edward,** 23 Christ Church Place, or **(17) Old Dublin,** 90/91 Francis St.

---

18. Tailor's Hall, erected in 1706, one of the few remaining Queen Anne buildings in the city and Dublin's oldest surviving guild-hall. This little lane ends at Patrick Street; take a right and follow Patrick Street south to:

19. St. Patrick's Cathedral, Dublin's second medieval cathe-dral, founded on this site in 1190 A.D., although not much remains from the cathedral's foundation days. It is mainly Early English in style, with a square medieval tower, a spire which was added in the 18th century, and a 300-foot long interior, which makes it the longest church in Ireland. St. Patrick's is closely associated with Jonathan Swift, who was dean here from 1713 to 1745 and who is buried within. From Patrick Street, turn left onto Patrick's Close and on the left is:

20. Marsh's Library, founded in 1701 and the oldest public library in Ireland with books dating back to 1472. This small street leads to Kevin Street where you will see the:

21. **Kevin Street Garda Station** (Police), formerly a medieval archbishop's palace. Now make a left and walk up Bridge Street and make another right onto Golden Lane, so named in medieval times because goldsmithing was practiced here, which becomes Stephen's Street. On Lower Stephen Street, make a left onto South William Street. On the right is the:

22. **Dublin Civic Museum,** located in the old City Assembly House, dating back to 1767, and now the home of an eclectic collection of memorabilia about the city. Across the street is the:

23. **Powerscourt Town House Centre,** formerly the town residence of Lord Powerscourt, built in 1771, and now a multilevel indoor shopping complex. This grand building contains some of the finest rococo plasterwork and wood carving in Ireland. Enter from the South William Street doorway and walk through the Powerscourt building to the Clarendon Street side. On the opposite side of this street is:

24. **St. Teresa's Church,** opened in 1810 and famed for its stained-glass windows and artistic statuary. From St. Teresa's side entrance, there is a side alley that leads directly to Grafton Street, Dublin's main shopping area. You can spend some time shopping or make a left turn and return to Trinity College or a right turn and end this tour at:

25. **St. Stephen's Green,** the oldest of Dublin's parklike squares. Dating back to medieval times, this 22-acre oasis of greenery was first enclosed in 1670 and formally laid out as a public park in 1880.

REFUELING STOPS Powerscourt Town House Centre offers a variety of self-service and full-service restaurants and snack bars including the **(26) Periwinkle Seafood Bar,** 59 S. William St. For a light snack or cup of coffee/tea stop into the **(27) Courtyard Café** at St. Teresa's Church, Clarendon Street. If you'd like to end the tour with dinner, restaurants in the area include **(28) Café Caruso,** 47 S. William St.; **(29) La Grenouille,** 64 S. William St.; **(30) Rajdoot Tandoori,** 26/28 Clarendon St.; and **(31) Pasta Fresca,** 3/4 Chatham St.

WALKING TOUR — The Georgian District

Start: The Grand Canal at Baggot Street.
Finish: St. Stephen's Green.
Time: Allow at least 3 to 4 hours, plus time for interior visits to museums, galleries, and public buildings.
Best Times: Mid-morning, mid-afternoon, or weekends.
Worst Times: Weekday rush hours.

(Map of the Georgian District of Dublin, showing numbered walking tour stops and streets including Merrion Square, St. Stephen's Green, Trinity College, Grafton Street, Fitzwilliam Square, Pembroke Street, Baggot Street, the River Liffey with its quays and bridges, St. Patrick's Park, and surrounding streets.)

1. Grand Canal
2. Baggot Street Bridge
3. Bank of Ireland complex
4. Fitzwilliam Square
5. ESB (Electricity Supply Board)
6. Number Twenty-Nine
7. St. Stephen's Church
8. Merrion Square
9. National Gallery of Ireland
10. Leinster House
11. Natural History Museum
12. St. Stephen's Green
13. Shelbourne Hotel
14. Gallery 22
15. Mitchell's Cellars
16. National Gallery restaurant
17. National Museum of Ireland
18. National Library
19. Heraldic Museum
20. Trinity College
21. Mansion House
22. Grafton Street
23. Bewley's Café
24. St. Stephen's Green Shopping Centre
25. Royal College of Surgeons
26. Harcourt Street
27. National University of Ireland
28. Newman House
29. Iveagh House
30. National Concert Hall
31. Leeson Street
32. Unicorn
33. Ante Room

This tour concentrates on many of Dublin's loveliest 18th-century streets, squares, and landmarks, many of which provide an attractive setting for the city's cultural and literary attractions. Start this day's walking at Baggot Street at Dublin's:

1. Grand Canal. Built in the 18th century to connect Dublin to the Shannon River and the Irish midlands, this is a major example of the engineering skills of the period. The towpath on either side of the canal has a rustic character, with terraces of small brick houses, wildfowl and swans on the water, and a series of curved 18th-century bridges. At:

2. Baggot Street Bridge, you will find the world headquarters of the Irish Tourist Board (Bord Failte), in case you wish to stop in for some information on Dublin or other parts of Ireland. Stroll northwest on Baggot Street, which is so named because it was where Baggotrath Castle stood until the early 19th century. In contrast, look to the right and see the modern:

3. Bank of Ireland complex. To view some perfect specimens of colorful Georgian doorways and homes, turn left and wander along Upper Fitzwilliam Street and around:

4. Fitzwilliam Square, dating back to the 1820s. It was the last and smallest of the great Georgian squares to be developed, and is also the only city-center park of its kind to remain private, for the use of the residents of the square only. The brick-faced Georgian buildings here, once the fashionable town homes of the Irish gentry, are now used primarily as offices by doctors, dentists, and creative professionals (such as advertising and public relations people). Return to Baggot Street, and proceed straight ahead through the traffic light onto Lower Fitzwilliam Street. On the right you will see the offices of the:

5. ESB (Electricity Supply Board); although relatively new brick-fronted buildings, they have been built in keeping with a Georgian style and theme. The ESB is also a cosponsor of:

6. Number Twenty-Nine, at 29 Lower Fitzwilliam St. on the corner of Upper Mount Street, a museum designed to reflect what a typical Georgian home looked like. On the other side of Upper Mount Street is:

7. St. Stephen's Church, a Greek Revival–style edifice dating back to 1824. It is known as the "Peppercanister Church" because of the form of the cupola that tops the bell tower. Across the street is the east side of:

8. Merrion Square, laid out in the 1760s and open to the public. Considered the core of the best-preserved section of Georgian Dublin, it is the setting for many historic and well-tended town houses. Over the years, many were the residences of Dublin's leading citizens. Walk around the square and you will find plaques commemorating former residents such as Daniel O'Connell (no. 58); William Butler Yeats (no. 82); George Russell, otherwise known as A. E. (no. 84); and Oscar Wilde and his parents, Sir William and Lady Speranza Wilde (no. 1). On the west side of Merrion Square is a trio of important public edifices starting with:

9. The National Gallery of Ireland. First opened in 1864, it contains a premier collection of paintings by Irish artists as well as works by such international masters as Fra Angelico, Rembrandt, Gainsborough, Manet, Degas, El Greco, Goya, Monet, Rubens, and Van Dyck, plus an important display of icons, and a room devoted totally to American painting. Next is:

10. Leinster House, a splendid Georgian mansion dating back to

1745. Standing in the center of a quadrangle, it is today the legislative hub of the Irish government—the meeting place of the Oireachtas (Irish Parliament), consisting of Dail Eireann (House of Representatives) and Seanad Eireann (Senate). If the lines of the building look a little familiar, that is because Leinster House was used as a model by James Hoban, the Irish architect who designed the White House. To the left of Leinster House is the:

11. **Natural History Museum of Ireland,** focusing on the zoological aspect of Irish history. Continue along Upper Merrion Street to Merrion Row and turn right. This small street leads to the north side of:

12. **St. Stephen's Green,** the oldest of Dublin's squares. A delightful 22-acre pedestrian park, it is called "Stephen's Green" or simply "the green" by Dubliners who flock to enjoy the flowers, trees, ponds, and free lunchtime concerts. Take a few steps along the this side of the green and on your right will be the:

13. **Shelbourne Hotel,** one of Dublin's landmark hotels dating back to 1824.

REFUELING STOPS If you would like a formal lunch, stop into the **Shelbourne Hotel** (no. 13 above) or the nearby **(14) Gallery 22** on St. Stephen's Green. For something light and creative, try **(15) Mitchell's Cellars** on Kildare Street or the **self-service restaurant** in the **(16) National Gallery,** on Merrion Square West.

Take a slight diversion off the green, turn right, and head up Kildare Street for a half block. On the right is the main entrance to the:

17. **National Museum of Ireland,** a building well worth visiting to gain an appreciation of Ireland's progress through the centuries. Here you'll see artwork from the first known appearance of man in Ireland, in the form of decorated stones from the megalithic tombs of 6,000 B.C., and items from the early-Christian, Viking, and Romanesque periods, as well as a comprehensive display of Irish silver, glass, ceramics, furniture, musical instruments, coins, medals, costumes, and lace. In addition, there is a suite of rooms aptly called "The Treasury" which contains such one-of-a-kind pieces as the Ardagh Chalice, Tara Brooch, Cross of Cong, and the Shrine of St. Patrick's Bell. Next to the museum is the Kildare Street entrance to Leinster House and then the:

18. **National Library,** the largest public library in Ireland. Founded in 1877, it is the repository for a half-million books, prints, and manuscripts. It also has an unrivaled collection of maps of Ireland, plus an extensive accumulation of Irish newspapers. The building next door is the:

19. **Heraldic Museum.** Its Irish Genealogical Office is an ideal starting point if you are trying to track down your ancestry. From Kildare Street, turn left onto Nassau Street, facing:

20. **Trinity College** (for a complete description, see "Walking Tour

1," above). On Nassau Street, you will encounter a row of fine souvenir, book, and clothing shops. You may wish to take some time out for shopping. Walk as far as Dawson Street and turn left. Dawson Street is lined with interesting bookshops and shops including the Royal Hibernian Way complex on the right. On the left, at the lower end of the street, is the:

21. **Mansion House,** a fanciful Queen Anne–style building erected by Joshua Dawson in 1710, and the home of the lord mayors of Dublin since 1715. Many important events have taken place here including the adoption of the Irish Declaration of Independence in 1919 and the signing of the truce that ended the Anglo-Irish hostilities in 1921. If your timing is right, you may also get a glimpse of the lord mayor's coach, a richly decorated horse-drawn carriage built by Dublin craftsmen in 1789 and restored in 1976. The body of the coach is carved and gilded, and the panels are painted with allegorical scenes relevant to the history of the city. Dawson Street then returns you to the north side of St. Stephen's Green. Walk 1 block and you have arrived at:

22. **Grafton Street,** the city's main shopping thoroughfare, considered as Dublin's equivalent of New York's Fifth Avenue or London's Bond Street. Recently pedestrianized, it is a continuous row of fashionable department stores, boutiques, and specialty shops. The best way to see it all is to walk up one side and down the other.

REFUELING STOP Don't miss **(23) Bewley's Café** in the center of Grafton Street, at the corner of Johnson Court. It's a Dublin tradition for coffee, tea, lunch, and snacks throughout the day.

When your exploration of Grafton Street is complete, return toward St. Stephen's Green and walk along the west side of the park. On your right will be:

24. **St. Stephen's Green Shopping Centre,** one of Dublin's newest indoor shopping malls, with a fanciful glassy Victorian facade. Next is the:

25. **Royal College of Surgeons,** Ireland's top medical college and one of the most notable Georgian buildings on the west side of the green. At the point where the south side of the green meets the west, you will come to:

26. **Harcourt Street,** a curving Georgian thoroughfare laid out in 1775 and named after the then-viceroy, Lord Harcourt. Take a look at no. 61, a fine brick building where George Bernard Shaw lived for a time, and no. 16, once the residence of Bram Stoker, the author of *Dracula*. Return to the south side of the green and you will pass the:

27. **National University of Ireland** buildings on the right including:

28. **Newman House,** the historic seat of the university, named for Cardinal John Henry Newman, 19th-century writer and theologian. Recently restored and opened to the public, the site is

actually a blend of two recently restored Georgian town houses, dating back to 1740. The basement also houses an elegant literary-themed restaurant. Next is:

29. **Iveagh House** at 80 St. Stephen's Green. Designed by Richard Castle in 1736, the house was originally built for a bishop, and later owned by the Guinness family of the brewery fame. It was presented to the Irish nation in 1939 and has since been used as offices for Ireland's Department of Foreign Affairs. As the south side of the green meets the east, you will see Earlsfort Terrace, the setting for Ireland's:

30. **National Concert Hall,** a turn-of-the-century building that was originally part of the National University. Here you will also encounter the beginning of:

31. **Leeson Street,** a strip known for its after-hours activity of all kinds, including an ever-changing parade of disco/nightclubs in the basements of restored Georgian town houses.

Stroll up the east side of the green now, returning toward the Shelbourne, or enter one of the gates of the park, amble over to one of the benches, and enjoy a rest in this sylvan setting after your walk.

REFUELING STOPS Depending on the time of day, you may wish to end your walk at the Shelbourne Hotel for a proper afternoon tea in the Georgian lounge or a drink in the equestrian-themed **Horseshoe Bar.** If you prefer to end with dinner, dine at the **Aisling Restaurant** of the Shelbourne, or enjoy a similarly elegant Georgian ambience at **The Commons Restaurant** at Newman House, 85/86 St. Stephen's Green. For an informal meal, try the nearby **(32) Unicorn** at 12B Merrion Court or the **(33) Ante Room** at 20 Lower Baggot St.

WALKING TOUR —— The North Side

Start: Parnell Square.
Finish: O'Connell Bridge.
Time: 3 to 4 hours, depending on interior visits of major buildings and museums.
Best Times: Weekdays or Saturday, from mid-morning through mid-afternoon.
Worst Times: Sunday when many shops and some attractions are closed.

The focal point of this tour is O'Connell Street, Dublin's broad main thoroughfare. Originally an elongated residential square known as Gardiner's Mall, it was extended and named Sackville Street in its early days. By the mid-19th century, it was renamed in honor of Daniel O'Connell, former lord mayor of Dublin and the champion of Catholic emancipation in Ireland. The adjoining bridge spanning the River Liffey was also rechristened in tribute to O'Connell.

Ranked among the grand ceremonial boulevards of Europe, O'Connell Street is one of the few broad two-way arteries in the city, with a center strip or mall dotted by a series of monuments and a fountain. Up until 25 years ago, O'Connell Street was considered the center of Dublin, "the place" to go and to be seen. Today much of the emphasis has shifted south of the River Liffey to the Grafton Street and St. Stephen's Green areas.

No visit to Dublin is complete, however, without devoting some time to the O'Connell Street area. It still has much to offer the walker in an historic and cultural vein, even though the local merchants have gone a little overboard on neon signs, fast-food cafés, and multiplex cinemas. Start your tour at the northernmost point of O'Connell Street at:

1. **Parnell Square.** This block-long landmark is named after Charles Stewart Parnell, a 19th-century Irish Protestant leader and advocate of Irish Home Rule who is fondly referred to as "the uncrowned king of Ireland." At the north end of the square is the:

2. **Garden of Remembrance,** a peaceful parklet dedicated to all those who died in the cause of Irish freedom. Directly opposite this serene patch of green is the:

3. **Hugh Lane Municipal Gallery of Modern Art,** housed in a building known as Charlemont House, one of Dublin's finest houses and often compared to a palace, erected between 1762 and 1765. The gallery itself was founded in 1908 by art collector Sir Hugh Lane, who subsequently died in the sinking of the *Lusitania* in 1915. With the Lane collection as its core, this museum also includes paintings from the impressionist and postimpressionist traditions and a collection of works by Irish artists. Next door to the gallery is one of Dublin's newest and most popular attractions, the:

4. **Dublin Writers Museum,** a multidimensional tribute to the city's great scribes. Housed in two restored 18th-century buildings, it offers literary exhibits focusing on Ireland's three Nobel Prize winners—Shaw, Yeats, and Beckett, as well as other famous Dublin writers from Swift and Wilde to O'Casey and Joyce. There is also a library, bookshop, literary gallery, and other changing exhibits. Before leaving the north side of Parnell Square, you may wish to turn right and take a slight detour for a half block to the:

5. **National Wax Museum,** which presents colorful tableaux of Irish historical and political figures, as well as world leaders and contemporary music stars, and fairy-tale characters to appeal to youngsters.

REFUELING STOPS Both the Hugh Lane Gallery of Contemporary Art and the Dublin Writers Museum have excellent **coffee shops,** suitable for a snack or light lunch; in the basement of the writers museum, there is also a top-notch restaurant for lunch or dinner, **Chapter One.**

Other buildings of note lining Parnell Square are the:

Map legend:

- ❶ Parnell Square
- ❷ Garden of Remembrance
- ❸ Hugh Lane Municipal Gallery of Modern Art
- ❹ Dublin Writers Museum
- ❺ National Wax Museum
- ❻ Gate Theatre
- ❼ Rotunda Hospital
- ❽ Parnell Monument
- ❾ James Joyce Cultural Centre
- ❿ Gresham Hotel
- ⓫ Father Theobald Matthew Statue
- ⓬ Dublin Tourism
- ⓭ Dublin Bus Offices
- ⓮ St. Mary's Pro-Cathedral
- ⓯ Tyrone House
- ⓰ Anna Livia Fountain
- ⓱ Henry Street
- ⓲ Moore Street
- ⓳ General Post Office (GPO)
- ⓴ Clerys
- ㉑ Statue of Jim Larkin
- ㉒ Abbey Theatre
- ㉓ Liberty Hall
- ㉔ Busaras
- ㉕ Custom House
- ㉖ P.O.E.T.S.
- ㉗ 101 Talbot
- ㉘ International Financial Services Centre
- ㉙ O'Connell Bridge
- ㉚ Four Courts
- ㉛ St. Michan's Church
- ㉜ Irish Whiskey Corner

Church ✝ Post Office ⊠ Information ⓘ

6. **Gate Theatre,** on the southeast corner. One of Dublin's leading stages, it was founded in 1928 by Hilton Edwards and Michael MacLiammoir, pioneers in contemporary Irish theater. On the southwest corner of Parnell Square is the:

7. **Rotunda Hospital.** Built in 1751–55, it is the oldest maternity hospital in Britain and Ireland and second oldest in the world, dating back to 1748. Built in the Palladian style, the complex

includes a chapel decorated in the baroque manner with very ornate and figurative plasterwork, unique for Dublin churches of the Georgian period. Leaving Parnell Square and returning to the northern tip of O'Connell Street, you will see the:

8. **Parnell Monument,** a statue dedicated to the 19th-century Irish leader for whom Parnell Square is also named. This section of O'Connell Street, from the monument to the juncture of Henry and North Earl Streets, is called "Upper" O'Connell Street. For a slight detour with a literary vein, depart Parnell Square at its southeast corner (onto Summerhill Street) and walk for 2 blocks to North Great George's Street and proceed for a half block to no. 35. Here you will see the:

9. **James Joyce Cultural Centre,** a new literary enclave commemorating the life and times and works of one of Dublin's most famous 20th-century writers. The center contains a museum, archive, and study area. Return to the north tip of Upper O'Connell Street and on the left side is the:

10. **Gresham Hotel,** founded in 1817 by Thomas Gresham and one of Dublin's great landmarks of hospitality. The hotel's beautiful Georgian interior is worth a detour. Outside of the Gresham, in the central mall, is the:

11. **Father Theobald Matthew statue.** This 19th-century priest was the founder of the Pioneer Total Abstinence movement in Ireland, a group of people who refrain from alcoholic drink and are known as "Pioneers." Continuing south on Upper O'Connell Street, you will pass the main office of:

12. **Dublin Tourism,** at 14 Upper O'Connell St. If you have not already done so, visit this office for the latest information on Dublin area activities. On the opposite side of the street are the:

13. **Dublin Bus Offices,** at 59 Upper O'Connell St. This is the departure point for many city sightseeing tours. After passing the tourist office, take a left at Cathedral Street and walk for 1 block to:

14. **St. Mary's Pro-Cathedral** on Marlborough Street, the seat of Roman Catholicism in Dublin, since the two main cathedrals, Christ Church and St. Patrick's, belong to Protestant denominations. Dedicated in 1825, it is a Doric-style edifice that combines a portico modeled after the Temple of Theseus in Athens, and an interior patterned after the church of St. Phillippe-le-Roule in Paris. It is noted for its Palestrina Choir, a group that spawned the great Irish tenor John McCormack at the turn of the century. Opposite the pro-cathedral is:

15. **Tyrone House,** an impressive 18th-century building erected for the Viscount Tyrone. It was acquired by the Irish government in 1835 and now houses the headquarters of the Irish Department of Education. Of particular note is the marble pietà statue outside, given to Ireland by the Italian government in gratitude for relief supplies sent during World War II. Return to the center of Upper O'Connell Street. Here you will see the:

16. **Anna Livia Fountain,** a multispouted monument erected during the city's millennium celebrations in 1988. It was designed to represent the River Liffey, the river of Dublin. Anna

Livia is the Irish name for the river and it was popularized in James Joyce's works. Cross to the other side of Upper O'Connell Street now and turn onto:

17. **Henry Street,** a busy pedestrianized shopping thoroughfare. There are several major department stores here as well as the huge ILAC shopping mall. A right turn off Henry Street will bring you to:

18. **Moore Street,** the city's largest al fresco market for fish, fruit, vegetables, and flowers. It is the home of Dublin's famous street barrow vendors, who peddle their wares in the tradition of Molly Malone. You'll be charmed by their persuasive salesmanship and their sharp wit and singsong voices, rich in the unique Dublin dialect. From Moore Street, return to O'Connell Street which, south of the Henry/North Earl Streets intersection, now becomes "Lower O'Connell Street," and on your right facing south is the:

19. **General Post Office (GPO).** Built between 1815 and 1818, this was one of the last great public buildings to be erected in the Georgian era. It is noted for its giant front Ionic portico, with six fluted columns topped by three stone figures, representing Mercury, Fidelity, and Hibernia. Besides being a place to buy stamps for your postcards, this great building was also a pivotal scene of Irish history. The Republic of Ireland was proclaimed here in 1916 when the Irish Volunteers commandeered the GPO as their headquarters. The building was shelled by a British gunboat anchored in the River Liffey and completely gutted by fire. Now fully restored, the GPO commemorates the Irish Rising in its main hall with a huge bronze statue of the dying *Cuchulainn,* a legendary Irish folk hero. Words from the Proclamation of the Irish Republic are also cut in stone on the building's facade. Opposite the GPO is:

20. **Clerys,** Ireland's largest department store, dating back to 1883. The monument in the central mall in front of Clerys is a:

21. **Statue of Jim Larkin,** champion of the working class and powerful orator, who organized the Irish Transport and General Workers Union in 1909 and the Workers Union of Ireland in 1924. Continue southward to Lower Abbey Street and turn left. Walk 1 block to the:

22. **Abbey Theatre,** Ireland's premier stage. Founded in 1904 by William Butler Yeats and Lady Augusta Gregory, the Abbey has given the world such classics as *The Playboy of the Western World* by John M. Synge, *Juno and the Paycock* by Sean O'Casey, *Philadelphia, Here I Come* by Brian Friel, and *Da* by Hugh Leonard. The present theater is modern (1966), having replaced the original, which burned down in 1951. Continue on Lower Abbey Street to a crescent-shaped street known as Beresford Place, make a right and see:

23. **Liberty Hall,** a 1960s addition to the Dublin scene and the closest thing to a skyscraper (16 stories) in this city. It's the headquarters of the Irish Transport and General Workers Union. Make a left and follow Beresford Place 2 blocks to Store Street to see:

24. **Busaras,** Dublin's central bus station and departure point for many sightseeing tours of the city and surrounding countryside, and the bus to the airport. Across the street is one of Dublin's foremost public buildings, the:

25. **Custom House.** Designed by James Gandon and completed in 1791, it is beautifully proportioned with a long classical facade of graceful pavilions, arcades, columns, and a central dome. Although burned to a shell in 1921, it has been masterfully restored.

REFUELING STOPS For a light snack or a full meal, try **(26) P.O.E.T.S.** on Beresford Place or **(27) 101 Talbot** at 101 Talbot St., 1 block north of Beresford Place.

A contrast in architecture is offered by the adjacent glassy and green-tinted facade of the:

28. **International Financial Services Centre,** a new government-sponsored headquarters for international banking and finance. One of the city's brightest stars in the sphere of urban renewal, it sits on a 27-acre site along the Custom House Docks and is earmarked for further expansion, with plans for a hotel, restaurants, theaters, and housing. Returning to the front of the Custom House, you are now on the quays overlooking the north bank of the River Liffey. Walk westward along Eden Quay and you come to:

29. **O'Connell Bridge** at the southern tip of O'Connell Street. Here stands a monument to Daniel O'Connell. Continuing west, next is Batchelor's Walk and Lower and Upper Ormond Quays, passing a variety of auction rooms, shops, and buildings in a state of transition. Continue to:

30. **The Four Courts** at Inns Quay. The headquarters of the Irish justice system, this huge 18th-century building has a distinctive vast lantern dome which makes it stand out on the Dublin skyline. It was also shelled during the warfare of the 1920s and was later restored. One block further west you will come to Church Street and:

31. **St. Michan's Church,** a 17th-century structure on the site of an 11th-century Danish chapel. It has some very fine woodwork, and an organ dated 1724 on which Handel is said to have played his *Messiah.* The most unique feature of this church, however, is the underground vaults. Because of the dry atmosphere, bodies have laid for centuries without showing signs of decomposition. If you touch the skin of these corpses, you'll find it to be soft, even though it is brown and leatherlike in appearance. If you "shake hands" with the figure known as The Crusader, it is said you will always have good luck. Turn left at Mary's Lane, north of St. Michan's, and the next right will bring you to Bow Street and the:

32. **Irish Whiskey Corner,** a museum with a series of exhibits explaining the history of Irish whiskey and how it is made. There is also an in-house pub offering samples of the products at the end of a daily tour (at 3:30pm Monday to Friday).

Return to the quays and walk along the pathway beside the River Liffey, enjoying the riverside sights and ending the tour at O'Connell Bridge (no. 27, above) and the foot of O'Connell Street.

CHAPTER 8

DUBLIN SHOPPING

1. THE SHOPPING SCENE

2. SHOPPING A TO Z

As a country known the world over for its handmade products and fine craftsmanship, Ireland is a shopper's paradise—and Dublin is a one-stop source for the country's best wares.

Dublin's shops are chock-full of handwoven tweeds from Donegal, Galway, and Wicklow; handcut glassware from Waterford, Cavan, Galway, Tipperary, Sligo, and the Fair City itself; delicate china and tableware produced in Galway and Donegal as well as over the border at Belleek in Northern Ireland; handknit sweaters from the Aran Islands and other rural parts of the West of Ireland; lace from Limerick and Monaghan; linens from Donegal and Northern Ireland; natural green marble products from Connemara; and much more.

1. THE SHOPPING SCENE

A good place to start a Dublin shopping spree is at the HQ Gallery on the top floor of the Powerscourt Town House Centre on South William Street in the heart of the city. Operated by the Craft Council of Ireland, this gallery provides a national showplace and a retail outlet for hundreds of craftworkers from all parts of the country. Products on display include knitwear and fashion accessories, ceramics, glass, leatherwork, jewelry, metalwork, furniture, woodwork, textiles, books, and souvenir gifts. The HQ Gallery also sells a very helpful guide to all of Ireland's crafts for £2 ($3.30).

HOURS In general, Dublin shops are open from 9am or 9:30am to 5:30pm or 6pm, Monday through Saturday, with late hours on Thursday until 8pm. There are exceptions, however, particularly in the tourist season (May through September or October), when many shops also post Sunday hours, usually mid-morning through 4pm or 5pm. Throughout the year, many book shops are also open on Sunday—check each listing for the prevailing schedule at presstime.

MAIN SHOPPING STREETS Dublin's "Fifth Avenue" is Grafton Street, displaying a parade of fine boutiques, fashionable department stores, and specialty shops. Smartly pedestrianized, Grafton Street often attracts street performers and sidewalk artists, giving it a festive atmosphere. The smaller streets radiating out from Grafton—**Duke Street, Dawson Street, Nassau Street,** and **Wicklow Street**—are also lined with fine small shops featuring books, handcrafts, and souvenirs.

Nearby is **Temple Bar,** the hub of Dublin's "Left Bank" artsy district, and the setting for art galleries, secondhand clothing stores, sports specialty shops, and a host of other interesting boutiques.

For antiques, the focal point is **Francis Street,** just west of St. Patrick's Cathedral, in the old section of the city.

On the north side of the Liffey, the **O'Connell Street** area is the main shopping nucleus, along with its nearby offshoots—**Abbey Street** for fine crafts, **Moore Street** known for its open-air markets, and **Henry Street,** a pedestrianized shopping mecca of department stores and indoor malls.

TAXES & TAX REFUNDS Before embarking on a Dublin shopping spree, you should know that your purchases will be subject to Irish sales tax, called VAT (value-added tax). This tax ranges from 16% on adult clothing and footwear—but there's no tax on children's clothing—to 21% on crystal, china, jewelry, pottery, heraldic crests, and most souvenirs. Books are not taxed. The VAT is usually already included in the prices quoted to you and on the price tags.

Fortunately, as a visitor, you can avoid paying this tax, *if* you follow a few simple procedures. The easiest way to make a VAT-free purchase is to arrange for a store to ship the goods directly abroad to your home; such a shipment is not liable to VAT. However, you do have to pay for shipping, so you may not save that much in the end. If you wish to take your goods with you, then you must pay the full amount for each item including all VAT charges. However, you can have that tax refunded to you in a number of ways. Here are the main choices:

Store Refund At the time of purchase, obtain a full receipt, print your own name and address on the receipt, and have the clerk indicate the VAT paid (cash register tally rolls are not acceptable by Customs); passports and other forms of identification (such as driver's license) may be required. When departing Ireland, go to the Customs office at the airport or ferryport to have receipts stamped and goods inspected. Stamped receipts should then be sent to the store of purchase, and the store will then issue a VAT refund check that is mailed to your home address. Most stores will deduct a small handling fee for this service.

Tax Back This is a private company that will do the paperwork for you for a flat fee of 1.5% on low VAT items (clothing and footwear) and 2% on high VAT items (jewelry, glassware, and other gifts). Simply make your purchases; obtain from the store a Tax Back form; and on departure from Ireland, send your receipts and forms in a postpaid envelope (obtainable free at most stores) to Tax Back, 93/95 Oliver Plunkett St., Cork City, Co. Cork (tel. 021/277010). If you charged your purchases on a credit card, Tax Back will arrange a credit to your account in the amount of the VAT refund; if you paid cash, then you will receive your refund by a check in U.S. dollars sent to your home.

Cashback This is a private company that will give you a cash refund (in the currency of your choice) as you depart from Dublin or Shannon airports. The fee for this service is calculated on the basis of 1.5% of the total amount spent plus £2.50 ($4.15) for each of the first two stores and 80p ($1.35) per store thereafter. A 60p ($1) charge applies for currency exchange other than Irish punts.

To obtain a refund, you must do the following:

1. Purchase items from stores displaying a Cashback sticker; and each time you make a purchase, you must obtain a Cashback voucher from a participating shop.
2. Fill out each form with your name, address, passport number, and other required details.
3. When departing Ireland, if you have any vouchers with a value of over Ł200 ($330), you must have them stamped and validated by a Customs official.
4. You can then go to the Cashback desk at Dublin airport (Departures Hall) or Shannon airport (in the Arrivals Hall), turn in your stamped Cashback forms, and receive cash payments in U.S. or Canadian dollars, British pounds sterling, or Irish punts—whatever you prefer.

If you are departing from Ireland via a ferryport, or if you don't have time to get to the Cashback desk before you leave, you can also mail your stamped receipts in postpaid preaddressed envelopes to the Cashback Headquarters at Spiddal Industrial Estate, Spiddal, County Galway (tel. 091/83258). Your refund, issued as a check, will be mailed to your home within 21 days. You can also request to have your VAT refund applied to your credit-card account.

Note: EC citizens are only entitled to a VAT refund on goods purchased with a gross value of more than Ł460 ($759) per item.

2. SHOPPING A TO Z

ANTIQUES

ANTHONY ANTIQUES, 7-9 Molesworth St., Dublin 2. Tel. 777222.
Although furniture is the focal point of this centrally located shop, there is also a great selection of small brass decorative pieces and heirlooms. **Open:** Mon–Sat 9:30am–5:30pm. **Transportation:** DART to Pearse Station or bus no. 10, 11A, 11B, 13, or 20B.

BITS AND PIECES, 78 Francis St., Dublin 8. Tel. 541178.
Located on the lower end of "antiques row," this shop carries a wide range of brass chandeliers, mirrors, and stained glass. **Open:** Mon–Sat 9:30am–6pm. **Bus:** No. 78A, 78B, or 21A.

CITY BRASS SHOP, 74 Francis St., Dublin 8. Tel. 542696.
As the name implies, brass in the form of candlesticks, curios, sconces, lamps, hardware, and trim of all descriptions are the specialty here. **Open:** Mon–Sat 9am–6pm. **Bus:** No. 78A, 78B, or 21A.

COOKE ANTIQUES, 79-85 Francis St., Dublin 8. Tel. 542057.
One of the largest shops along "antiques row," this long-

established place is known for larger pieces, such as 18th-century Georgian and 19th-century Victorian decorative furniture, marble fireplaces, and architectural fittings. There is also a picture gallery, and restoration work is a specialty. **Open:** Mon–Sat 9am–6pm. **Bus:** No. 78A, 78B, or 21A.

DENIS CUSACK ANTIQUE DEALER, 13-14 Harcourt Rd., Dublin 2. Tel. 753537.

⭐ This shop specializes in smaller gift-type antiques including silver, pieces of ivory, curios, china, glass, paintings, lace, candelabras, clocks, and crystal, as well as furniture. **Open:** Mon–Sat 9:30am–6pm. **Bus:** No. 62.

FRANCIS STREET ANTIQUE ARCADE, 59 Francis St., Dublin 8. Tel. 534255.

Come to this shop for a good selection of antique lamps, china, plates, glass, vases, silver, and copper. **Open:** Mon–Sat 9:30am–6pm. **Bus:** No. 78A, 78B, or 21A.

LANTERN ANTIQUES, 57 Francis St., Dublin 8. Tel. 534593.

⭐ Framed old pub posters, prints, and mirrors are a special find here, as are one-of-a-kind cash registers, curio jugs, and recycled church furnishings. There is also a good selection of books. **Open:** Mon–Sat 9:30am–6pm. **Bus:** No. 78A, 78B, or 21A.

ROXANE MOORHEAD ANTIQUES, 77 Francis St., Dublin 8. Tel. 533962.

⭐ Located at the very southern tip of "antiques row," this lovely little shop is packed with silver, glass, dishes, and hard-to-find Victorian curios and bric-a-brac, such as small perfume bottles and urns, cheese dishes, and sardine boxes. **Open:** Mon–Sat 9:30am–6pm. **Bus:** No. 21A, 49A, 65A, 65B, 78A, or 78B.

ART

COMBRIDGE FINE ARTS, 24 Suffolk St., Dublin 2. Tel. 774652.

In business for over 100 years and centrally located near Trinity College, this shop often features works by modern Irish artists, such as Colin Gibson, George Gillespie, Norman McCaig, and Fergal Nally, as well as framed quality reproductions of classic Irish art and cold-cast bronze reproductions of great Irish sculpture pieces. **Open:** Mon–Sat 9:30am–5:30pm. **Transportation:** DART to Pearse Station or bus no. 15A, 15B, 15C, 55, or 83.

THE DAVIS GALLERY, 11 Capel St., Dublin 1. Tel. 726969.

Located just a block north of the River Liffey, this shop offers a wide selection of Irish watercolors and oil paintings, with emphasis on Dublin scenes, seascapes, river views, and the Irish countryside, as well as a fine array of wildlife and flora. **Open:** Mon–Fri 10am–4:45pm, Sat 11am–4:45pm. **Bus:** No. 34, 70, or 80.

BOOKS

CATHACH BOOKS, 10 Duke St., Dublin 2. Tel. 718676.

This small shop, between Grafton and Dawson Streets, stocks hard-to-find antiquarian books of Irish interest, from history and geography to literature, music, and biography. There is also a good selection of Irish-related prints and maps. **Open:** Mon–Sat 9:30am–6pm. **Transportation:** DART to Pearse Station or bus no. 10, 11A, 11B, 13, or 20B.

CELTIC BOOKSTORE [AN SIOPA LEABHAR], 6 Harcourt St., Dublin 2. Tel. 783814.

Located on the ground level of Chonradh na Gaeilge (the organization that fosters the use of the Irish language), this shop features a large selection of books in the Irish language and how to learn the language, as well as books focusing on Gaelic and Celtic literature and history. **Open:** Mon–Fri 9:30am–1:30pm and 2–5:30pm, Sat 10am–1:30pm and 2–4pm. **Bus:** No. 62.

EASON & SON LTD., 40-42 Lower O'Connell St., Dublin 1. Tel. 733811.

For more than 100 years, Eason's has been a leading bookseller at this central location and at its many branches throughout Ireland. This huge store offers a particularly comprehensive selection of books and maps about Dublin and Ireland, as well as Irish literature, folklore, sport, and music. There are also sections devoted to periodicals, best-sellers, fiction, stationery, art materials, games, toys, and children's books. **Open:** Mon–Sat 8:30am–6:15pm. **Transportation:** DART to Connolly Station or bus no. 25, 34, 37, 38A, 39A, 39B, 66A, or 67A.

FRED HANNA LTD., 27-29 Nassau St., Dublin 2. Tel. 771255.

Located across from Trinity College, this is a good bookshop for academic texts, as well as new, used, and antiquarian volumes on all topics. There are also strong art, architecture, and "Irish Interest" sections, and a paperback shop. **Open:** Mon–Sat 9am–5:30pm. **Transportation:** DART to Pearse Station or bus no. 5, 7A, 8, or 62.

GREENES BOOKSHOP LTD., 16 Clare St., Dublin 2. Tel. 762554.

Established in 1843 and close to Trinity College, this is one of Dublin's treasures for bibliophiles. It is chock-full of new and secondhand books on every topic from modern novels to religion, as well as school texts and a very comprehensive selection of books about Ireland. The staff is very helpful and will gladly track down a hard-to-find volume. **Open:** Mon–Sat 9am–5:30pm. **Transportation:** DART to Pearse Station or bus no. 5, 7A, 8, or 62.

HOGGIS FIGGIS, 57/58 Dawson St., Dublin 2. Tel. 774754.

This three-story landmark store has great charm and browse appeal. Although all topics are covered, there are particularly good sections on Irish literature, Celtic studies, folklore, and cooking, as well as a comprehensive selection of maps of Ireland. It's less than half a block south of Trinity College. **Open:** Mon–Fri 9am–8:30pm, Sat 9am–6:30pm, Sun 11am–6pm. **Transportation:** DART to Pearse Station or bus no. 10, 11A, 11B, 13, or 20B.

TRINITY COLLEGE LIBRARY SHOP, Nassau St., Dublin 2. Tel. 772941, ext. 1171.
Located in the heart of the college campus, this shop carries books related to Ireland's and Dublin's history, attractions, and literature, as well as texts illustrating and commentating on the Book of Kells and other early Christian manuscripts. There are also maps, atlases, posters, postcards, T-shirts, and souvenirs related to Trinity College. **Open:** Mon–Fri 9:45am–4:45pm, Sat 9:45am–noon. **Transportation:** DART to Pearse Station or bus no. 5, 7A, 8, 15A, 15B, 46, 55, 62, 63, 83, or 84.

VERITAS, 7-8 Lower Abbey St., Dublin 1. Tel. 788177.
This is a particularly good source of books on Ireland's Christian heritage, especially volumes on Irish saints and scholars, from St. Patrick to the many monks who went forth in the Middle Ages to found some of the great monasteries of Europe. You'll also find Irish religious music tapes and videos, as well as souvenir items with Christian traditions, such as Celtic crosses and St. Brigid's Cross, Connemara marble rosaries, and inspirational postcards and stationery. **Open:** Mon–Sat 9am–5:30pm. **Transportation:** DART to Connolly Station or bus no. 28, 29A, or 30.

WATERSTONE'S, 7 Dawson St., Dublin 2. Tel. 679-1415 or 679-1260.
⭐ Less than a block south of Trinity College, this large literary emporium has a good section of books on Irish interests, and also offers a cross section of titles on art, antiques, biography, the classics, crime, gay literature, health, new age, religion, sport, travel, women's studies, and wine. Books on tape are also stocked here. **Open:** Mon–Fri 8:30am–9pm, Sat 9:30am–7pm, Sun noon–7pm. **Transportation:** DART to Pearse Station or bus no. 10, 11A, 11B, 13, or 20B.

BRASS

KNOBS AND KNOCKERS, 19 Nassau St., Dublin 2. Tel. 710495 or 710609.
If you find yourself enamored by the polished brass door knockers on the Georgian entranceways of Fitzwilliam Street or Merrion Square, this shop makes it possible to buy your own to take home. You can also purchase brassy door knobs, decorative door handles and Victorian cupboard knobs, as well as the popular Claddagh-ring door knocker. **Open:** Mon–Fri 9:30am–6pm, Sat 9:30am–5pm. **Transportation:** DART to Pearse Street or bus no. 5, 7A, 8, 15A, 15B, 46, 55, 62, 63, 83, or 84.

CHINA & CRYSTAL

CHINA SHOWROOMS, 32/33 Abbey St., Dublin 1. Tel. 786211.
⭐ Established in 1939, this shop is a one-stop source of fine china, such as Belleek, Aynsley, Royal Doulton, and Rosenthal. It also offers varied selections of handcut crystal from Waterford, Tipperary, and Tyrone, and handmade Irish pottery.

Open: Mon–Sat 9:30am–5:30pm. **Transportation:** DART to Connolly Station or bus no. 27B or 53A.

DUBLIN CRYSTAL GLASS COMPANY, Brookfield Terrace, Carysfort Ave., Blackrock, Co. Dublin. Tel. 288-7932.
This is Dublin's own distinctive handcut crystal business, founded in 1764 and revived in 1968. Visitors are welcome to browse in the factory shop and to see the glassmaking and engraving processes. **Open:** Mon–Fri 10am–6pm, Sat 10am–1pm. **Transportation:** DART to Blackrock Station or bus no. 6 or 6A.

COINS & COLLECTIBLES

COINS & MEDALS, 10 Cathedral St., Dublin 1. Tel. 744033.
Wedged between O'Connell and Marlborough Streets, this small shop is the definitive source for Irish and foreign coins, medals, and books. Owner Emil Szauer is considered an internationally known numismatic expert. **Open:** Mon 2–5pm, Tues–Sat 9:30am–5pm. **Transportation:** DART to Connolly Station or bus no. 28, 29A, or 30.

PHILATELIC BUREAU, GPO Arcade, Henry St., Dublin 1. Tel. 721263.
Housed in a small arcade in the General Post Office, this shop sells all types of Irish stamps and commemorative covers. It's a must visit for any philately enthusiast. **Open:** Mon–Sat 9:30am–5:30pm. **Transportation:** DART to Connolly Station or bus no. 25, 34, 37, 38A, 39A, 39B, 66A, or 67A.

THOMAS READ AND COMPANY, 4 Parliament St., Dublin 2. Tel. 771487.
⭐ Established in 1670, this is said to be Dublin's oldest shop, specializing in cutlery. It began as a knife- and sword-making shop/forge, originally located on Blind Quay, then on Crane Lane, and moved to its present premises opposite City Hall in 1765. Several James Joyce works, including *Ulysses,* mention this place as a hub of early commerce. Today it is both a museum and a shop— items on display include a cutlery collection ranging from the world's smallest scissors to the world's largest knife, containing 576 blades, as well as old swords, guns, model ships, and historic documents. Besides knives and scissors of all types, you can also purchase silver pitchers and goblets, copper cups, shaving mugs and brushes, and money clips. **Open:** Mon–Fri 9am–5pm. **Bus:** No. 21A, 78A, or 78B.

CRAFT COMPLEXES

POWERSCOURT TOWN HOUSE CENTRE, 59 S. William St., Dublin 2. Tel. 679-4144.
⭐ As soon as you enter this restored 1774 town house, you'll probably feel as if you are in Dublin's version of Ghirardelli Square or South Street Seaport. It consists of a central skylit courtyard where a pianist or harpist often plays gentle background music, surrounded by four floors and balconies with more than 60

boutiques, craft shops, art galleries, snackeries, wine bars, and restaurants. The wares include all kinds of crafts, antiques, oil paintings, old prints, ceramics, graphics, leatherwork, silver and gold jewelry, clothing, perfume, hand-dipped chocolates, and farmhouse cheeses. **Open:** Mon–Sat 9am–6pm. **Bus:** No. 10, 11A, 11B, 13, 16A, 19A, 20B, 22A, 55, or 83.

TOWER DESIGN CENTRE, Pearse St., off Grand Canal Quay, Dublin 2. Tel. 775655.

Located along the banks of the Grand Canal, this 1862 sugar refinery was beautifully restored in 1983 and developed into a nest of craft workshops. Watch the artisans at work and then purchase a special souvenir—from fine-art greeting cards and hand-marbled stationery, to pewter, ceramics, pottery, knitwear, hand-painted silks, copper-plate etchings, all-wool wall hangings, silver and gold Celtic jewelry, and heraldic gifts. **Open:** Mon–Fri 9:30am–5:30pm. **Transportation:** DART to Pearse Station or bus no. 2 or 3.

DEPARTMENT STORES

ARNOTTS, 12 Henry St., Dublin 1. Tel. 721111.

Located on the north side of the River Liffey just around the corner from the General Post Office, this store offers moderately priced goods. The 30 departments, spread over four floors, include a range of high-quality Irish goods, from fashion garments, handwoven tweeds, Aran knit sweaters, Irish crystal (from Waterford, Cavan, and Galway), linen, lace, and china, to records, tapes, toys, and sporting goods. **Open:** Mon–Wed and Fri–Sat 9am–5:30pm, Thurs 9am–8pm. **Transportation:** DART to Connolly Station or bus no. 25, 26, 28, 29A, 30, 37, or 38A. Also located at 112 Grafton St., Dublin 2 (tel. 721033).

BROWN THOMAS, 15-20 Grafton St., Dublin 2. Tel. 679-5666.

With a very distinctive old-world shopfront facade and entrances on Grafton, Duke, and Dawson Streets, this is one of Dublin's most fashionable and varied stores. Departments include Burberrys, Callaghan's Country Wear, Ralph Lauren, and Jaeger, as well as Irish designers Paul Costelloe and Louise Kennedy. A focal point of the ground floor is a Food and Wine Hall with an amazing array of Irish and European specialties from teas to truffles; and an adjacent Bloomingdale's-style Presents of the Mind shop with hundreds of unusual gifts. There is also a restaurant, men's hairdressing salon, and an information desk that also books tickets for the Gate and Focus Theatres and for special events such as the Dublin Horse Show. **Open:** Mon–Wed and Fri–Sat 9:30am–6pm, Thurs 9:30am–8pm. **Transportation:** DART to Pearse Station or bus no. 10, 11A, 11B, 13, or 20B.

CLERYS, Lower O'Connell St., Dublin 1. Tel. 786000.

Standing out on the city's main thoroughfare opposite the General Post Office, this is Ireland's largest store, with four floors and 70 different departments. Items for sale include Irish-made leather shoes and finely crafted Jonathan Richards' hats, as well as Aran sweaters, crystal from Waterford, Galway, and Tyrone, china from Belleek and Royal Tara, linens and tweeds from Donegal. On the ground floor, there is a helpful information desk, a foreign exchange bureau, a branch of Western Union, and a VAT-refund desk, enabling shoppers to take care of all the paperwork on the spot. **Open:** Mon–Wed and Fri–Sat 9:30am–6pm, Thurs 9:30am–8pm. **Transportation:** DART to Connolly Station or bus no. 25, 34, 37, 38A, 39A, 39B, 66A, or 67A.

MARKS AND SPENCER, 28 Grafton St., Dublin 2. Tel. 679-7855.

As its name suggests, this is a branch of the famous British chain, known for its competitive prices. It offers a broad range of Irish clothing, household items, and souvenir products. **Open:** Mon–Wed and Fri–Sat 9am–6pm, Thurs 9am–8pm. **Transportation:** DART to Pearse Station or bus no. 10, 11A, 11B, 13, or 20B. Also located north of the River Liffey at 24 Mary St., Dublin 1 (tel. 728833).

SWITZERS, 92 Grafton St., Dublin 2. Tel. 776821.

A shopper's landmark, this store is known for its ground-floor display of crystal and china featuring the well-known names of Waterford, Belleek, Ciro, Doulton, Spode, and Wedgwood. Other highlights include departments for linens, knitwear, and rainwear, as well as a hairdressing salon and restaurant. There is an information desk on second floor. **Open:** Mon–Wed and Fri–Sat 9am–6pm, Thurs 9am–8pm. **Transportation:** DART to Pearse Station or bus no. 10, 11A, 11B, 13, or 20B.

DOLLS & TOYS

THE DOLLS STORE, 62 S. Great George's St., Dublin 2. Tel. 783403.

Dolls of all sizes and types are for sale here, from antique dolls to contemporary dolls, as well as the largest selection of porcelain dolls in Ireland. Other items include prams and buggies, miniature furniture, dolls' clothing, and dollhouse kits. In addition, there is a doll dressmaking service and a doll hospital and teddy bear clinic. **Open:** Mon–Sat 10am–5pm. **Transportation:** DART to Pearse Station or bus no. 22A.

MEMOIRS, 21 S. Anne St., Dublin 2. Tel. 679-1544.

Located between Grafton and Dawson Streets, this little shop specializes in "nostalgic gifts," with a particular emphasis on dolls, teddy bears, carved animals, and dollhouse furniture. There is also a good selection of miniature frames, Victorian-style cards and stationery, and mobiles. **Open:** Mon–Sat 9:30am–6pm. **Transportation:** DART to Pearse Station or bus no. 10, 11A, 11B, 13, or 20B.

FASHION & DESIGNERS — FOR WOMEN

CLEO, 18 Kildare St., Dublin 2. Tel. 761421.

⭐ For more than 50 years, the Joyce family has been creating designer ready-to-wear clothing in a rainbow of vibrant tweed colors. Elegant ponchos, capes, peasant skirts, coat-sweaters, decorative crios belts (traditional, colorful, handmade string belt from the west of Ireland), and brimmed hats are just a few of the unique high-fashion items that bear the Cleo label. **Open:** Mon–Sat 9:30am–5:30pm. **Transportation:** DART to Pearse Station or bus no. 10, 11A, 11B, 13, or 20B.

IB JORGENSEN, 29 Molesworth St., Dublin 2. Tel. 619758.

This unique couture boutique, situated three doors from the revered Buswells Hotel, presents made-to-measure day and evening fashions for women, created in an art gallery setting amid a selection of 19th- and 20th-century paintings and drawings. **Open:** Mon–Sat 10am–5pm. **Transportation:** DART to Pearse Station or bus no. 10, 11A, 11B, 13, or 20B.

JIMMY HOURIHAN, 28 Blackwater Rd., Dublin Industrial Estate, Glasnevin, Dublin 9. Tel. 300033.

Although this factory shop is a little off the beaten track opposite Glasnevin Cemetery on the north side, it is worth the trip for stylish ready-to-wear women's coats, suits, jackets, skirts, and knits, as well as men's overcoats, car coats, and sports jackets. **Open:** Mon–Sat 10am–5pm. **Bus:** No. 34 or 38A.

PAT CROWLEY, 3 Molesworth Place, Dublin 2. Tel. 615580.

This designer is noted for her use of lace, silk, and hand-crochet in making frilly dresses and blouses. **Open:** Mon–Fri 9am–6pm, Sat 10am–4pm. **Transportation:** DART to Pearse Station or bus no. 10, 11A, 11B, 13, or 20B.

PIA BANG, 46 Grafton St., Dublin 2. Tel. 715065.

Contemporary ready-to-wear women's fashions are the keynote here, with special emphasis on bright colors—canary yellow, citrus orange, and lotus green for suits, dresses and hats that stand out in a crowd. **Open:** Mon–Wed and Fri–Sat 9am–6pm, Thurs 9am–8pm. **Transportation:** DART to Pearse Station or bus no. 10, 11A, 11B, 13, or 20B.

RICHARD ALAN, 58 Grafton St., Dublin 2. Tel. 775149.

Synonymous with smartly tailored women's ready-to-wear fashions, this shop offers a wide selection of the latest European designers, from Akris and Escada to Mani and Valentino, in dresses, suits, hats, and accessories. **Open:** Mon–Wed and Fri–Sat 9am–5:30pm, Thurs 9am–8pm. **Transportation:** DART to Pearse Station or bus no. 10, 11A, 11B, 13, or 20B.

SYBIL CONNOLLY, 71 Merrion Sq., Dublin 2. Tel. 767281.

⭐ Irish high fashion is synonymous with this world-renowned made-to-measure designer. Evening wear and Irish linen creations are a specialty. **Open:** Mon–Fri 10am–5pm and by appointment. **Transportation:** DART to Pearse Station or bus no. 5, 7A, or 8.

THOMAS WOLFANGEL, 158 Pembroke Rd., Ballsbridge, Dublin 4. Tel. 604069.

⭐ A gold-medal winner in the London Tailor and Cutter Exhibition, this designer specializes in made-to-measure women's suits and coats made of wools, silks, and Irish tweeds. He can produce a garment in 2 days, with two fittings on the first day and delivery by the end of the second day. This town house salon is located opposite the American embassy near Jurys Hotel. **Open:** Mon–Sat 10–4 or by appointment. **Transportation:** DART to Lansdowne Road Station or bus no. 46, 63, or 84.

FASHION & TAILORS — FOR MEN

F. X. KELLY, 48 Grafton St., Dublin 2. Tel. 778211.
A long-established men's ready-to-wear shop, this place blends old-fashioned charm with modern design. It offers a handsome selection of styles, many from designer names like Armani, Boss, Jet Set, and Joseph Abboud, with emphasis on conventional clothing as well as creased-linen suits, painted ties, and trendy sportswear. **Open:** Mon–Wed and Fri–Sat 9:30am–6pm, Thurs 9:30am–8pm. **Transportation:** DART to Pearse Station or bus no. 10, 11A, 11B, 13, or 20B.

KENNEDY & McSHERRY, 39 Nassau St., Dublin 2. Tel. 778770 or 716015.
Established in 1890 and located opposite Trinity College, this men's ready-to-wear shop offers lightweight rain coats and a wide range of overcoats and jackets in cashmere and Donegal handwoven tweed, as well as formal wear and accessories, including shirts, knitwear, casual wear, ties, gloves, scarves, hats, and caps. **Open:** Mon–Sat 8:30am–5:30pm. **Transportation:** DART to Pearse Station or bus no. 5, 7A, 8, 15A, 15B, 46, 55, 62, 63, 83, or 84.

KEVIN AND HOWLIN, 31 Nassau St., Dublin 2. Tel. 770257.

⭐ Located opposite Trinity College, this shop has treated men's tailoring as an art for over five decades, custom-making Donegal tweed suits, overcoats, and jackets for all sizes. In addition, there is a wide selection of men's ready-to-wear tweed jackets, as well as Gatsby and Sherlock Holmes caps, Rally and Paddy hats, and, as a sign of the times, a few jackets for women also. **Open:** Mon–Sat 9am–5:30pm. **Transportation:** DART to Pearse Station or bus no. 5, 7A, 8, 15A, 15B, 46, 55, 62, 63, 83, or 84.

LOUIS COPELAND, 39-41 Capel St., Dublin 1. Tel. 721600 or 721868.

⭐ With a dark wood old-world-style shopfront, this store stands out on the north side of the River Liffey in a busy commercial section at the corner of Mary Street. The interior is equally distinctive—with lots of decorative brass and a fireplace with mantel and chiming clock, all setting the tone for the high-quality work in made-to-measure and ready-to-wear men's suits, coats, and shirts.

Open: Mon–Wed and Fri–Sat 9am–5:30pm, Thurs 9am–8pm.
Bus: No. 34, 70, or 80. Also located at 30 Pembroke St., Dublin 2
(tel. 610110 or 767620), and 18 Wicklow St., Dublin 2 (tel. 777038 or
777331).

GIFTS & GENERAL SELECTION

**BEST OF IRISH, Harry St., off Grafton St., Dublin 2. Tel.
679-1233.**
Located next to the entrance of the Westbury Hotel, this shop has
a wide range of Irish-made products, from handknits, linens, lace,
pewter, family crests and shillelaghs, to Royal Tara china, Belleek,
and Waterford crystal. **Open:** Mon–Sat 9am–6pm, Sun 11am–5pm.
Transportation: DART to Pearse Station or bus no. 10, 11A, 11B,
13, or 20B. Also located at 5 Nassau St., Dublin 2 (tel. 679-9117).

**DUBLIN CRAFT, 59 S. William St., Dublin 2. Tel. 679-
9233.**
Situated on the top floor of Powerscourt Town House Centre, this
shop specializes in original handcrafted items by local Dublin area
artisans. Items available range from hand-forged iron candlesticks, to
jewelry, pewter, pottery, leathers, colored glass, cards, crochet, knits,
candles, and wood, copper, and marble products. **Open:** Mon–Sat
9am–6pm. **Bus:** No. 10, 11A, 11B, 13, 16A, 19A, 20B, 22A, 55, or
83.

**FERGUS O'FARRELL WORKSHOP, 62 Dawson St., Dublin
2. Tel. 770862.**
Ireland's design work from the 5th to the 15th centuries has
been the inspiration for much of the craft work at this unique
shop. These conversation-piece souvenirs range from Book of
Kells art and bog-oak figurines to hand-carved fish boards and
beaten-copper wall hangings, as well as Irish road signs, handmade
dolls and animals, metallic jewelry, brass door knockers, walking
sticks, pottery, posters, tin whistles, and T-shirts with an Irish literary
theme. **Open:** Mon–Sat 10am–5:30pm. **Transportation:** DART
to Pearse Station or bus no. 10, 11A, 11B, 13, or 20B.

**HOUSE OF IRELAND, 37-38 Nassau St., Dublin 2. Tel.
714543.**
Located opposite Trinity College, this shop is a treasure trove
of European and Irish products, from Waterford and Belleek
to Wedgwood and Lladró, as well as tweeds, linens, knitwear,
Celtic jewelry, mohair capes, shawls, kilts, blankets, and Molly
Malone dolls. **Open:** Mon–Sat 9:30am–6pm, Sun (Apr–Oct only)
10:30am–5:30pm. **Transportation:** DART to Pearse Station or bus
no. 5, 7A, 15A, 15B, 46, 55, 62, 63, 83, or 84.

**THE KILKENNY SHOP, 6-10 Nassau St., Dublin 2. Tel.
777066.**
A sister operation of the Blarney Woolen Mills, this modern
multilevel shop is a showplace for original Irish designs and
quality products, including pottery, glass, candles, woolens,
pipes, knitwear, jewelry, books, and prints. There is also a first-rate
café on the premises, ideal for coffee and pastries or a light lunch.

Open: Mon–Wed and Fri–Sat 9am–6pm, Thurs 9am–8pm. **Transportation:** DART to Pearse Station or bus no. 5, 7A, 15A, 15B, 46, 55, 62, 63, 83, or 84.

HERALDRY

HERALDIC ARTISTS, 3 Nassau St., Dublin 2. Tel. 679-7020 or 679-5313.

For over 20 years, this shop has been known for helping visitors locate their family roots. In addition to tracing surnames, it also sells all of the usual heraldic items, from parchments and mahogany wall plaques to crests and scrolls, as well as Irish flags, jewelry, ogham art (from the ancient Celtic alphabet), and books on researching ancestry. **Open:** Mon–Sat 9am–6pm. **Transportation:** DART to Pearse Station or bus no. 5, 7A, 8, 15A, 15B, 46, 55, 62, 63, 83, or 84.

HOUSE OF NAMES, 26 Nassau St., Dublin 2. Tel. 679-7287.

This company offers a wide selection of Irish, British, and European family names, crests, and mottoes, affixed onto plaques, shields, parchments, jewelry, glassware, and sweaters. It also stocks books and maps designed to help visitors trace the origins of family surnames. **Open:** Mon–Sat 9am–5:30pm, Sun noon–4pm. **Transportation:** DART to Pearse Station or bus no. 5, 7A, 8, 15A, 15B, 46, 55, 62, 63, 83, or 84. Also located at 8 Fleet St., Dublin 2 (tel. 777034).

MULLINS HERALDIC HOUSE, 36 Upper O'Connell St., Dublin 1. Tel. 741133.

On the city's north side near the Gresham Hotel, this is a long-established source for heraldic crests and family name coats-of-arms. **Open:** Mon–Sat 9–6pm. **Transportation:** DART to Connolly Station or bus no. 51A.

KNITWEAR

BLARNEY WOOLLEN MILLS, 21-23 Nassau St., Dublin 2. Tel. 710068.

A branch of the highly successful Cork-based enterprise of the same name, this shop is ideally located opposite the south side of Trinity College. Known for its competitive prices, it stocks a wide range of woolen knitwear made at the home base in Blarney. In addition, there are all the visitor favorites including crystal, china, pottery, and souvenirs. **Open:** Mon–Wed and Fri–Sat 9am–6pm, Thurs 9am–8pm, Sun 11am–6pm. **Transportation:** DART to Pearse Station or bus no. 5, 7A, 8, 15A, 15B, 46, 55, 62, 63, 83, or 84.

DUBLIN WOOLLEN MILLS, 41 Lower Ormond Quay, Dublin 1. Tel. 770301 or 775014.

Since 1888, this Roche family enterprise has been a leading source of Aran handknit sweaters, vests, hats, jackets, and scarves. Other goods include lambswool sweaters, kilts, ponchos, and tweeds.

Situated on the north side of the River Liffey, it is next to the city's famous Ha'penny Bridge. **Open:** Mon–Sat 9am–6pm. **Bus:** No. 70 or 80.

MONAGHAN'S, 15-17 Grafton Arcade, Grafton St., Dublin 2. Tel. 770823.

✪ Established in 1960 and enthusiastically operated by two generations of the Monaghan family, this store is known as a prime source of cashmere sweaters for men and women—both cardigans and pullovers, with the best selection of colors, sizes, and styles of anywhere in Ireland. Other items stocked include traditional Aran knits, lambswool, crochet, and Shetland wool products. **Open:** Mon–Sat 8:30am–6pm. **Transportation:** DART to Pearse Station or bus no. 10, 11A, 11B, 13, or 20B. Also located at 4/5 Royal Hibernian Way, off Dawson Street (tel. 679-4451).

SWEATER SHOP, 9 Wicklow St., Dublin 2. Tel. 713270.

This store specializes in quality manufactured Irish knitwear made of natural fibers of pure new wool, cotton, and linen. There is a vast selection of sweaters in solid colors and in unique multicolor designs of floral, geometric, and scenic patterns. **Open:** Mon–Sat 9am–6pm. **Transportation:** DART to Pearse Station or bus no. 5, 7A, 8, 15A, 15B, 46, 55, 62, 63, 83, or 84.

INTERNATIONAL DESIGNER PRODUCTS

AQUASCUTUM OF LONDON, 51 Dawson St., Dublin 2. Tel. 770522.

Located opposite the Mansion House, this attractive shop offers all the usual designs associated with the manufacturer, in coats, suits, jackets, and accessories for men and women. **Open:** Mon–Sat 9am–5:30pm. **Transportation:** DART to Pearse Station or bus no. 10, 11A, 11B, 13, or 20B.

BALLY, 43 Grafton St., Dublin 2. Tel. 770333.

This shop offers the famous shoes from Switzerland, along with handbags and other leather accessories. **Open:** Mon–Sat 9am–5:30pm. **Transportation:** DART to Pearse Station or bus no. 10, 11A, 11B, 13, or 20B.

LA COSTE, 12 Wicklow St., Dublin 2. Tel. 716015.

This store carries all the usual sport fashions associated with the famous alligator symbol. **Open:** Mon–Sat 9am–5:30pm. **Transportation:** DART to Pearse Station or bus no. 5, 7A, 8, 15A, 15B, 46, 55, 62, 63, 83, or 84.

LAURA ASHLEY, 60 Grafton St., Dublin 2. Tel. 679-5433.

This is the Irish branch for the famous English designer's products, offering a full selection of women's and children's clothes, home furnishings, and accessories. **Open:** Mon–Wed and Fri 9:30am–6pm, Thurs 9:30am–8pm, Sat 9am–6pm. **Transportation:** DART to Pearse Station or bus no. 10, 11A, 11B, 13, or 20B.

YVES ST. LAURENT, 36 Molesworth St., Dublin 2. Tel. 614600.

In a lovely location near Leinster House (home of the Irish

Parliament), this boutique features all the women's fashions associated with this designer. **Open:** Mon–Sat 9:30am–5:30pm. **Transportation:** DART to Pearse Station or bus no. 10, 11A, 11B, 13, or 20B.

MALLS & ARCADES

ILAC CENTRE, Henry St., Dublin 1.

Situated in the heart of the north side's main pedestrianized shopping area, this huge skylit complex has 60 components including two department stores known for budget prices, Dunne's and Roche's. It also offers a variety of smaller shops as well as a chapel and a library on the premises. Information is available at several self-help computer stations. **Open:** Mon–Wed and Fri–Sat 9am–6pm, Thurs 9am–8pm. **Transportation:** DART to Connolly Station or bus no. 25, 34, 37, 38A, 39A, 66A, or 67A.

ROYAL HIBERNIAN WAY, 49/50 Dawson St., Dublin 2.

Standing at the juncture of Molesworth Street, this mall-style collection of shops and boutiques occupies the site that was formerly the Royal Hibernian Hotel. The wares for sale include buttons, candies, clothing, gifts, jewelry, and silver. There is also a branch of Monaghan's (see above) for cashmere sweaters, a hairdressing salon, newsstand, and a 1-hour photo service. **Open:** Mon–Sat 9am–6pm. **Transportation:** DART to Pearse Station or bus no. 10, 11A, 11B, 13, or 20B.

ST. STEPHEN'S GREEN SHOPPING COMPLEX, St. Stephen's Green, Dublin 2.

✪ Adding a fanciful Victorian-style facade to the south end of Grafton Street, this huge three-story complex offers a wide array of shops and stalls, in a skylit and banner-filled airy atmosphere. Items for sale range from Donegal tweeds and Irish gifts to balloons, candy, T-shirts, ties, cards, shoes, toys, records, and art and hobby supplies. In addition, there is an on-premises pub, Sinnott's, a dome-style restaurant, sandwich and ice-cream stands, a sport shop, hairdressing salon, and a lottery ticket bureau. **Open:** Mon–Wed and Fri–Sat 9am–6pm, Thurs 9am–8pm. **Transportation:** DART to Pearse Station or bus no. 10, 11A, 11B, 13, or 20B.

MARKETS

CHRIST CHURCH MARKET, Christchurch Place, High St., Dublin 8.

Situated in the shadow of the landmark cathedral of the same name, this market sells primarily antiques and secondhand books. **Open:** Sat–Sun 10am–5:30pm. **Bus:** No. 21A, 78A, or 78B.

IVEAGH MARKET, Francis St. at Dean Swift Sq., Dublin 8. Tel. 545413.

Located along "antiques row" in the heart of the Liberties area, this is Dublin's only purpose-built secondhand market. Funded and commissioned by the earl of Iveagh (of the Guinness family) in 1907 to house displaced street vendors, today it provides a setting for a host of dealers of used clothing, bric-a-brac, antiques, curios, and furniture. New items arrive daily from all parts of Ireland, so it's always worth a browse for a one-of-a-kind souvenir. **Open:** Tues–Sat 10:30am–6pm. **Bus:** No. 21A, 78A, or 78B.

MOORE STREET MARKET, Moore St., off Henry St., Dublin 1.

For a flashback of what life was like for fishmonger Molly Malone, don't miss this Dublin enclave, full of streetside barrow vendors, and plenty of local color and chatter. It's the principal open-air fruit, flower, fish, and vegetable market of the city. **Open:** Mon–Sat 9am–6pm. **Transportation:** DART to Connolly Station or bus no. 25, 34, 37, 38A, 66A, or 67A.

MOTHER REDCAPS MARKET, Back Lane, off High St., Dublin 8.

Located in the heart of Old Dublin opposite the two St. Audeon's Churches, this enclosed market is one of Dublin's best. The various stalls offer everything from antiques and used books and coins, to silver, handcrafts, leather products, knitwear, music tapes, furniture, and even a fortune teller! It's worth a trip here just to sample the wares at the Ryefield Foods stall (farmmade cheeses, baked goods, marmalades, and jams) and the Gallic Kitchen stall (gourmet take-out puff-pastry snacks, pâtés, and pastries). **Open:** Most stalls, Wed–Sun 10am–5pm; Gallic Kitchen, Fri–Sun 10am–5pm. **Bus:** No. 21A, 78A, or 78B.

SOUTH CITY MARKET ARCADE, Drury and Castle Sts., off S. Great George's St., Dublin 2.

This sheltered arcade, just 1 block west of the Powerscourt Town House Centre, offers various stalls with an ever-changing assortment of used goods, from books and prints to jewelry and plants, as well as antique clothing from Jenny Vander. **Open:** Mon–Sat 10am–6pm. **Bus:** No. 22A.

MUSICAL INSTRUMENTS

McCULLOGH PIGOTT MUSICAL INSTRUMENTS, 11/13 Suffolk St., Dublin 2. Tel. 773138 or 773161.

Over 150 years in business and located just a block from Trinity College, this shop attracts many students and young musicians. The inventory includes a wide selection of modern musical equipment, such as guitars and drums, as well as more traditional instruments from tin whistles and flutes to harps, bodhrans, and uileann pipes. There is also a good selection of sheet music, books about music and musicians, and stave pages and pads to pen your own music. **Open:** Mon–Sat 9:30am–6pm. **Transportation:** DART to Pearse Station or bus no. 15A, 15B, 15C, 55, or 83.

WALTON'S MUSICAL INSTRUMENT GALLERIES LTD., 2/5 N. Frederick St., Dublin 1. Tel. 747805.

If you hanker for a harp or want to buy some bagpipes, this is Dublin's quintessential music store. You'll find large and small instruments, from pianos to tin whistles or harmonicas, as well as very traditional bodhrans (goatskin drums). This is also a good source for sheet music of your favorite Irish tunes. **Open:** Mon–Sat

9am–5:30pm. **Transportation:** DART to Connolly Station or bus no. 1, 36A, 40A, 40B, or 40C.

MUSIC — TAPES, RECORDS & CDs

HMV, 65 Grafton St., Dublin 2. Tel. 795332.

Located at the intersection of Chatham Street near the Gaiety Theatre, this shop offers a wide variety of contemporary tapes, CDs, and records, with a good section on Irish music. You can also buy tickets to the latest shows and concerts at the on-premises ticket desk. **Open:** Mon–Wed and Fri–Sat 9:30am–6pm, Thurs 9:30am–8pm. **Transportation:** DART to Pearse Station or bus no. 10, 11A, 11B, 13, or 20B. Also at 18 Henry St., Dublin 1 (tel. 732899).

VIRGIN MEGASTORE LTD., 14-18 Aston Quay, Dublin 2. Tel. 777361.

Situated along the southern bank of the River Liffey and 1 block west of O'Connell Bridge, this huge emporium carries an up-to-date selection of tapes, CDs, cassettes, records, and videos of every genre, from popular rock hits to Irish folk music. Shoppers are encouraged to use a set of earphones to listen to featured albums before making a decision to buy. Entertainment magazines and software are also for sale, as are games, books, posters, and T-shirts. **Open:** Mon–Wed and Fri–Sat 9:30am–6pm, Thurs 9am–8pm, Sun 2–6pm. **Bus:** No. 21A, 46A, 46B, 51B, 51C, 68, 69, or 86.

PENS & WRITING SUPPLIES

THE PEN CORNER LTD., 12 College Green, Dublin 2. Tel. 679-3641.

Recognized as fountain pen specialists since 1927, this shop sells all types of pens and writing supplies, as well as calligraphic supplies, artistically designed writing cards and stationery, and Irish art postcards. It also offers a pen-repair service. It is located at the corner of Trinity Street, 1 block west of Trinity College. **Open:** Mon–Fri 9am–5:30pm, Sat 10am–5pm. **Transportation:** DART to Tara Street Station or bus no. 5, 7A, 8, 15A, 15B, 46, 55, 62, 63, 83, or 84.

THE PEN SHOP LTD., 36 Nassau St., Dublin 2. Tel. 679-1633.

Dating back to 1935, this small shop is tucked into a small premises opposite Trinity College. It offers a feast of writing instruments of all sizes and types. **Open:** Mon–Sat 9am–5:30pm. **Transportation:** DART to Pearse Station or bus no. 5, 7A, 8, or 62.

PIPES & TOBACCO

KAPP & PETERSON, 117 Grafton St., Dublin 2. Tel. 714652.

Located opposite Trinity College, this shop has been a tradition since 1875. It offers a complete selection of pipes, tobaccos, cigars, lighters, writing instruments, giftware, and souvenirs. **Open:** Mon–

Sat 9–5:30pm. **Transportation:** DART to Pearse Station or bus no. 15A, 15B, 46, 55, 63, or 83.

SHEEPSKINS & LEATHERS

SHEEPSKIN SHOP, 20 Wicklow St., Dublin 2. Tel. 719585.

As its name indicates, this is a good place to find sheepskin jackets, hats, and moccasins, as well as suede coats and lambskin wear. **Open:** Mon–Sat 9am–6pm. **Transportation:** DART to Pearse Station or bus no. 5, 7A, 8, 15A, 46, 55, 62, 63, 83, or 84.

SHOES

TUTTY'S HANDMADE SHOES LTD., 59 S. William St., Dublin 2. Tel. 679-6566.

Located on the top floor of the Powerscourt Town House Center, this tiny shop specializes in made-to-measure shoes and boots, crafted from the finest leathers. Shoes are also repaired on the premises by master shoemakers. **Open:** Mon–Sat 9am–5pm. **Bus:** No. 10, 11A, 11B, 13, 16A, 19A, 20B, 22A, 55, or 83. Also at Friary Rd., Naas, Co. Kildare (tel. 04576879).

SPORTING GOODS

PATRICK CLEERE & SON LTD., 5 Bedford Row, Dublin 2. Tel. 777406.

If you intend to do a little fishing in the River Liffey or other nearby waters, this Temple Bar district shop is just the spot to stock up on fishing tackle, rods, reels, flies, hats, boxes, and bags. Salmon and trout flies are a specialty. **Open:** Mon–Sat 9am–5:30pm, Sat 9am–5pm. **Transportation:** DART to Tara Street Station or bus no. 78A or 78B.

RORY'S FISHING TACKLE, 17A Temple Bar, Dublin 2. Tel. 772351.

Tucked inconspicuously into the Temple Bar district between Fownes Street and Adsill Row, this shop has prospered for over 35 years. It sells a wide range of freshwater and sea-fishing tackle, reels, spools, rods, lures, flies, and fly lines, as well as trout bags, boots, and clothing. **Open:** Mon–Sat 9:30am–6pm. **Transportation:** DART to Tara Street Station or bus no. 78A or 78B.

WATTS BROTHERS LTD., 18 Upper Ormond Quay, Dublin 7. Tel. 778574.

Situated on the north side of the River Liffey near the Four Courts, this shop was established in 1946. For the fisherman or fisherwoman, it offers a full range of fly-tying equipment and tools, rods, reels, and hooks. Archery equipment and guns are also for sale, as is country clothing, boots, and hats. **Open:** Tues–Sat 9am–5:30pm. **Bus:** No. 34, 70, or 80.

UMBRELLAS & WALKING STICKS

H. JOHNSTON, 11 Wicklow St., Dublin 2. Tel. 771249.

Just in case it rains, this centrally located shop is a good source for durable umbrellas. And if you are looking for an Irish blackthorn stick, otherwise known as a shillelagh, this spot has been specializing in them for more than 110 years. There is also a good selection of luggage, belts, and handbags. **Open:** Mon–Sat 9:30am–5:30pm. **Transportation:** DART to Pearse Station or bus no. 5, 7A, 8, 15A, 46, 55, 62, 63, 83, or 84.

CHAPTER 9

DUBLIN NIGHTS

1. THE PERFORMING ARTS

2. THE CLUB & MUSIC SCENE

3. THE PUBS

As the home of more than 1,000 pubs plus the legendary Abbey Theatre and dozens of other entertainment venues, Dublin is lively and gregarious at night. Turn any corner and there is music or laughter in the air.

The best way to find out what is going on is to ask for current calendar listings at the Dublin Tourism office at 14 Upper O'Connell St. (tel. 747733), or consult the entertainment/leisure pages of the *Irish Times* and other daily newspapers.

In addition, the tourist office and most hotels distribute copies of the biweekly *Dublin Event Guide,* a free newspaper listing entertainment and theater programs. Two other biweekly publications, for sale at most newsstands, also feature nightlife—*In Dublin* (£1.50, or $2.50), a magazine that give details of theaters, concerts, music clubs, and pubs; and *Hot Press* (£1.25, or $2.10), a newspaper concentrating on the rock music scene.

Unlike London's West End or New York's Broadway, Dublin's theatrical venues are not concentrated in one area but are spread throughout the city, both north and south of the River Liffey and in the suburbs. Consequently, there is no central ticket office or booking agency for all productions. Each theater operates its own box office for ticket sales or accepts credit-card bookings over the phone.

In addition, tickets for some theaters can be purchased during normal business hours in the following music/record or department stores: **HMV** at 18 Henry St. (tel. 732899), and at 65 Grafton St. (tel. 679-5334), sells tickets for the Point Depot Theatre, RDS, Olympia Theatre, Gaiety Theatre, and Tivoli Theatre; **McCullough Pigott,** 11-13 Suffolk St. (tel. 773138 or 773161), sells tickets for the Olympia Theatre and occasionally for other venues; and **Brown Thomas,** 15-20 Grafton St. (tel. 679-5666), books tickets for the Focus and Gate Theatres and for special events.

Prices for most seats at Dublin's theaters and concert halls average less than $20, far below other major capital cities offering comparable entertainment. Consequently, there is no half-price ticket booth operating in the city. If you are looking for a bargain, however, watch newspaper advertisements announcing "previews," usually priced £2 ($3.30) less than the lowest-price regular ticket. Depending on demand, some theaters also chop off £2 to £4 ($3.30 to $6.60) from ticket prices for all shows on Monday.

1. THE PERFORMING ARTS

THE MAJOR CONCERT/PERFORMANCE HALLS

NATIONAL CONCERT HALL (AN CEOLARAS NAISIUNTA), Earlsfort Terrace, Dublin 2. Tel. 711533.

⭐ Located downtown just off St. Stephen's Green, this magnificent 1,200-seat hall, restored in 1981, is the setting for the classical music of the Concert Orchestra of Irish Television and the Irish Chamber Orchestra, as well as a variety of international performers. In addition, there are also evenings of Gilbert and Sullivan, opera, jazz, and recitals.

Open: Box office Mon–Sat 11am–7pm, Sun (if concert scheduled) from 7pm. Performances at 7:30pm or 8pm.

Admission: £5–£15 ($8.25–$24.75). **Transportation:** DART to Pearse Station or bus no. 14A, 46A, 46B, or 86.

THE POINT DEPOT THEATRE, East Link Bridge, North Wall Quay, Dublin 1. Tel. 363633.

With a seating capacity of 3,000, this is Ireland's newest large theater and concert venue, attracting top Broadway-caliber shows and international stars.

Open: Box office Mon–Sat 10am–6pm; matinees at 2:30pm and evening shows at 8pm.

Admission: £10–£30 ($16.50–$49.50). **Transportation:** DART to Connolly Station or bus no. 53A.

ROYAL DUBLIN SOCIETY (RDS), Merrion Rd., Ballsbridge, Dublin 2. Tel. 680645.

Although best known as the venue for the Dublin Horse Show, this huge show-jumping arena is also the setting for major music concerts, with seating/standing room for more than 6,000 people.

Open: Box office hours vary according to events; shows at 8pm.

Admission: £10–£30 ($16.50–$49.50). **Transportation:** DART to Lansdowne Road Station or bus no. 5, 7, 7A, or 45.

ROYAL HOSPITAL, Military Rd., Kilmainham, Dublin 8. Tel. 718666.

This beautifully restored 17th-century building with its open-air quadrangle courtyard provides the setting for frequent concerts by well-known international performers and Irish artists. The program includes classical, chamber, and modern music.

Open: Box office hours vary according to events; evening shows at 8pm.

Admission: £4–£20 ($6.60–$33). **Bus:** No. 24, 79, or 90.

THEATERS

ABBEY THEATRE, Lower Abbey St., Dublin 1. Tel. 787222.

MAJOR CONCERT & PERFORMANCE HALL BOX OFFICES

Abbey Theatre Tel. 787222
Gaiety Theatre Tel. 771717
The Gate Tel. 744045
National Concert Hall Tel. 711533
Olympia Tel. 777744
The Point Depot Theatre Tel. 363633
Royal Dublin Society Tel. 680645

⭐ Celebrating its 90th birthday in 1994, the Abbey is the national theater of Ireland and home of the world-famed Abbey Players. The original theater, destroyed in a 1951 fire, was replaced in 1966 by the current modern 600-seat building. Names like Yeats, Synge, O'Casey, Beckett, Behan, and most recently, Tony Award–winner Hugh Leonard, are but a few of the revered Irish playwrights whose works have been staged here.

Open: Box office Mon–Sat 10:30am–7pm; shows Mon–Sat at 8pm.

Admission: £8–£12 ($13.20–$19.80). **Transportation:** DART to Connolly Station or bus no. 27B or 53A.

ANDREWS LANE THEATRE, 12/16 Andrews Lane, Dublin 2. Tel. 679-5720.

Relatively new to the Dublin scene and within 2 blocks of Trinity College, this showplace consists of a 220-seat main theater that presents contemporary work from home and abroad, and a 76-seat studio that is geared for experimental productions.

Open: Box office Mon–Sat 10:30am–7pm; shows Mon–Sat at 8pm in theater and 8:15pm in studio.

Admission: £6–£12 ($9.90–$19.80). **Transportation:** DART to Pearse Station or bus no. 15A, 15B, 15C, 46, 55, 63, or 83.

CITY ARTS CENTRE, 23/25 Moss St. at City Quay, Dublin 2. Tel. 770643.

Opened in 1989, this is one of Dublin's newest lively arts venues, backed by the Irish Arts Council and the rock group U2. Situated in a fast-developing area on the south bank of the Liffey across from the new Dublin Financial Centre, it presents a varied program, from local drama groups performing original new plays, to theatrical discussions, comedies, readings by local writers, and touring companies from other parts of Ireland and abroad. The four-story complex also houses two galleries for rotating exhibits, a coffee shop with a river view, and rehearsal and recording studios for young rock musicians.

Open: Box office opens at 7:30pm; reservations can be made in advance by phone only Mon–Sat 9am–6pm; shows Mon–Sat at 8pm or later.

Admission: £2–£6 ($3.30–$9.90). **Transportation:** DART to Tara Street Station or bus no. 1 or 3.

FOCUS THEATRE, 6 Pembroke Place, off Pembroke St., Dublin 2. Tel. 763071.

Nestled in a secluded alley 2 blocks south of St. Stephen's Green, this small 70-seat theater presents a surprisingly varied repertoire of Irish and international plays including the great classics.

Open: Box office Mon–Sat 10am–7:30pm; shows Mon–Sat at 8pm.

Admission: £7–£8 ($11.55–$13.20). **Transportation:** DART to Pearse Station or bus no. 46A, 46B, or 86.

GAIETY THEATRE, S. King St., Dublin 2. Tel. 771717.

The Dublin Grand Opera Society performs its spring (April) and winter (December) seasons here. During the rest of the year, this very fine 19th-century 1,100-seat theater stages musical comedy, ballet, revue, pantomime, and drama, all with Irish and international talent. It is well located within a block from Grafton Street and St. Stephen's Green.

Open: Box office Mon–Sat 11am–7pm; shows Mon–Sat at 8pm.

Admission: £7–£16 ($11.55–$26.40). **Transportation:** DART to Pearse Station or bus no. 10, 11A, 11B, 13, or 20B.

THE GATE, 1 Cavendish Row, Dublin 1. Tel. 744045 or 743722.

⭐ Situated just north of O'Connell Street off Parnell Square, this recently restored 370-seat theater was founded in 1928 by Hilton Edwards and Michael MacLiammoir to provide a showing for a broad range of plays. This policy prevails today, with a program that includes a blend of modern works, as well as some classics of sophisticated comedy written by Irish greats like Goldsmith, Wilde, Sheridan, and Shaw.

Open: Box office Mon–Sat 11am–7pm; shows Mon–Sat at 8pm.

Admission: £9–£12 ($14.85–$19.80). **Transportation:** DART to Connolly Station or bus no. 1, 40A, 40B, or 40C.

LAMBERT MEWS PUPPET THEATRE, 5 Clifden Lane, Monkstown, Co. Dublin. Tel. 280-0974.

Founded by master ventriloquist Eugene Lambert, this 300-seat suburban theater presents puppet shows designed to delight audiences who are both young and young-at-heart. During intermission, you can also browse in the on-premises puppet museum.

Open: No box office; book by phone daily; shows Sat–Sun at 3:30pm.

Admission: £3–£4 ($4.95–$6.60). **Transportation:** DART to Salthill Station or bus no. 7, 7A, or 8.

NEW EBLANA THEATRE, Store St., Dublin 1. Tel. 679-8404.

Housed in the basement of Busaras (the central bus station), this 230-seat midtown theater presents a varied program of modern plays and events.

Open: Box office (at Andrews Lane Theatre) Mon–Sat 10:30am–6pm, tickets also on sale on day of show if available from 7pm; shows Mon–Sat at 8pm.

Admission: Ł6–Ł12 ($9.90–$19.80). **Transportation:** DART to Connolly Station or bus no. 27A, 42B, 42C, or 43.

OLYMPIA, 72 Dame St., Dublin 2. Tel. 777744.

⭐ Dating back to the 1800s, this Victorian music hall–style theater has a capacity of 1,300. It presents an eclectic schedule of variety shows, musicals, operettas, concerts, ballet, comedy, and drama. As a variation, for the late-night crowd, live bands are often featured after regular programs.

Open: Box office Mon–Sat 10am–6pm; shows Mon–Sat at 8pm; late-night shows Fri–Sat midnight–2am.

Admission: Ł7.50–Ł15 ($12.40–$24.75) for regular programs; Ł6–Ł9 ($9.90–$14.85) for late-night live bands. **Transportation:** DART to Tara Street Station or bus no. 50, 50A, 56A, 78, or 78A.

PEACOCK, Lower Abbey St., Dublin 1. Tel. 787222.

In the same building as the Abbey, this small 150-seat theater features contemporary plays and experimental works including poetry readings and one-person shows, and plays in the Irish language.

Open: Box office Mon–Sat 10:30am–7pm; shows Mon–Sat at 8:15pm.

Admission: Ł8–Ł10 ($13.20–$16.50). **Transportation:** DART to Connolly Station or bus no. 27B or 53A.

PROJECT ARTS CENTRE, 39 E. Essex St., Dublin 2. Tel. 712321.

Located in the burgeoning Temple Bar district, this contemporary theater is part of a multipurpose arts complex. With a capacity of 150 to 180 seats, it specializes in experimental and new works, as well as performances by the Irish Modern Dance Theatre troupe. Depending on demand, it schedules lunchtime or late-night shows.

Open: Box office Mon–Sat 10am–6pm; shows Mon–Sat at 8pm.

Admission: Ł6–Ł8 ($9.90–$13.20). **Transportation:** DART to Tara Street Station or bus no. 50, 50A, 56A, 78, or 78A.

RIVERBANK THEATRE, 13-14 Merchant's Quay, Dublin 2. Tel. 773370.

Situated on the south bank of the River Liffey less than a block from the historic Brazen Head pub and opposite the Four Courts, this modern theater presents contemporary plays and new works by Irish and international authors. It is a little out-of-the-way, but it has a parking lot at the rear of the theater and good bus service.

Open: Box office Mon–Fri 10am–6pm, Sat 10am–1pm; shows Tues–Sun at 8pm, Sat–Sun at 3pm.

Admission: Ł6–Ł10 ($9.90–$16.50). **Bus:** No. 51B, 51C, 68, 69, or 79, or take a taxi.

TIVOLI THEATRE, 135-138 Francis St., Dublin 8. Tel. 544472.

Situated in the older part of Dublin known as the Liberties and along the street considered as "antiques row" for shoppers, this 500-seat theater was originally a movie house that was refurbished and reopened in 1987. It presents Broadway and West End musicals and dramas. Facilities include a secure car park and an on-premises bar.

Open: Box office Mon–Sat 10am–6pm; shows Mon–Sat at 8pm; late-night performances Fri–Sat at 11pm.

Admission: £8–£15 ($13.20–$24.75). **Bus:** No. 21A, 78A, or 78B, or take a taxi.

DINNER SHOWS

ABBEY TAVERN, Abbey Rd., Howth, Co. Dublin. Tel. 390307.

Irish ballad music, with its blend of fiddles, pipes, tin whistles, and spoons, is on tap at this authentic old-world tavern, with open turf fireplaces, stone walls, flagged floors, and gas lights. A night at the Abbey Tavern includes a complete traditional four-course meal, plus a 2-hour musical show.

If you prefer a more leisurely à la carte dinner, the Abbey Tavern provides another option. There is also a small gourmet restaurant upstairs, offering a top-class seafood menu in romantic candlelit surroundings (see "Suburbs—North" in Chapter 5). You can dine at your leisure, and, if you wish, join in the ballad session later in the evening, or you can just come for the music and drinks.

Open: Box office Mon–Sat 9am–5pm; dinner/show daily Mar–Oct and Mon–Sat Nov–Feb; dinner at 7pm, show at 9pm.

Admission: Dinner/entertainment £29 ($47.85); entertainment and two drinks £11 ($18.15). **Transportation:** DART to Howth Station or bus no. 31.

DOYLE'S IRISH CABARET, Upper Leeson St., Dublin 4. Tel. 605222, ext. 1162.

Staged in the ballroom of the Burlington Hotel, this colorful dinner/show features some of Ireland's top performers in a 2½-hour program of Irish music, dancing, ballad singing, and storytelling. The evening starts with a traditional dinner of Irish potato soup, salmon or steak, colcannon, and Irish liqueur soufflé.

Schedule: May–early Oct, Mon–Sat dinner at 7pm, show at 8pm.

Admission: Dinner/show £28.90 ($47.70); show with two drinks £17.50 ($28.90). **Bus:** No. 11A, 11B, 13, or 18.

JURY'S IRISH CABARET, Pembroke Rd., Ballsbridge, Dublin 4. Tel. 605000.

As Ireland's longest-running show (over 30 years), this 2½-hour benchmark production has been enjoyed by an accumulated total of more than two million people in the ballroom of Jurys Hotel. It is a unique mix of traditional Irish and international music, rousing ballads and Broadway classics, toe-tapping set-dancing and graceful ballet, humorous monologues and telling recitations, and audience participation—all designed to appeal to visitors and natives alike. The five-course dinner offers a choice of main courses such as corned beef and cabbage, seafood, or steak.

Schedule: May–mid-Oct, Tues–Sun, dinner at 7:15pm, show at 8pm.

Admission: Dinner/show £29.50 ($48.70); show with two drinks £17.50 ($28.90). **Transportation:** DART to Lansdowne Road Station or bus no. 5, 7A, 8, 46, 63, or 84.

LOCAL CULTURAL ENTERTAINMENT

CULTURLANN NA hEIREANN, 32 Belgrave Sq., Monkstown, Co. Dublin. Tel. 280-0295.

⭐ This is the home of Comhaltas Ceoltoiri Eireann, an Irish cultural organization that has been the prime mover in encouraging a renewed appreciation of and interest in Irish traditional music. Located in a residential area near the seaside suburb of Dun Laoghaire, it is an informal gathering place with several music/meeting rooms, a small theater, and bar. The year-round entertainment programs include old-fashioned ceili dances on Friday and informal music sessions on Friday and Saturday. In the summer months, an authentic fully costumed show featuring traditional music, song, and dance is staged. No reservations are necessary for any of the events.

Schedule: Year-round, ceili dances Fri 9:30pm–12:30am, informal music sessions Fri–Sat 9:30–11:30pm; June–Sept, Sat–Thurs traditional music stage show 9–10:30pm.

Admission: Ceilis £4 ($6.60); informal music sessions £1.50 ($2.50); stage shows £5 ($8.25). **Transportation:** DART to Salthill Station or bus no. 7, 7A, or 8.

2. THE CLUB & MUSIC SCENE

Although it has never been known as a nightlife mecca, Dublin has spawned a surprising number of new after-hours clubs in recent years. Lower Leeson Street, a strip of Georgian refurbished town houses just south of St. Stephen's Green, is known for its collection of about a dozen basement-level disco clubs.

These premises tend to change names and themes with the seasons, so it is difficult to recommend reliable clubs. However, if you stroll along this 1-block area anytime between midnight and 6am, you are bound to find some lively spots. Most of these clubs do not have a cover charge but drinks are expensive, from £15 ($24.75) for a bottle of champagne or wine, to £5 ($8.25) for a jug of orange juice or £2 ($3.30) for a glass of mineral water.

Beyond Lower Leeson Street, the more well-established clubs usually do have a cover charge, but it often includes a buffet or light meal. Some dependable choices follow.

Note: Since Dublin's public transport ends before midnight, recommended transportation for late-night premises in every case is via taxi.

NIGHTCLUBS/DISCOS

ANNABEL'S, Upper Leeson St., Dublin 4. Tel. 605222.

Located in the Burlington Hotel just south of the famed Lower Leeson Street nightclub strip, this club is one of the most long-lasting in town. It welcomes a mix of tourists and locals of all ages to a disco party atmosphere. Annabel's is south of the Grand Canal, off Morehampton Road.

Open: Tues–Sat 10pm–2am.
Admission: Ł7 ($11.55).

CLUB M, Anglesea St., Dublin 2. Tel. 715622.

Housed in the basement of Blooms Hotel in the trendy Temple Bar district and close to Trinity College, this club boasts Ireland's largest "hydraulic moving" laser-lighting system. It offers either disco or live music, for the over-23 age bracket. The club is located downtown, next to the Bank of Ireland, between Fleet Street and College Green.

Open: Tues–Sun 10pm–2am.
Admission: Ł4–Ł8 ($6.60–$13.20).

LILLIE'S BORDELLO, 45 Nassau St., Dublin 2. Tel. 679-7539 or 679-9204.

One of Dublin's newest "in" spots as we go to press, this place is designed to convey the fun-filled, slightly decadent atmosphere of yesteryear, with the music beats of today. It's located downtown, at Adams Court, off Grafton Street.

Open: Daily 10pm–1am or later.
Admission: Weekdays Ł7 ($11.55), weekends Ł8 ($13.20).

McGRATTANS' DINERS CIRCLE, 76 Fitzwilliam Lane, Dublin 2. Tel. 618808.

Housed upstairs at McGrattan's restaurant, this is Dublin's version of a supper club, with live music of the blues and torch-song genres. It is a cozy setting, with comfortable banquette seating, fireplaces, and candlelight. Dublin vocalist Joan Daly serves as hostess and performer. The menu, which is an abbreviated version of the main restaurant's fare, offers substantially more than the usual snacks, buffets, or fast food provided at other late-night clubs. It's located off Lower Baggot Street, between Merrion and Fitzwilliam Streets.

Open: Tues–Sat 10pm–2am.
Admission: No cover charge; main courses Ł9.50–Ł11.95 ($15.70–$19.75).

THE PINK, Setenta Centre, S. Frederick St., Dublin 2. Tel. 775876.

Situated downtown less than a block south of Trinity College, between Molesworth and Nassau Streets, this well-established club has been in business for over a dozen years, offering a choice of disco music on three floors.

Open: Daily 11pm–3am.

Admission: Sun–Thurs £5 ($8.25), Fri–Sat £8 ($13.20).

COMEDY CLUBS

THE COMEDY CELLAR, 23 Wicklow St., Dublin 2. Tel. 779250.

In spite of its name, this informal midtown club is located upstairs at the International Bar, an old-world pub with splendid carved-wood fixtures. The sessions blend guest artists with "open mike" opportunities for guests.

Open: Wed only 9–11pm.

Admission: £2.50–£3.50 ($4.15–$5.80). **Transportation:** DART to Pearse or Tara Street Station or bus no. 15A, 15B, 15C, 46, 55, 63, or 83.

THE GASWORKS INTERNATIONAL COMEDY CLUB, 14/15 Sir John Rogerson's Quay, Dublin 2. Tel. 778466.

Located off the beaten track along the docks at the Waterfront (a riverside bar known for its usual agenda of rock music), this club offers performances by leading local and visiting comedians from London and abroad, as well as "open mike" comedy searches and contests for local talent.

Open: Fri–Sat from 8pm; show at 9pm.

Admission: £4–£6 ($6.60–$9.90). **Transportation:** DART to Tara Street Station or bus no. 1 or 3.

COUNTRY

BAD BOB'S BACKSTAGE BAR, 35-37 E. Essex St., Dublin 2. Tel. 775482.

If country music stars like Garth Brooks, Reba McIntyre, or Randy Travis are in Dublin, this is where they will be. Located in the heart of the city's artsy Temple Bar district, this place specializes in live country music 7 nights a week, drawing top international and local talent. It is situated next to the Project Arts Centre at Sycamore Street, and said to be a favorite haunt of Dublin's police and nurses.

Open: Daily 10pm–2am.

Admission: £6–£8 ($9.90–$13.20). **Transportation:** DART to Tara Street Station or bus no. 50, 50A, 56A, 78, or 78A.

JAZZ/BLUES/CAJUN/SOUL

BRUXELLES BLUES CLUB, 7 Harry St., off Grafton St., Dublin 2. Tel. 775362.

Located next to the Westbury Hotel, this is a well-preserved Victorian pub with a touch of European ambience. In addition to the weekly session of blues music, it's worth a visit here just to see the owner's collection of old tankards and historic hats from around the world.

Open: Mon 8:30–11:30pm.

Admission: No cover charge for music. **Transportation:** DART to Pearse Station or bus no. 10, 11A, 11B, 13, or 20B.

NIGHT TRAIN, 7 Lower Mount St., Dublin 2. Tel. 761717.
Located in the basement of the traditional-style O'Dwyer's Pub, this enclave presents a varied program of jazz, Cajun, blues, soul, and rock, attracting a mostly over-25 crowd. It's located between Merrion Square East and the Grand Canal.
Open: Daily 11pm–2am. **Transportation:** DART to Pearse Station or bus no. 46 or 84.
Admission: £6–£8 ($9.90–$13.20).

WHELANS, 25 Wexford St., Dublin 2. Tel. 780766.
Situated in a slightly off-the-beaten-track location between Camden and Aungier Streets yet within a block of St. Stephen's Green, this pub draws big crowds for its nightly programs of Cajun, blues, country, and other types of music.
Open: Daily 9pm onward.
Admission: £3–£5 ($4.95–$8.25). **Bus:** No. 55 or 83.

ROCK

BAGGOT INN, 143 Lower Baggot St., Dublin 2. Tel. 761430.
Located east of St. Stephen's Green, this pub has long been a podium for emerging rock musicians and bands, including U2 in their early days. Rockers of all ages assemble here as gigs are held in the ground-floor bar and upstairs.
Open: Daily; shows from 9pm.
Admission: £3–£5 ($4.95–$8.25). **Transportation:** DART to Pearse Station or bus no. 10.

CHARLIE'S BAR, 2 Aungier St., Dublin 2. Tel. 755895.
Located just 2 blocks west of St. Stephen's Green off Grafton Street, this slightly out-of-the-way pub offers a regular program of disco music and live local and international rock acts.
Open: Daily; shows from 9pm.
Admission: £3 ($4.95). **Bus:** No. 16A, 19A, 22A, 55, or 83.

ROCK GARDEN, Crown Alley, Dublin 2. Tel. 679-9773.
Live contemporary rock music, with emphasis on up-and-coming bands, is presented at this lively spot, ideally located in the heart of the youth-oriented Temple Bar district. It's behind the Central Bank, between Cope Street and Temple Bar.
Open: Daily 11pm–2am or later.
Admission: £3–£6 ($4.95–$9.90) and up.

THE WATERFRONT, 14/15 Sir John Rogerson's Quay, Dublin 2. Tel. 679-9258.
It is not surprising that a rock bar should spring up in this location, just a block from the Windmill Lane recording studios of U2. The music ranges from contemporary rock dance bands to classic funk and hip hop. It's located on the south bank of the Liffey in the docks area; take a taxi there and back.
Open: Thurs–Sun 11pm–2am.

Admission: Ł4–Ł6 ($6.60–$9.90).

3. THE PUBS

The mainstay of Dublin social life—both by night and by day—is unquestionably the pub. With more than 1,000 specimens spread throughout the city, there are pubs on every street, at every turn. It was in *Ulysses* that James Joyce referred to the puzzle of trying to cross Dublin without passing by a pub, but then he abandoned the quest as fruitless, preferring instead to sample a few in his path. Needless to say, every visitor should heed his advice.

The origin of pubs harks back several centuries ago to a time when there were no hotels or restaurants. In those days, neighbors would gather in a kitchen, often to sample some home brew. As a certain spot grew popular, word spread and people would come from all directions, always assured of a warm welcome.

Such places gradually became known as "public houses" or "pubs," for short. In time, the name of the person who tended a public house was mounted over the doorway, and hence many pubs still bear a family or proprietor's name, such as Doheny & Nesbitt, Mulligan's, or W. Ryan.

Many pubs have been in the same family for generations and have changed little in the last 200 years. A few may have added televisions, pool tables, and dart boards to their decor, but the true Irish pub is still basically a homey place—a unique hybrid of open hearth, news depot, and gathering spot.

In recent years, many pubs have shown their versatility by introducing "pub grub," an inexpensive food service, primarily at lunchtime. Pubs have also led the way in providing musical entertainment in the evenings, whether it be spontaneous traditional tunes or a staged contemporary program.

Most of all, however, the Dublin pub is a friendly place where the art of conversation is king and strangers soon become friends.

Pub Etiquette Before you set foot into one of these hallowed establishments, it is helpful to know about local habits. Rarely do people sit or drink alone in a pub. If you don't have your own family and friends traveling with you, you'll find that Dubliners will draw you into their own conversations. If so, be warned that the "round system" often prevails. That means that each person in a group or conversation takes a turn buying a round of drinks; this can require great stamina if you happen to be in a large party. You also pay as you go, not running up a tab.

Pub Hours May through September from 10:30am to 11:30pm on Monday through Saturday, closing a half hour earlier during the rest of the year. On Sunday bars are open from 12:30pm to 2pm and from 4 to 11pm all year.

Drink Prices Charges are more or less standardized throughout the city, with hotel bar prices sometimes slightly higher than the norm. Pints of draft beer or stout average Ł2 ($3.30); bottled beer, from Ł1.30 to Ł1.90 ($2.15 to $3.15); a measure of whiskey,

Ł1.65 to Ł2.05 ($2.75 to $3.40); brandy, from Ł2.30 ($3.80); or a glass of wine, Ł1.60 to Ł2.15 ($2.65 to $3.55). Keep in mind that 50% of the price goes back to the government as tax!

Raising a Glass The official toast is "Slainte!" (*slawn-che*)—an Irish or Gaelic word meaning "To your health!"

So head for a few pubs—and "Slainte!" to you.

PUBS FOR CONVERSATION & ATMOSPHERE

THE BAILEY, 2 Duke St., Dublin 2. Tel. 773055 or 770600.

Located just off Grafton Street, this is one of Dublin's best-known pubs, with a striking Edwardian facade and interior. The classy atmosphere makes it a favorite with artists, writers, musicians, and the young and successful singles set. A good conversation-starter on display here is the door marked 7 Eccles St., referred to in James Joyce's *Ulysses*.

Transportation: DART to Pearse Station or bus no. 10, 11A, 11B, 13, or 20B.

BRAZEN HEAD, 20 Lower Bridge St., Dublin 8. Tel. 679-5186.

⭐ This brass-filled and lantern-lit pub claims to be the city's oldest—and with good reason, considering it was licensed in 1661 and it occupies the site of an earlier tavern dating from 1198. Nestled on the south bank of the River Liffey, it is at the end of a cobblestone courtyard and was once the meeting place of Irish freedom fighters such as Robert Emmet and Wolfe Tone. There is live music (from traditional to blues) on Wednesday through Sunday nights and a good selection of pub grub at lunchtime, but the ambience is the big draw to this secluded spot.

Transportation: Bus no. 51B, 51C, 68, 69, or 79, or take a taxi.

DAVY BYRNES, 21 Duke St., Dublin 2. Tel. 775217.

Referred to as a "moral pub" by James Joyce in *Ulysses*, this imbibers' landmark has drawn poets, writers, and lovers of literature ever since. Located just off Grafton Street, it actually dates back to 1873 when Davy Byrnes first opened the doors. He presided here for more than 50 years, and visitors today can still see his likeness on one of the turn-of-the-century murals hanging over the bar.

Transportation: DART to Pearse Station or bus no. 10, 11A, 11B, 13, or 20B.

DOHENY AND NESBITT, 5 Lower Baggot St., Dublin 2. Tel. 762945.

The locals call this Victorian-style pub simply "Nesbitts." Situated about 1 block from either St. Stephen's Green or Merrion Square, it's frequented by government officials and a sprinkling of lawyers, doctors, and architects. There are two fine specimens of "snugs" (a small room with a trapdoor where women were served a drink in days of old).

Transportation: DART to Pearse Station or bus no. 10.

FLANNERY'S TEMPLE BAR, 48 Temple Bar, Dublin 2. Tel. 773807 or 773808.

Nestled in the heart of the trendy Temple Bar district on the corner of Temple Lane, this small three-room pub was established in 1840. The decor is an interesting mix of crackling fireplaces, globe ceiling lights, old pictures on the walls, and shelves filled with local memorabilia.

Transportation: DART to Tara Street Station or bus no. 21A, 46A, 46B, 51B, 51C, 68, 69, or 86.

THE LONG HALL, 51 S. Great George's St., Dublin 2. Tel. 751590.

⭐ Tucked into a busy commercial street, this is one of the city's most photographed pubs, with a beautiful Victorian decor of filigree-edged mirrors, polished dark woods, and traditional snugs. The hand-carved bar is said to be the longest counter in the city.

Bus: No. 22A.

MULLIGAN'S, 8 Poolbeg St., Dublin 2. Tel. 775582.

Established in 1782, this is a typical man's pub known for its superb pints and smokey Old Dublin atmosphere. The decor is rich in solid mahogany wood, gas lamps, and large wall mirrors. It's a favorite with journalists (two newspaper offices are nearby), dockworkers, and students from Trinity College.

Transportation: DART to Tara Street Station or bus no. 44B, 45, 47A, 47B, 48A, or 62.

NEARY'S, 1 Chatham St., Dublin 2. Tel. 778586.

Adjacent to the back door of the Gaiety Theatre, this celebrated enclave is a favorite with stage folk and theatergoers. Trademarks here are the pink-and-gray marble bar and the brass hands which support the globe lanterns at the entrance. Evening chatter almost always revolves around show business.

Transportation: DART to Pearse Station or bus no. 10, 11A, 11B, 13, or 20B.

THE OLD STAND, 37 Exchequer St., Dublin 2. Tel. 777220.

A sporting atmosphere with lots of camaraderie is the sine qua non here. It's a favorite meeting place for participants and followers of rugby, horse racing, and Gaelic games.

Transportation: DART to Pearse Station or bus no. 10, 11A, 11B, 12, 20B, or 22A.

P. McCORMACK & SONS, 67 Lower Mounttown Rd., off York Rd., Dun Laoghaire. Tel. 280-5519.

⭐ If you rent a car and head toward the city's southern seaside suburbs, this is a great pub (with its own parking lot) to stop for refreshment, with a choice of three different atmospheres. The main section has an old-world feeling, with globe lamps, stained-glass windows, books and jugs on the shelves, and lots of nooks and crannies for a quiet drink. For a change of pace, there is a skylit and plant-filled conservatory area where classical music fills the air, and outdoors you'll find a festive courtyard beer garden. The pub grub here is top-notch, with a varied buffet table of lunchtime salads and meats.

Transportation: Bus no. 46A or drive.

PALACE BAR, 21 Fleet St., Dublin 2. Tel. 779290.

A favorite with the staff of the *Irish Times* and other literati, this old charmer is decorated with local memorabilia, cartoons, and paintings that tell the story of Dublin through the years. It has a convenient midtown location off Westmoreland Street, near the River Liffey and Trinity College.

   Transportation: DART to Tara Street Station or bus no. 21A, 46A, 46B, 51B, 51C, 68, 69, or 86.

THE QUEENS, 12/13 Castle St., Dalkey, Co. Dublin. Tel. 285-4569.

If you venture south of the city in the Dun Laoghaire direction, this is a good pub to know in a delightful seaside suburb with palm trees. Situated on the main street, it has a decidedly 18th-century atmosphere, with a decor of dark wood beams and pillars; oak and pine furnishings; floors of polished tile, rough timber, and coarse flag; and an authentic collection of memorabilia from copper jugs and urns to lanterns and nautical bric-a-brac, all scattered amid nooks and alcoves and on fireplace mantels. In warm weather, seating is also offered on an outside umbrella-shaded patio.

   Transportation: DART to Dalkey Station or bus no. 8.

STAG'S HEAD, 1 Dame Court, off Dame St., Dublin 2. Tel. 679-3701.

Mounted stags' heads and eight stag-themed stained-glass windows dominate the decor here, as its name implies, but there are also wrought-iron chandeliers, polished Aberdeen granite, old barrels, skylights, and ceiling-high mirrors. Established in 1895, it was one of the first pubs to use electricity, although that appears to be the only concession to modernity.

   Transportation: DART to Tara Street Station or bus no. 15A, 15B, 15C, 46, 55, 63, or 83.

W. RYAN, 28 Parkgate St., Dublin 7. Tel. 776097.

Three generations of the Ryan family have contributed to the success of this gem of a public house, located on the north side of the River Liffey near Phoenix Park. Some of Dublin's best traditional pub features are a part of the scene here, from a metal ceiling and a domed skylight, to beveled mirrors, etched glass, brass lamp holders, a mahogany bar, and four old-style snugs.

   Bus: No. 10, 25, or 26.

PUBS WITH TRADITIONAL/FOLK MUSIC

AN BEAL BOCHT, 58 Charlemont St., off Harcourt St. at Albert Place West, Dublin 2. Tel. 755614.

Located between St. Stephen's Green and the Grand Canal, this cozy vintage pub offers a varied program of Irish traditional music on most nights and on Sunday from 12:30 to 2pm. This is also the only pub in Dublin to devote 1 night a week exclusively to the music of women (Monday). On many nights, plays by Irish authors are also staged by Priory Productions in a back room at 8:30pm.

   Admission: No cover charge for traditional music; £2–£5 ($3.30–$8.25) for plays. **Bus:** No. 14A, 15A, 15B, 15C, or 62.

BARRY FITZGERALDS, 90/92 Marlborough St., Dublin 1. Tel. 740685.

Named for the Abbey actor who became a Hollywood movie star, this place offers live traditional music every night, with Irish ballads on Friday and karaoke on Saturday. Located within a block of the Abbey Theatre, it is also a good pub for theatrical atmosphere, with lots of thespian memorabilia lining the walls and alcoves.

Admission: No cover charge for music. **Transportation:** DART to Connolly Station or bus no. 28, 29A, 30, 31A, 31B, 32A, 32B, or 44A.

KITTY O'SHEA'S, 23/25 Upper Grand Canal St., Dublin 4. Tel. 609965 or 608050.

Situated just south of the Grand Canal, this pub is named after the sweetheart of 19th-century Irish statesman Charles Stewart Parnell. Like its namesake, it abounds with a warm and friendly charm, attracting a mixed clientele of executives and assistants, journalists, sports fans, and visitors. The decor reflects the Parnell era, with ornate oak paneling, stained-glass windows, old political posters, cozy alcoves, and brass railings. The pub grub is top-notch, especially Sunday brunch (complete with zesty Bloody Marys). Traditional Irish music is on tap every night.

Admission: No cover charge for music. **Transportation:** DART to Pearse Station or bus no. 45 or 84.

THE HARCOURT, 60 Harcourt St., Dublin 2. Tel. 783677.

Although this place offers a mix of country, jazz, and disco music on many nights, it is best known for its sessions of Irish traditional music, drawn from Ireland's 32 counties, every Monday night at 8:30pm.

Admission: £4 ($6.60). **Bus:** No. 15A, 15B, 15C, or 62.

O'DONOGHUE'S, 15 Merrion Row, Dublin 2. Tel. 614303 or 607194.

Tucked between St. Stephen's Green and Merrion Street, this smoke-filled enclave is widely heralded as the "granddaddy" of traditional music pubs. At almost any time of the day or night, a spontaneous session is likely to erupt. Consequently, it's often very crowded, with different musical groups vying for attention in a stand-up and lined-up-out-the-door atmosphere.

Admission: No cover charge for music. **Transportation:** DART to Pearse Station or bus no. 10.

O'SHEA'S MERCHANT PUB, 12 Lower Bridge St., Dublin 8. Tel. 793797.

Located in the oldest section of the city on the south bank of the Liffey off Merchant's Quay, this pub offers authentic Irish ceili music on Saturday from 8:30pm or 9pm.

Admission: £3–£3.50 ($4.95–$5.80). **Bus:** No. 51B, 51C, 68, 69, or 79, or take a taxi.

SEAN O'CASEY, 105 Marlborough St., Dublin 1. Tel. 744294.

Located a block from the Abbey Theatre and named for one of Dublin's great playwrights, this Tudor-style pub is appropriately decorated with playbills and posters. There is some kind of music on nightly, with traditional music on Wednesday from 9:15 to 11:30pm.

Admission: £1 ($1.65) music cover charge. **Transportation:** DART to Connolly Station or bus no. 28, 29A, 30, 31A, 31B, 32A, 32B, or 44A.

SLATTERY'S, 129/130 Capel St., Dublin 1. Tel. 727971.

Located on the north side of the River Liffey in the busy commercial corridor between Henry and Abbey Streets, this pub stands out with a classic old-world facade and an interior that is rich in brass trim, dark wood, gas lamps, mirrors, and church-pew benches. On Sunday, between 12:30 and 2pm, it is a focal point for traditional Irish music and ballads, with as many as 20 musicians playing in an informal session in the main bar. On Wednesday to Sunday nights, rock and blues music is featured in the upstairs lounge, from 9 to 11:30pm.

Admission: No cover charge for Irish music sessions; £3–£4 ($4.95–$6.60) cover charge for rock or blues. **Bus:** No. 34 or 34A.

WEXFORD INN, 26 Wexford St., Dublin 2. Tel. 751588 or 780391.

Tucked between Camden and Aungier Streets on a small slightly out-of-the-way street, this place is known for its Irish traditional music sessions in its large barnlike lounge, from 9pm nightly.

Admission: No cover charge for Irish music. **Bus:** No. 55 or 83.

CHAPTER 10

EASY EXCURSIONS FROM DUBLIN

1. COUNTY WICKLOW
2. COUNTIES LOUTH & MEATH
3. COUNTY KILDARE

Whether you head north or south or west, Dublin is the gateway to some of Ireland's most historic and scenic countryside. In fact, because Ireland is so small, Dublin can be a stepping stone to just about any corner of the Emerald Isle.

To help you choose your destinations in the most practical way, however, we have narrowed the choices to the best places that are less than 50 miles away, enabling you to return to Dublin each day in time for dinner and overnight.

The ideal way to reach most of these areas is by car (see "Getting Around" in Chapter 3), but, in some cases, you can take a train or bus, or a half- or full-day escorted tour.

For further information about public transportation or tours, contact the following:

Bus Eireann, Busaras/Central Bus Station, Store Street, Dublin 1 (tel. 01/366111). Operates daily bus service to most destinations and seasonal (May to September) escorted sightseeing tours to scenic and historic areas.

Irish Rail, Connolly Station, Amiens Street, Dublin 1 (tel. 01/363333). Operates daily train service to major towns and cities.

Gray Line Tours, 3 Clanwilliam Terrace, Grand Canal Quay, Dublin 2 (tel. 01/619666). Offers seasonal (May to October) escorted sightseeing bus tours to scenic and historic areas.

INFORMATION For information about Counties Kildare, Louth, Meath, and Wicklow, contact the **Midlands—East Regional Tourism Organization, Ltd.,** Dublin Road, Mullingar, Co. Westmeath (tel. 044/48761), or the Irish Tourist Board offices (see "Sources of Information" in Chapter 2).

---

1. COUNTY WICKLOW

12–40 miles S of Dublin City

GETTING THERE **By Train** Irish Rail provides daily train service between Dublin and Bray and Wicklow.

By Bus Bus Eireann operates daily express bus service to Arklow, Bray, and Wicklow towns. Both Bus Eireann and Gray Line Tours offer seasonal (May to September) sightseeing tours to Glendalough, Wicklow, and Powerscourt Gardens.

By Car Take N11 south from Dublin City and follow turnoff signs for major attractions.

Situated directly south of Dublin, County Wicklow offers a gentle contrast to the bustling capital city. Aptly described as the "Garden of Ireland," Wicklow is a collage of tree-lined country lanes and nature trails, sloping hills and domed granite mountains, gentle glens and wooded river valleys, glistening lakes and sandy seascapes, and picturesque little villages with names such as Annamoe, Ballinalea, Enniskerry, Laragh, Shillelagh, and Hollywood—yes, County Wicklow even has a Hollywood! Equally alluring are windswept mountain passes called Sally Gap, the Devil's Punch Bowl, Glenmalure, and Glen of the Downs.

This verdant county is also home to many stately 18th-century estate houses and award-winning gardens, Ireland's third-highest mountain—Lugnaquilla (3,039 ft.), and a 6th-century monastic site at Glendalough, as well as a hand-weaving craft center dating back to 1723 at Avoca, and the highest village in Ireland at Roundwood (780 ft.). Best of all, County Wicklow's borders start just a dozen miles south of downtown Dublin.

WHAT TO SEE & DO

ARKLOW POTTERY, South Quay, Arklow, Co. Wicklow. Tel. 0402/32401.

Situated in a busy seaside town, this is Ireland's largest pottery factory, and the home of Noritake's Kelt Craft and Misty Isle lines. The pottery produced here ranges from earthenware, porcelain, and bone china tableware to decorated teapots, casseroles, and gifts, using both modern and traditional designs. Free tours are available mid-June through August with the exception of the last week of July and first 2 weeks August when the factory is closed for annual staff vacation.

Admission: Free.

Open: Daily 9:30am–4:45pm. **Directions:** In the heart of town, signposted along the waterfront.

AVOCA HANDWEAVERS, Avoca, Co. Wicklow. Tel. 0402/35105 or 35284.

Dating back to 1723, this cluster of whitewashed stone buildings comprises the oldest surviving hand-weaving company in Ireland. A wide range of tweed clothing, knitwear, and accessories is produced here, with dominant tones of mauve, aqua, teal, and heather, reflecting the landscape of the surrounding County Wicklow countryside. Visitors are welcome to watch as craftspeople weave strands of yarn that has been carded, dyed, and spun from the wool from local sheep. Facilities also include a retail outlet and coffee shop. A second outlet/shop is located on the main N11 road at Kilmacanogue, Bray, Co. Wicklow (tel. 01/286-7466).

Admission: Free.

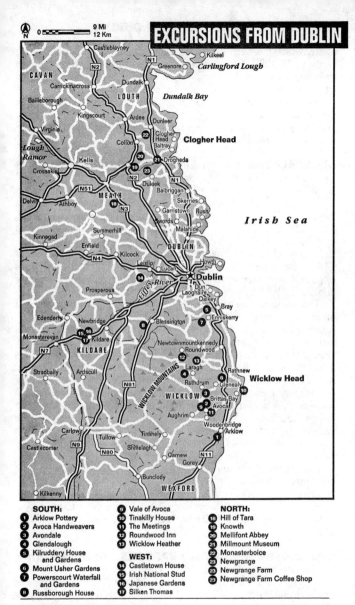

EXCURSIONS FROM DUBLIN

0 — 9 Mi
0 — 12 Km
N

SOUTH:
1. Arlow Pottery
2. Avoca Handweavers
3. Avondale
4. Glendalough
5. Kilruddery House and Gardens
6. Mount Usher Gardens
7. Powerscourt Waterfall and Gardens
8. Russborough House
9. Vale of Avoca
10. Tinakilly House
11. The Meetings
12. Roundwood Inn
13. Wicklow Heather

WEST:
14. Castletown House
15. Irish National Stud
16. Japanese Gardens
17. Silken Thomas

NORTH:
18. Hill of Tara
19. Knowth
20. Mellifont Abbey
21. Millmount Museum
22. Monasterboice
23. Newgrange
23. Newgrange Farm
23. Newgrange Farm Coffee Shop

Open: Mon–Fri 9:30am–5:30pm, Sat–Sun 10am–6pm. **Directions:** In center of town.

AVONDALE, Rathdrum, Co. Wicklow. Tel. 0404/46111.

Nestled in a fertile valley between Glendalough and the Vale of Avoca, this is the former home of Charles Stewart Parnell (1846–91), one of the country's great political leaders of the 19th century. The house, built in 1777, is filled with Parnell memorabilia and furnishings, but the main focus of attention is the surrounding 523-acre estate, which has been developed into a training school for the Irish Forest and Wildlife Service, and is considered as the cradle of modern Irish forestry. Visitors can enjoy flowers, shrubs, trees and signposted nature trails along the Avondale River.

Admission: £2 adults ($3.30), £1 ($1.65) seniors and children under 16.

Open: Year-round, daily 11am–5pm. **Directions:** One mile south of the village of Rathdrum.

GLENDALOUGH, Co. Wicklow. Tel. 0404/45325 or 45352.

⭐ Derived from the Irish or Gaelic phrase, "Gleann Da Locha" meaning "The Glen of the Two Lakes," this secluded tree-shaded setting was chosen in the 6th century by St. Kevin for a monastery. Over the centuries, it became a leading center of learning, with thousands of students enrolling from Ireland, Britain, and all over Europe. In the 12th century, St. Lawrence O'Toole was among the many abbots to follow Kevin and spread the influence of Glendalough. But, like so many early Irish religious sites, the glories of Glendalough came to an end by the 15th century because of plundering by Anglo-Norman invaders.

Today visitors can stroll from the upper lake to the lower lake and quietly contemplate what it must have been like in St. Kevin's day. Although much of the monastic city is in ruins, the remains do include a nearly perfect round tower, 103 feet high and 52 feet around the base, as well as hundreds of timeworn Celtic crosses, plus a variety of churches including St. Kevin's chapel, often called St. Kevin's Kitchen, a fine specimen of an early Irish barrel-vaulted oratory, with its own miniature round tower belfry rising from a stone roof. A new visitor center at the entrance to the site provides a helpful orientation and background via exhibits focusing on the archeology, history, folklore, and wildlife of the area. There is no charge to walk around Glendalough, but there is a fee to view the exhibits.

Admission: £1 adults ($1.65), 70p ($1.15) seniors, 40p (65¢) children and students under 16.

Open: Mid-Mar to mid-June and mid-Sept to Oct, daily 10am–5pm; mid-June to mid-Sept, daily 10am–7pm; Nov to mid-Mar, Tues–Sun 10am–4:30pm. **Directions:** One mile west of the village of Laragh.

KILRUDDERY HOUSE AND GARDENS, Kilruddery, Bray, Co. Wicklow. Tel. 01/286-3405.

The seat of the earl of Meath since 1618, this main structure of this mansion dates mainly from 1820. Although the house boasts a Victorian conservatory that is modeled after the Crystal Palace in London, the real focal point of the estate is the gardens, said to be the only surviving 17th-century layout in Ireland. The highlights include beech hedge "angles," twin canals stretching for over 500 feet in length, a sylvan theater, and a maze of ponds and fountains, with a variety of foreign trees and exotic shrubs.

Admission: House and garden tour, £2.50 ($4.15) adults, £1.50 ($2.50) seniors and students over 12; garden only, £1 ($1.65) adults, 50p (85¢) seniors and students over 12.

Open: May–June and Sept, daily 1–5pm. **Directions:** Off the main (N11) road, 1 mile south of Bray.

MOUNT USHER GARDENS, Ashford, Co. Wicklow. Tel. 0404/40116.

Spread out along 20 acres beside the River Vartry, this sylvan site is distinguished for its collection of more than 5,000 different species of rare trees and plants, gathered from all parts of the world. The specimens include spindle trees from China, North American swamp cypress, and Burmese juniper trees, as well as fiery rhododendrons, fragrant eucalyptus trees, meandering green creepers, pink magnolias, and snowy camellias.

Admission: £2 ($3.30) adults, £1.30 ($2.15) seniors, students and children under 12.

Open: Mar 17–Oct, Mon–Sat 10:30am–6pm, Sun 11am–6pm. **Directions:** On the main (N11) road, 30 miles south of Dublin.

POWERSCOURT WATERFALL AND GARDENS, Enniskerry, Co. Wicklow. Tel. 01/286-7676.

Nestled beside the River Dargle about 12 miles south of Dublin, this is a 14,000-acre estate which has been open to the public for over 50 years. It is a fine example of an aristocratic garden with Italian and Japanese themes, plus herbaceous borders, ornamental lakes, splendid statuary, decorative ironwork, a pet cemetery, and a park with herds of roaming deer. Nearby is a waterfall, the highest in Ireland and Britain, which tumbles downward from a 400-foot-high cliff. Up until 1974, there also stood a fine 18th-century manor house, until it was gutted by fire; there are plans to restore it by 1994.

Admission: Gardens £2.50 ($4.15) adults, £2 ($3.30) seniors and students, £1.50 ($2.50) children aged 5–16; free for children under 5. Waterfall £1.50 ($2.50) adults, £1 ($1.65) seniors and students, 80p ($1.35) children aged 5–16; free for children under 5.

Open: Gardens Mar–Oct, daily 9am–5:30pm; waterfall, summer, daily 9:30am–7pm, winter 10:30am–dusk. **Directions:** Signposted from Bray, off main (N11) road.

RUSSBOROUGH HOUSE, Blessington, Co. Wicklow. Tel. 045/65239.

Built between 1740 and 1750, this Georgian house is designed in the Palladian style. Although it is full of European furniture, silver, bronzes, tapestries, and carpets, and contains some fine examples of Francini plasterwork, Russborough's main claim to fame is that it houses the world-famous Beit Art Collection of paintings including work by Vernet, Guardi, Bellotto, Gainsborough, Rubens, Reynolds, and many others.

Admission: £2.50 ($4.15) adults, £1.50 ($2.50) seniors and students.

Open: Easter–May and Sept–Oct, Sun 10:30am–5:30pm; June–Aug, daily 10:30am–5:30pm. **Directions:** 25 miles southwest of Dublin, off N81, 1 mile south of Blessington.

VALE OF AVOCA, Route 755, Avoca, Co. Wicklow.

Immortalized in the writings of Ireland's 19th-century poet,

Thomas Moore, this place is famed as the setting for "Meeting of the Waters," the tranquil confluence where the Avonmore and Avonbeg Rivers join to form the Avoca River. Although it is basically a peaceful riverbank, the prime tourist attraction here is Tom Moore's Tree, under which the poet is supposed to have sat looking for inspiration—and penned the now famous lines, "There is not in the wide world a valley so sweet, as the vale in whose bosom the bright waters meet . . ." The tree is a sorry sight now, however, as it has been picked almost bare by souvenir hunters. There is also an adjacent pub with Moore memorabilia on display (see The Meetings, below).

Admission: Free.

Directions: Three miles north of Avoca village.

WHERE TO EAT

Expensive

TINAKILLY HOUSE, Rathnew, Co. Wicklow. Tel. 0404/69274.

Cuisine: NEW IRISH/INTERNATIONAL. **Reservations:** Recommended. **Directions:** Two miles south of the village of Rathnew, off main road (N11) and local road R750.

$ **Prices:** Set lunch from £16.50 ($27.25); set dinner from £25 ($41.25). AE, DC, MC, V.

Open: Lunch daily 12:30–2pm; dinner daily 7:30–9:30pm.

For a big splurge, don't miss dining at this elegantly restored 19th-century Victorian mansion, built for Capt. Robert Halpin, commander of the *Great Eastern*, the ship that laid the first telegraph cable linking Europe to America. The kitchen offers a varied menu, using the finest beef, lamb, game, and freshly caught fish from local waters, as well as vegetables, fruits, and herbs from the house gardens. Breads are baked fresh daily on the premises.

Moderate/Inexpensive

THE MEETINGS, Avoca, Co. Wicklow. Tel. 0402/35226.

Cuisine: IRISH/PUB FOOD. **Reservations:** Not required. **Directions:** Beside the Vale of Avoca, three miles north of Avoca.

$ **Prices:** Appetizers £1–£3 ($1.65–$4.95); main courses £3–£7 ($4.95–$11.55). MC, V.

Open: Daily 11am–10pm.

This pub restaurant serves food all day, in a Tudor-style country cottage atmosphere overlooking the "Meeting of the Waters" at Avoca, the site associated with Ireland's famous poet, Thomas Moore. The interior is chock-full of Moore memorabilia including an 1889 copy of a book of his poems. The menu features soups and sandwiches as well as steaks, mixed grills, and local seafood, including a specialty of smoked salmon and brown bread. There is an open-air ceili with Irish traditional music every Sunday afternoon.

ROUNDWOOD INN, Main St., Roundwood, Co. Wicklow. Tel. 01/282-8107 or 282-8125.

Cuisine: IRISH/CONTINENTAL. **Reservations:** Not required for lunch, recommended for dinner. **Directions:** In the middle of village on main road (R755).

$ **Prices:** Appetizers £1–£5 ($1.65–$8.25); lunch main courses £1.65–£9.75 ($2.75–$16); £10–£15 ($16.50–$24.75) dinner main courses. MC, V.

Open: Lunch Tues–Sat 1–2:30pm; dinner Tues–Sat 7:30–9:30pm.

Dating back to 1750, this old coaching inn is the focal point of an out-of-the-way spot high in the mountains called Roundwood, said to be the highest village in Ireland. The old-world atmosphere includes open log fireplaces and antique furnishings. Menu choices range from steaks and sandwiches to traditional Irish stew, fresh lobster or smoked salmon salads, oysters on the half shell, rollmops, and pickled herring, as well as Hungarian goulash, smoked trout, and gravlax. Food is served all day in the bar, besides the normal meal times in the restaurant.

WICKLOW HEATHER, Laragh, Co. Wicklow. Tel. 0404/ 45157.

Cuisine: IRISH/INTERNATIONAL. **Reservations:** Required on weekends. **Directions:** On the main street between Laragh and Glendalough.

$ **Prices:** Appetizers £1–£4 ($1.65–$6.60); lunch main courses £3.50–£7.95 ($5.80–$13.15); dinner main courses £8.50–£11.95 ($14–$19.75). MC, V.

Open: Apr–Oct, daily 9am–11pm.

Situated just down the road from the entrance to Glendalough, this little cottage is surrounded by colorful rose gardens and offers seating indoors or on picnic tables outside. The menu emphasizes local favorites such as Irish stew, sausage and beans, pork chops, and mixed grills, as well as lighter international fare such as smoked trout, pâté, salads, soups, and sandwiches. Reduced-price tourist menus are also available at certain times of the day.

---

2. COUNTIES LOUTH & MEATH

30–40 miles NW of Dublin

GETTING THERE By Train Irish Rail provides daily train service between Dublin and Drogheda.

By Bus Bus Eireann operates daily express bus service to Slane, Collon, Navan, and Drogheda. Both Bus Eireann and Gray Line Tours offer seasonal (May to September) sightseeing tours to Newgrange and/or the Boyne Valley.

By Car Take N1 north from Dublin City to Drogheda and then N51 west to Boyne Valley; N2 northwest to Slane and east on N51 to Boyne Valley; or N3 northwest via Hill of Tara to Navan, and then east on N51 to Boyne Valley.

Within a hour's drive of Dublin is the River Boyne, surrounded by the rich and fertile countryside of Counties Meath and Louth.

More than any other river in the country, this meandering body of water has been at the center of Irish history.

The banks of the Boyne are literally lined with reminders from almost every phase of Ireland's past—from the prehistoric passage tombs, dating back to 3,000 B.C., to the early Christian sites associated with the preachings of St. Patrick, and the royal seats of Irish high kings. This land was also the setting for the infamous Battle of the Boyne in 1690, when King William of Orange crushed James II and so changed the course of English and Irish history that the effects are still felt today.

Local history is also reflected in the ancient town of Drogheda (pronounced *Drah-ah-da*). A complex of medieval walls, gates, and churches, Drogheda was established as a permanent fortified settlement by the Danes in 911 and quickly ranked with Dublin and Wexford as a trading center. By the 14th century, it was one of the four principal towns in Ireland, and continued to prosper until Oliver Cromwell took it by storm in 1649 and massacred its 2,000 inhabitants. Happily, the population has grown to 10 times that number today, and the town is a thriving port and industrial center.

Although many of the places along the valley of the River Boyne are nothing more than grassy mounds or ruins today, visitors flock to see the sites and walk the pathways of long ago. If the River Boyne could talk, what a story it would tell.

WHAT TO SEE & DO

HILL OF TARA, Navan, Co. Meath. Tel. 046/25903.
Although it had been an important site since the late Stone Age, this glorious hill is best remembered as the religious and cultural capital of Ireland in the early centuries after Christ. It was here, every three years, that a *feis* (great national assembly) was held—laws were passed, tribal disputes were settled, and matters of peace and defense were decided. By the end of the 6th century, the Tara monarchy had become the most powerful of Ireland's five kingdoms. As the old song goes, "The harp that once through Tara's halls, the soul of music shed. . . ."

If you rally to Tara's halls today, however, you won't see any towers and turrets, or moats and crown jewels; in fact, you won't even see any halls. Be advised not to come to Tara at all, unless you can use your imagination (and bring some good walking shoes). All that remains of Tara's former glories are grassy mounds and occasional ancient pillar stones. As you look around, however, you can see for miles, and surely the vistas are just as awesome as they were 1,500 years ago.

Note: In a way, Tara can take the credit for the shamrocks seen every March 17th. It all started in the 5th century when St. Patrick began to preach from Tara's heights. In an effort to convert High King Laoire to Christianity, Patrick plucked a three-leaf clover, or shamrock, from the grass to illustrate the doctrine of the Trinity. The spellbinding saint made such an impression that the shamrock has since become synomous with Ireland and the Irish all over the world.
Admission: Free; no access to interior.

Open: Mid-June to Sept, daily 9:30am–6:30pm; winter, daily 10am–dusk. **Directions:** Six miles south of Navan, off the main Dublin road (N3).

KNOWTH, Slane, Co. Meath.

Dating from the Stone Age and currently under excavation, this great mound is believed to have been a site for the burial of the high kings of Ireland, with evidence of occupation from 3000 B.C. to 1200 A.D. It is more complex than Newgrange (see below), with two passage tombs, surrounded by another 18 smaller satellite ones. Knowth has the greatest collection of passage-tomb art ever uncovered in Western Europe. Although work is in progress, and at time of press there is not yet access to the interior, you may still stroll the grounds.

Admission: £1 ($1.65) adults, 70p ($1.15) seniors, 40p (65¢) students and children under 12.

Open: June–Sept, daily 9:30am–6:30pm. **Directions:** Between Drogheda and Slane, 1 mile northwest of Newgrange.

MELLIFONT ABBEY, Collon, Co. Louth. Tel. 041/26459.

Referred to as "The Big Monastery," this was Ireland's first Cistercian monastery, founded in 1142 by St. Malachy of Armagh on the banks of the Mattock River. Although little more than the foundations remain, there are still remnants of a 14th-century chapter house, an octagonal lavabo dating back to around 1200, and several arches of Romanesque design. It's worth a visit just to pause a few moments in this tranquil setting.

Admission: 80p ($1.35) adults, 55p (90¢) seniors, 30p (40¢) students and children under 12.

Open: Mid-June to mid-Sept, daily 10am–6pm. **Directions:** Located 6 miles west of Drogheda on a signposted secondary road off T25.

MILLMOUNT MUSEUM, Duleek St., Drogheda, Co. Louth. Tel. 041/36391.

Located in the courtyard of 18th-century Millmount Fort along the south bank of the River Boyne, this museum offers a range of exhibits about the local history of Drogheda and the Boyne Valley area. Among the items on display are a Bronze Age coracle, medieval tiles, and a collection of 18th-century guild banners, as well as early kitchen butter churns and utensils; spinning, weaving, and brewing equipment; and antique gramophones, mousetraps, coins, movie posters, bottles, shop bells, and hot-water jars.

Admission: 50p (85¢) adults, 20p (35¢) children under 12.

Open: May–Sept, Tues–Sun 2–6pm; Oct–Apr, Wed and Sat–Sun 3–5pm. **Directions:** At the south entrance to Drogheda, off the main Dublin road (N1).

MONASTERBOICE, near Collon, Co. Louth.

Once a great monastery and now little more than a peaceful cemetery, this site is dominated by Muiredach's High Cross, 17 feet tall and one of the most perfect specimens in Ireland. Dating back to the 922 A.D., the cross is ornamented with sculptured panels of biblical scenes from the Old and New Testaments. The monastery grounds also feature the remains of a round tower, two churches, two early grave-slabs, and a sundial.

Admission: Free.

Open: Daily daylight hours. **Directions:** Six miles northwest of Drogheda on a signposted secondary road off N1.

NEWGRANGE, Slane, Co. Meath. Tel. 041/24488.

Set overlooking the Boyne River and known in Gaelic as "Brugh na Boinne" (The Palace of the Boyne), this is Ireland's best-known prehistoric monument and one of the finest archeological wonders of western Europe.

Dating back to 3000 B.C., it is 500 years older than the Pyramids of Egypt and 1,500 years older than Britain's Stonehenge. It consists of a huge mound 36 feet high and 280 feet in diameter, built from 200,000 tons of stone, with a 6-ton capstone, and other stones up to 16 tons each—many of the stones are believed to have been hauled from as far away as County Wicklow and the Mountains of Mourne. Each stone fits perfectly in the overall pattern and the result is a watertight structure. It was built as a passage tomb in which Stone Age men buried the cremated remains of the dead nearly 5,000 years ago.

In addition to being an amazing feat of engineering, it offers specimens of early art carved into the stones, with examples of spirals, diamonds, and concentric circles. Curiosity about Newgrange reaches a peak each mid-December, as light suddenly flows into the passage, timed to coincide with the winter solstice, as the sun rises to the southeast at 8:58am. The sun pierces the inner chamber with an orange-toned light for about 17 minutes. This occurrence is so unique that there is already a waiting list for viewing through the year 2004. Admission by guided tour only.

Admission: £1.50 ($2.50) adults, 60p ($1) students and children over 12.

Open: Nov to mid-Mar, Tues–Sun 10am–1pm and 2–4:30pm; mid-Mar to May and mid-Sept–Oct, daily 10am–1pm and 2–5pm; June to mid-Sept, daily 10am–7pm. **Directions:** Two miles east of Slane, sign-posted off N51.

NEWGRANGE FARM, Slane, Co. Meath. Tel. 041/24119.

In contrast to all the surrounding antiquity, this busy 333-acre farm in the midst of the Boyne Valley is a 20th-century attraction well worth visiting. Farmer Willie Redhouse and his family invite visitors to tour their working farm, which currently grows wheat, oats, barley, oil seed rape, corn, and linseed (flax), and to lend a hand in some of its activities, such as throwing feed to the ducks, grooming a calf, or bottle-feeding the baby lambs or kid goats. You can also hold a newborn chick, pet a pony, play with the pigs, or view the aviaries of rare birds, pheasants, and poultry, and the fields of donkeys, horses, and rare Jacob sheep.

In addition, there are daily demonstrations of sheepdog working, threshing, spinning, and farrier work, as well as displays of farm tools and horse-drawn equipment outside. Within the farm buildings, many of which date back to the 17th century, there are butter churners and molds, blackberry pickers, tabletop churns, spinning wheels, irons, and other early farm implements collected from throughout the valley. The Redhouses also spin and dye their own wool, and have put together an exhibit of the fibers produced and the methods of making natural vegetable-dye colors from beets, carrots, gorse, yew, and sage. The 1½-hour tour ends at the herb garden, with a pick-your-own lesson on unusual plants and herbs. Facilities include a coffee shop (see below) and indoor and outdoor picnic areas.

Note: April to June and September are the busiest months for tours, booked in advance by local school groups, so it is wise to phone in advance for best times to visit. In July and August, there is usually spontaneous Irish music at the farm, provided by the Franklins, a local family of five who play the harp, flute, violin, piano, and hammered dulcimer (old Irish instrument).

Admission: Ł1.75 ($2.90) per person; special reduced rates for parents with children.

Open: Apr–June and Sept, Mon–Fri 10am–5:30pm, Sun 2–5:30pm; July–Aug, Mon–Fri 10am–5:30pm, Sat–Sun 2–5:30pm.

Directions: Two miles east of Slane, signposted off N51 and directly west of Newgrange.

WHERE TO EAT

Inexpensive

NEWGRANGE FARM COFFEE SHOP, Slane, Co. Meath. Tel. 041/24119.

Cuisine: IRISH. **Reservations:** Not required. **Directions:** At Newgrange Farm, 2 miles east of Slane, signposted off N51 and directly west of Newgrange.

$ Prices: 95p–Ł2.50 ($1.60–$4.15). No credit cards.

Open: Apr–Sept, daily 10am–5:30pm.

Located on the premises of a working farm (see above), this family-run restaurant is housed in a converted cowhouse, now whitewashed and skylit with an open fireplace and local art on the walls. Ann Redhouse and her family oversee the baking and food preparation each day, using many ingredients grown on the farm or locally. The ever-changing blackboard menu ranges from homemade soups and hot scones or biscuits to sandwiches, with tempting dessert choices such as apple tart and cream, carrot cake, and fruit pies. Food can also be enjoyed in an outdoor picnic area, and there is often live Irish traditional music as a background in the summer months.

3. COUNTY KILDARE

30 miles W of Dublin

GETTING THERE By Train Irish Rail provides daily train service to Kildare town.

By Bus Bus Eireann operates daily express bus service to Kildare.

By Car Take a main Dublin-Limerick road (N7) west of Dublin to Kildare; or the main Dublin-Galway road (N4) to Celbridge, turning off on local road R403.

Just as Ireland and the horse are synonymous, Kildare and horse racing go hand in hand, or, should we say, neck and neck.

Home of the Curragh racetrack (see "Sports and Recreation" in Chapter 6) where the Irish Derby is held each June and other smaller tracks at Naas and Punchestown, County Kildare is also the heartland of Ireland's flourishing bloodstock industry. Many of the country's 300 stud farms are nestled in this veritable panorama of open grasslands and fertile turf.

WHAT TO SEE & DO

CASTLETOWN HOUSE, Celbridge, Co. Kildare. Tel. 01/ 628-8582.

Although a little removed from the heart of Kildare horse country, this great house deserves a detour. One of Ireland's architectural gems, it is a Palladian-style mansion designed by Italian architect Alessandro Galilei and built in 1722 for William Connolly, then speaker of the Irish House of Commons. Preserved and restored by the Irish Georgian Society, Castletown is known for its long gallery laid out in the Pompeian manner and hung with Venetian chandeliers; main hall and staircase with elaborate Italian plasterwork; and an 18th-century print room. The interior is also a showcase of Georgian-era Irish furniture and paintings.

Admission: £2.50 ($4.15) adults, £2 ($3.30) seniors and students, £1 ($1.65) children under 12.

Open: Apr–Sept, Mon–Fri 10am–6pm, Sat 11am–6pm, Sun 2–6pm; Oct, Mon–Fri 10am–5pm, Sun 2–5pm; Nov–Mar, Sun 2–5pm. **Directions:** En route to Kildare, it is 10 miles northeast of Naas, off the main road (N7) and via local routes R407 and R403; or 13 miles west of Dublin via the main Galway road (N4) and turn off at R403.

IRISH NATIONAL STUD, Tully, Co. Kildare. Tel. 045/ 21617.

In this horse-happy county, this is one of the chief visitor attractions—a government-sponsored stud farm and a prototype for all others throughout the land. Some of Ireland's most famous horses have been bred and raised on these grounds; and visitors are welcome to walk around and watch the noble steeds being exercised and groomed.

In addition to the outdoor sights, there is an indoor museum which aims to bring to life the history of the horse in Ireland, with exhibits dating from the Bronze Age to the present. There are also displays on horses in transport, racing, steeplechasing, hunting, and show jumping, plus the skeleton of Arkle, one of Ireland's most famous equine heroes, and an authentic jockey's weighing-in chair.

Admission: £2 ($3.30) adults, £1.50 ($2.50) seniors, students, and children over 12.

Open: Easter–Oct, Mon–Fri 10am–5pm, Sat 10am–6pm, Sun

2–6pm. **Directions:** Off the main Dublin-Limerick road (N7), 1 mile southeast of Kildare.

JAPANESE GARDENS, Tully, Co. Kildare. Tel. 045/ 21251.

Designed to symbolize the life of man, this is an authentic Japanese garden, first laid out in 1906–10, and considered to be among the oldest and finest Asian gardens in Europe. This is one place in Ireland where the bonsai trees outnumber the shamrocks.

Admission: Ł2 ($3.30) adults, Ł1.50 ($2.50) students, Ł1 ($1.65) children under 12.

Open: Easter–Oct, Mon–Fri 10:30am–5pm, Sat 10:30am–5:30pm, Sun 2–5:30pm. **Directions:** Adjacent to the Irish National Stud, off the main Dublin-Limerick road (N7), 1 mile southeast of Kildare.

WHERE TO EAT

Moderate/Inexpensive

SILKEN THOMAS, The Square, Kildare, Co. Kildare. Tel. 045/22232.

Cuisine: IRISH/INTERNATIONAL. **Reservations:** Not required for lunch. **Directions:** On the main square in Kildare town.

$ Prices: Appetizers Ł1–Ł3 ($1.65–$4.85); lunch main courses Ł3–Ł5 ($4.95–$8.25); dinner main courses Ł5–Ł10 ($8.25–$16.50). MC, V.

Open: Lunch Mon–Sat 12:30–2:30pm, Sun 12:30–2pm; dinner Mon–Sat 6–10pm, Sun 6–9pm.

Formerly known as the Leinster Lodge, this historic inn offers an old-world-style pub-restaurant, with an open fireplace and dark woods. It is named after a character in Irish history, a member of the Norman Fitzgerald family, whose stronghold was in Kildare. He led an unsuccessful rebellion against Henry VIII and some of the decor recalls his efforts. The menu offers a good selection of soups, sandwiches, and salads as well as steaks, roasts, and fresh seafood.

APPENDIX

A. METRIC MEASURES

LENGTH

1 millimeter (mm)	=	.04 inches (*or* less than 1/16 in.)
1 centimeter (cm)	=	.39 inches (*or* just under ½ in.)
1 meter (m)	=	39 inches (*or* about 1.1 yards)
1 kilometer (km)	=	.62 miles (*or* about ⅔ of a mile)

To convert kilometers to miles, multiply the number of kilometers by .62. Also use to convert kilometers per hour (kmph) to miles per hour (m.p.h.).

To convert miles to kilometers, multiply the number of miles by 1.61. Also use to convert from m.p.h. to kmph.

CAPACITY

1 liter (l)	=	33.92 fluid ounces = 2.1 pints = 1.06 quarts
	=	.26 U.S. gallons
1 Imperial gallon	=	1.2 U.S. gallons

To convert liters to U.S. gallons, multiply the number of liters by .26.

To convert U.S. gallons to liters, multiply the number of gallons by 3.79.

To convert Imperial gallons to U.S. gallons, multiply the number of Imperial gallons by 1.2.

To convert U.S. gallons to Imperial gallons, multiply the number of U.S. gallons by .83.

WEIGHT

1 gram (g)	=	.035 ounces (*or* about a paperclip's weight)
1 kilogram (kg)	=	35.2 ounces
	=	2.2 pounds
1 metric ton	=	2,205 pounds (1.1 short ton)

To convert kilograms to pounds, multiply the number of kilograms by 2.2.

To convert pounds to kilograms, multiply the number of pounds by .45.

TEMPERATURE

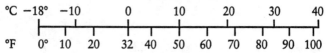

To convert degrees Celsius to degrees Fahrenheit, multiply °C by 9, divide by 5, and add 32 (example: 20°C × 9/5 + 32 = 68°F).

To convert degrees Fahrenheit to degrees Celsius, subtract 32 from °F, multiply by 5, then divide by 9 (example: 85°F − 32 × 5/9 = 29.4°C).

B. SIZE CONVERSIONS

The following charts should help you to choose the correct clothing sizes in Ireland. However, sizes can vary, so the best guide is simply to try things on.

WOMEN'S DRESSES, COATS & SKIRTS

American	3	5	7	9	11	12	13	14	15	16	18
British	8	10	11	12	13	14	15	16	17	18	20

WOMEN'S BLOUSES & SWEATERS

American	10	12	14	16	18	20
British	32	34	36	38	40	42

WOMEN'S STOCKINGS

American	8	8½	9	9½	10	10½
British	8	8½	9	9½	10	10½

WOMEN'S SHOES

American	5	6	7	8	9	10
British	3½	4½	5½	6½	7½	8½

MEN'S SUITS

American	34	36	38	40	42	44	46	48
British	34	36	38	40	42	44	46	48

MEN'S SHIRTS

American	14½	15	15½	16	16½	17	17½	18
British	14½	15	15½	16	16½	17	17½	18

MEN'S SHOES

American	7	8	9	10	11	12	13
British	6	7	8	9	10	11	12

MEN'S HATS

American	6⅞	7⅛	7¼	7⅜	7½	7⅝
British	6¼	6⅞	7⅛	7¼	7⅜	7½

CHILDREN'S CLOTHING

American	3	4	5	6	6X
British	18	20	22	24	26

CHILDREN'S SHOES

American	8	9	10	11	12	13	1	2	3
British	7	8	9	10	11	12	13	1	2

INDEX

GENERAL INFORMATION

SIGHTS & ATTRACTIONS

DUBLIN

Note: * indicates author's favorite.

EXCURSION AREAS

ACCOMMODATIONS

DUBLIN

Key to Abbreviations: *B* = Budget; *E* = Expensive; *I* = Inexpensive; *M* = Moderate; *VE* = Very Expensive; * = Author's favorite; $ = Super-value choice.

RESTAURANTS

DUBLIN

Key to Abbreviations: *B* = Budget; *E* = Expensive; *I* = Inexpensive; *M* = Moderate; *VE* = Very Expensive; * = Author's favorite; $ = Super-value choice.

EXCURSION AREAS

Now Save Money on All Your Travels by Joining
FROMMER'S ™ TRAVEL BOOK CLUB
The World's Best Travel Guides at Membership Prices

FROMMER'S TRAVEL BOOK CLUB is your ticket to successful travel! Open up a world of travel information and simplify your travel planning when you join ranks with thousands of value-conscious travelers who are members of the FROMMER'S TRAVEL BOOK CLUB. Join today and you'll be entitled to all the privileges that come from belonging to the club that offers you travel guides for less to more than 100 destinations worldwide. Annual membership is only $25 (U.S.) or $35 (Canada and all foreign).

The Advantages of Membership

1. Your choice of three free FROMMER'S TRAVEL GUIDES. You can pick two from our FROMMER'S COUNTRY and REGIONAL GUIDES (listed under Comprehensive, $-A-Day, and Family) and one from our FROMMER'S CITY GUIDES (listed under City and City $-A-Day).
2. Your own subscription to **TRIPS & TRAVEL** quarterly newsletter.
3. You're entitled to a **30% discount** on your order of any additional books offered by FROMMER'S TRAVEL BOOK CLUB.
4. You're offered (at a small additional fee) our **Domestic Trip Routing Kits.**

Our quarterly newsletter **TRIPS & TRAVEL** offers practical information on the best buys in travel, the "hottest" vacation spots, the latest travel trends, world-class events and much, much more.

Our **Domestic Trip Routing Kits** are available for any North American destination. We'll send you a detailed map highlighting the best route to take to your destination—you can request direct or scenic routes.

Here's all you have to do to join:
Send in your membership fee of $25 ($35 Canada and foreign) with your name and address on the form below along with your selections as part of your membership package to FROMMER'S TRAVEL BOOK CLUB, P.O. Box 473, Mt. Morris, IL 61054-0473. Remember to check off 2 FROMMER'S COUNTRY and REGIONAL GUIDES and 1 FROMMER'S CITY GUIDE on the pages following.

If you would like to order additional books, please select the books you would like and send a check for the total amount (please add sales tax in the states noted below), plus $2 per book for shipping and handling ($3 per book for all foreign orders) to:

**FROMMER'S TRAVEL BOOK CLUB
P.O. Box 473
Mt. Morris, IL 61054-0473
1-815-734-1104**

[ ] YES. I want to take advantage of this opportunity to join FROM-MER'S TRAVEL BOOK CLUB.

[ ] My check is enclosed. Dollar amount enclosed_____*
(all payments in U.S. funds only)

Name_____

Address_____

City_____ State_____ Zip_____

To ensure that all orders are processed efficiently, please apply sales tax in the following areas: CA, CT, FL, IL, NJ, NY, TN, WA, and CANADA.

*With membership, shipping and handling will be paid by FROMMER'S TRAVEL BOOK CLUB for the three free books you select as part of your membership. Please add $2 per book for shipping and handling for any additional books purchased ($3 per book for all foreign orders).

Allow 4-6 weeks for delivery. Prices of books, membership fee, and publication dates are subject to change without notice.

Please Send Me the Books Checked Below

FROMMER'S COMPREHENSIVE GUIDES
(Guides listing facilities from budget to deluxe, with emphasis on the medium-priced)

	Retail Price	Code		Retail Price	Code
☐ Acapulco/Ixtapa/Taxco 1993–94	$15.00	C120	☐ Jamaica/Barbados 1993–94	$15.00	C105
☐ Alaska 1990–91	$15.00	C001	☐ Japan 1992–93	$19.00	C020
☐ Arizona 1993–94	$18.00	C101	☐ Morocco 1992–93	$18.00	C021
☐ Australia 1992–93	$18.00	C002	☐ Nepal 1992–93	$18.00	C038
☐ Austria 1993–94	$19.00	C119	☐ New England 1993	$17.00	C114
☐ Austria/Hungary 1991–92	$15.00	C003	☐ New Mexico 1993–94	$15.00	C117
☐ Belgium/Holland/ Luxembourg 1993–94	$18.00	C106	☐ New York State 1992–93	$19.00	C025
☐ Bermuda/Bahamas 1992–93	$17.00	C005	☐ Northwest 1991–92	$17.00	C026
☐ Brazil, 3rd Edition	$20.00	C111	☐ Portugal 1992–93	$16.00	C027
☐ California 1993	$18.00	C112	☐ Puerto Rico 1993–94	$15.00	C103
☐ Canada 1992–93	$18.00	C009	☐ Puerto Vallarta/ Manzanillo/ Guadalajara 1992–93	$14.00	C028
☐ Caribbean 1993	$18.00	C102	☐ Scandinavia 1993–94	$19.00	C118
☐ Carolinas/Georgia 1992–93	$17.00	C034	☐ Scotland 1992–93	$16.00	C040
☐ Colorado 1993–94	$16.00	C100	☐ Skiing Europe 1989–90	$15.00	C030
☐ Cruises 1993–94	$19.00	C107	☐ South Pacific 1992–93	$20.00	C031
☐ DE/MD/PA & NJ Shore 1992–93	$19.00	C012	☐ Spain 1993–94	$19.00	C115
☐ Egypt 1990–91	$15.00	C013	☐ Switzerland/ Liechtenstein 1992–93	$19.00	C032
☐ England 1993	$18.00	C109	☐ Thailand 1992–93	$20.00	C033
☐ Florida 1993	$18.00	C104	☐ U.S.A. 1993–94	$19.00	C116
☐ France 1992–93	$20.00	C017	☐ Virgin Islands 1992–93	$13.00	C036
☐ Germany 1993	$19.00	C108	☐ Virginia 1992–93	$14.00	C037
☐ Italy 1993	$19.00	C113	☐ Yucatán 1993–94	$18.00	C110

FROMMER'S $-A-DAY GUIDES
(Guides to low-cost tourist accommodations and facilities)

	Retail Price	Code		Retail Price	Code
☐ Australia on $45 1993–94	$18.00	D102	☐ Israel on $45 1993–94	$18.00	D101
☐ Costa Rica/ Guatemala/Belize on $35 1993–94	$17.00	D108	☐ Mexico on $50 1993	$19.00	D105
			☐ New York on $70 1992–93	$16.00	D016
☐ Eastern Europe on $25 1991–92	$17.00	D005	☐ New Zealand on $45 1993–94	$18.00	D103
☐ England on $60 1993	$18.00	D107	☐ Scotland/Wales on $50 1992–93	$18.00	D019
☐ Europe on $45 1993	$19.00	D106	☐ South America on $40 1993–94	$19.00	D109
☐ Greece on $45 1993–94	$19.00	D100			
☐ Hawaii on $75 1993	$19.00	D104	☐ Turkey on $40 1992–93	$22.00	D023
☐ India on $40 1992–93	$20.00	D010	☐ Washington, D.C. on $40 1992–93	$17.00	D024
☐ Ireland on $40 1992–93	$17.00	D011			

FROMMER'S CITY $-A-DAY GUIDES
(Pocket-size guides with an emphasis on low-cost tourist accommodations and facilities)

	Retail Price	Code		Retail Price	Code
☐ Berlin on $40 1992–93	$12.00	D002	☐ Madrid on $50 1992–93	$13.00	D014
☐ Copenhagen on $50 1992–93	$12.00	D003	☐ Paris on $45 1992–93	$12.00	D018
☐ London on $45 1992–93	$12.00	D013	☐ Stockholm on $50 1992–93	$13.00	D022

FROMMER'S TOURING GUIDES
(Color-illustrated guides that include walking tours,
cultural and historic sights, and practical information)

	Retail Price	Code		Retail Price	Code
☐ Amsterdam	$11.00	T001	☐ New York	$11.00	T008
☐ Barcelona	$14.00	T015	☐ Rome	$11.00	T010
☐ Brazil	$11.00	T003	☐ Scotland	$10.00	T011
☐ Florence	$ 9.00	T005	☐ Sicily	$15.00	T017
☐ Hong Kong/Singapore/ Macau	$11.00	T006	☐ Thailand	$13.00	T012
			☐ Tokyo	$15.00	T016
☐ Kenya	$14.00	T018	☐ Venice	$ 9.00	T014
☐ London	$13.00	T007			

FROMMER'S FAMILY GUIDES

	Retail Price	Code		Retail Price	Code
☐ California with Kids	$17.00	F001	☐ San Francisco with Kids	$17.00	F004
☐ Los Angeles with Kids	$17.00	F002	☐ Washington, D.C. with Kids	$17.00	F005
☐ New York City with Kids	$18.00	F003			

FROMMER'S CITY GUIDES
(Pocket-size guides to sightseeing and tourist accommodations
and facilities in all price ranges)

	Retail Price	Code		Retail Price	Code
☐ Amsterdam 1993–94	$13.00	S110	☐ Minneapolis/St. Paul, 3rd Edition	$13.00	S119
☐ Athens, 9th Edition	$13.00	S114			
☐ Atlanta 1993–94	$13.00	S112	☐ Montréal/Québec City 1993–94	$13.00	S125
☐ Atlantic City/Cape May 1991–92	$ 9.00	S004	☐ New Orleans 1993–94	$13.00	S103
☐ Bangkok 1992–93	$13.00	S005	☐ New York 1993	$13.00	S120
☐ Barcelona/Majorca/ Minorca/Ibiza 1993–94	$13.00	S115	☐ Orlando 1993	$13.00	S101
			☐ Paris 1993–94	$13.00	S109
☐ Berlin 1993–94	$13.00	S116	☐ Philadelphia 1993–94	$13.00	S113
☐ Boston 1993–94	$13.00	S117	☐ Rio 1991–92	$ 9.00	S029
☐ Cancún/Cozumel/ Yucatán 1991–92	$ 9.00	S010	☐ Rome 1993–94	$13.00	S111
			☐ Salt Lake City 1991–92	$ 9.00	S031
☐ Chicago 1993–94	$13.00	S122	☐ San Diego 1993–94	$13.00	S107
☐ Denver/Boulder/ Colorado Springs 1990–91	$ 8.00	S012	☐ San Francisco 1993	$13.00	S104
			☐ Santa Fe/Taos/ Albuquerque 1993–94	$13.00	S108
☐ Dublin 1993–94	$13.00	S128	☐ Seattle/Portland 1992–93	$12.00	S035
☐ Hawaii 1992	$12.00	S014			
☐ Hong Kong 1992–93	$12.00	S015	☐ St. Louis/Kansas City 1993–94	$13.00	S127
☐ Honolulu/Oahu 1993	$13.00	S106	☐ Sydney 1993–94	$13.00	S129
☐ Las Vegas 1993–94	$13.00	S121	☐ Tampa/St. Petersburg 1993–94	$13.00	S105
☐ Lisbon/Madrid/Costa del Sol 1991–92	$ 9.00	S017			
			☐ Tokyo 1992–93	$13.00	S039
☐ London 1993	$13.00	S100	☐ Toronto 1993–94	$13.00	S126
☐ Los Angeles 1993–94	$13.00	S123	☐ Vancouver/Victoria 1990–91	$ 8.00	S041
☐ Madrid/Costa del Sol 1993–94	$13.00	S124	☐ Washington, D.C. 1993	$13.00	S102
☐ Mexico City/Acapulco 1991–92	$ 9.00	S020			
☐ Miami 1993–94	$13.00	S118			

Other Titles Available at Membership Prices

SPECIAL EDITIONS

	Retail Price	Code		Retail Price	Code
☐ Bed & Breakfast North America	$15.00	P002	☐ Where to Stay U.S.A.	$14.00	P015
☐ Caribbean Hideaways	$16.00	P005			
☐ Marilyn Wood's Wonderful Weekends (within a 250-mile radius of NYC)	$12.00	P017			

GAULT MILLAU'S "BEST OF" GUIDES
(The only guides that distinguish the truly superlative from the merely overrated)

	Retail Price	Code		Retail Price	Code
☐ Chicago	$16.00	G002	☐ New England	$16.00	G010
☐ Florida	$17.00	G003	☐ New Orleans	$17.00	G011
☐ France	$17.00	G004	☐ New York	$17.00	G012
☐ Germany	$18.00	G018	☐ Paris	$17.00	G013
☐ Hawaii	$17.00	G006	☐ San Francisco	$17.00	G014
☐ Hong Kong	$17.00	G007	☐ Thailand	$18.00	G019
☐ London	$17.00	G009	☐ Toronto	$17.00	G020
☐ Los Angeles	$17.00	G005	☐ Washington, D.C.	$17.00	G017

THE REAL GUIDES
(Opinionated, politically aware guides for youthful budget-minded travelers)

	Retail Price	Code		Retail Price	Code
☐ Able to Travel	$20.00	R112	☐ Kenya	$12.95	R015
☐ Amsterdam	$13.00	R100	☐ Mexico	$11.95	R016
☐ Barcelona	$13.00	R101	☐ Morocco	$14.00	R017
☐ Belgium/Holland/Luxembourg	$16.00	R031	☐ Nepal	$14.00	R018
			☐ New York	$13.00	R019
☐ Berlin	$11.95	R002	☐ Paris	$13.00	R020
☐ Brazil	$13.95	R003	☐ Peru	$12.95	R021
☐ California & the West Coast	$17.00	R121	☐ Poland	$13.95	R022
			☐ Portugal	$15.00	R023
☐ Canada	$15.00	R103	☐ Prague	$15.00	R113
☐ Czechoslovakia	$14.00	R005	☐ San Francisco & the Bay Area	$11.95	R024
☐ Egypt	$19.00	R105			
☐ Europe	$18.00	R122	☐ Scandinavia	$14.95	R025
☐ Florida	$14.00	R006	☐ Spain	$16.00	R026
☐ France	$18.00	R106	☐ Thailand	$17.00	R119
☐ Germany	$18.00	R107	☐ Tunisia	$17.00	R115
☐ Greece	$18.00	R108	☐ Turkey	$13.95	R027
☐ Guatemala/Belize	$14.00	R010	☐ U.S.A.	$18.00	R117
☐ Hong Kong/Macau	$11.95	R011	☐ Venice	$11.95	R028
☐ Hungary	$14.00	R118	☐ Women Travel	$12.95	R029
☐ Ireland	$17.00	R120	☐ Yugoslavia	$12.95	R030
☐ Italy	$13.95	R014			